Cheryl Robson

Series Editor

Cheryl Robson is an award-winning writer and editor who has created the celebrated, independent publishing company Aurora Metro Books and has spent three decades bringing the work of diverse writers to publication with works translated from more than 20 languages. Her many accolades include winning the Pandora Award (1990), the Arts Council's Raymond Williams Publishing Award (1992), Gourmand World Cookbook Awards including a Special Jury Prize for Peace, (2005 & 2012), finalist in the Independent Publisher Guild's Diversity Awards (2019 & 2020) and a finalist in the ITV National Diversity Awards for Lifetime Achievement (2019) and as Entrepreneur of the Year (2022). She has also campaigned successfully to erect a statue of the literary icon, Virginia Woolf, in Richmond-upon-Thames in UK.

Having trained at the BBC as a filmmaker after leaving university, Robson has also made a number of films, including the multi-award-winning feature documentary *Rock 'n' Roll Island* which aired on BBC4 in 2020 and was a *Sunday Times* Critics' Choice programme. www.cherylrobson.net

50 Women in Sport is part of a series of books exploring women of achievement in culture, media, technology and sport. www.aurorametro.com

First published in the UK in 2022 by Supernova Books, an imprint of Aurora Metro Publications Ltd.

67 Grove Avenue, Twickenham, TW1 4HX www.aurorametro.com info@aurorametro.com

t: @aurorametro F: facebook.com/AuroraMetroBooks

50 Women in Sport edited by Cheryl Robson copyright © 2022 Supernova Books/Aurora Metro Publications Ltd.

Front cover L-R: Junko Tabei, Serena Williams, Smriti Mandhana, Fu Yuanhui, Nicola Adams, Megan Rapinoe.

Cover design: copyright © Supernova Books 2022/ Aurora Metro Publications Ltd.

Edited by Cheryl Robson.

Pioneers and Legends copyright © Supernova Books 2022/ Aurora Metro Publications Ltd.

Biography research and interviews compiled by Emily Dominey and Cheryl Robson

Early Sports Pioneers copyright © 2022 Jean Williams

Women in Sport: Post-War to Today copyright © 2022 Jean Williams

Great Paralympians copyright © 2022 Gemma Lumsdaine

Photographs courtesy of: Contributors' own photos, CC., wikimedia, flickr; Team GB, World Netball, Red Sky, swimming.org, Red Sox, Getty, Wasps, Wisden, IOC, AFP, Time, Smithsonian, Library of Congress, White House, Morning Star, localwiki.org/oakland, BT, Hans Bezard, Rach, Olympic Team Canada, Lorie Schaull, Anders Henrikson, Eugene Everson, Mansoor Ahmed, Chris Cox, JS Sports Photography, IPC/World Para Swimming, Georgie Kerr/British Swimming, Libby Mudditt, UK Sport, Kurt Arrigo, EOC, WAO, RFU, Phil Williams, Sarah Bunt, Craig Maccubbin, Australian Paralympics Committee, BBC, Ludovic Peron, US Ski Team/Doug Haney, James Boyes, Jaan Kunnup, Wang Lama Humla, Gage Skidmore, Angela George, Jason Pini, Amplified 2010, Sander van Ginkel, Oleg Bkhambri, Fernando Frazão, Chris Carmichael, Chris Kirkham, Edwin Martinez, Evening Standard, Troy Williams.

All the photographs in this volume are reprinted with permission or presumed to be in the public domain. Every effort has been made to ascertain and acknowledge copyright status, but should there have been any oversight on our part, we will endeavour to rectify the error in subsequent printings.

Aurora Metro Books would like to thank: Alice Billington, Alison Kervin

All rights are strictly reserved. For rights enquiries please contact the publisher: info@aurorametro.com

No part of this publication may be reproduced, stored in or introduced into a retrieval system, or transmitted in any form, or by any means (electronic, mechanical, photocopying, recording or otherwise) without the prior permission of the publisher. Any person who does any unauthorised act in relation to this publication may be liable to criminal prosecution and civil claims for damages.

This paperback is sold subject to the condition that it shall not, by way of trade or otherwise, be lent, resold, hired out, or otherwise circulated without the publisher's prior consent in any form of binding or cover other than that in which it is published and without a similar condition being imposed on the subsequent purchaser.

We gratefully acknowledge financial assistance for this book from SporTedd, Teddington, UK.

Printed by Short Run Press, Exeter, UK on sustainably resourced paper.

ISBNs: 978-1-913641-01-6 (print)
ISBN 978-1-913641-02-3 (ebook)

Lindsey Vonn, skier, with Olympic medals and eight Crystal Globes, 2010 at the World Cup Finals in Garmisch-Partenkirchen, Germany.
Photo: US Ski Team/Doug Haney

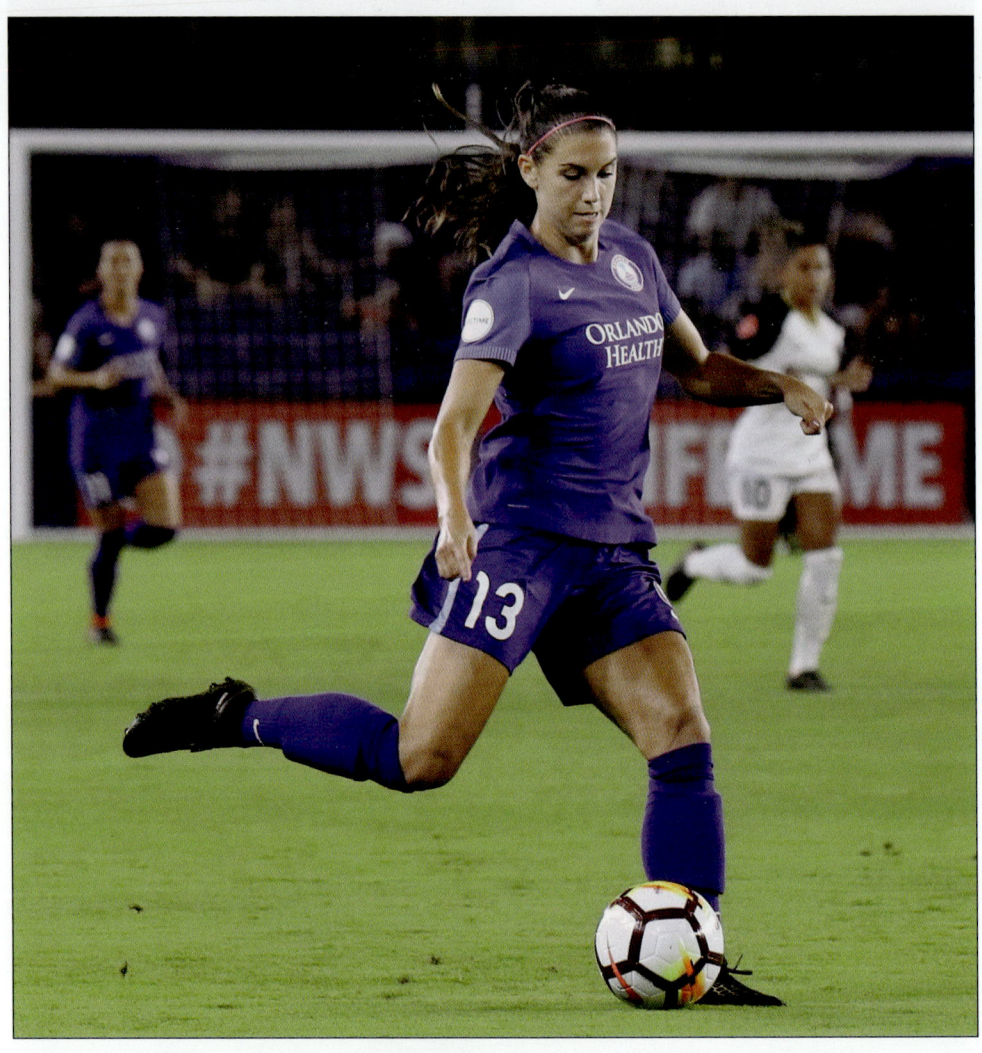
Footballer Alex Morgan, with the Orlando Pride of the NWSL, in May 2018.
Photo: Jamie Smed

50 WOMEN
IN SPORT

SUPERNOVA BOOKS

Mithali Raj, one of India's greatest batters, gets record fifty as India complete a 2-1 win over England, 2018. Photo:Wisden

CONTENTS

EARLY SPORTS PIONEERS — 11
Jean Williams

WOMEN IN SPORT: POST-WAR TO TODAY — 21
Jean Williams

GREAT PARALYMPIANS — 35
Gemma Lumsdaine

PIONEERS AND LEGENDS

Toni Stone	42
Althea Gibson	44
Barbara Buttrick	46
Larisa Latynina	48
Krystyna Chojnowska-Liskiewicz	50
Junko Tabei	52
Billie Jean King	54
Jayne Torvill	56
Luan Jujie	58
Jackie Joyner-Kersee	60
Nawal El Moutawakel	62
Natalia Molchanova	64
Lisa Leslie	66
Cathy Freeman	68
Ellen MacArthur	70
Serena Williams	72
Janica Kostelić	74
Nicola Adams	76
Megan Rapinoe	78
Marta	80
Rachael Blackmore	82
Saina Nehwal	84
Laura Kenny	86
Fu Yuanhui	88
Simone Biles	90

50 WOMEN IN SPORT

WOMEN IN SPORT IN THEIR OWN WORDS

Chemmy Alcott	94
Cat Carr	101
Ellie Challis	107
Pamela Cookey	113
Alice Dearing	119
Tracy Edwards	125
Menna Fitzpatrick	130
Katherine Grainger	135
Steph Houghton	143
Julie Kitchen	147
Meg Lanning	152
Gabby Logan	156
Yaroslava Mahuchikh	163
Eve Muirhead	168
Liz Nicholl	173
Celia Quansah and Megan Jones	178
Aries Susanti Rahayu	188
Jawahir Roble	192
Kate Shortman and Izzy Thorpe	198
Barbara Slater	206
Bianca Smith	212
Zoe Smith	215
Maria Toorpakai	220

INDEX   228

England Women v New Zealand Women June 2019
Photo: James Boyes

Mosaic of women exercising at the Villa Romana del Casale, Sicily c. 4th century.

EARLY SPORTS PIONEERS

Jean Williams

What makes a sporting pioneer? Someone who is physically adventurous, who creates their own opportunities and who does not shy from discomfort in the pursuit of excellence? We often hear sports stars today say that they have shown 'character,' and most of the early women sporting pioneers, whatever their discipline, were dedicated and single-minded in their careers. As the title of the seminal 1973 work *Hidden Histories: Three Hundred Years of Women's Oppression* by Sheila Rowbotham implied, both women's work and leisure were part of a 'hidden history', until fifty years ago. This gives the impression that women working in sport-related roles was a twentieth century innovation. But this notion is far from the reality.

When Dame Juliana Berners, a member of the Order of Saint Benedictine, published a treatise on hunting and hawking in 1486, it became one of the earliest examples of sporting literature in the printed word. Juliana Berners, high-born and educated, enjoyed field sports, including fishing, as part of her status before joining Sopwell Nunnery, near St Albans. She authored *Treatyse on Fysshynge wyth an Angle,* a how-to fishing manual. Berners gave a moral dimension to sport which enabled the contemplative angler the opportunity to appreciate God's glory through an appreciation of nature; she also argued for environmental conservation, healthy eating, and etiquette. While modern feminists argue that 'the personal is political,' Berners agreed that the choice of how to spend one's leisure was an embodied and spiritual practice, in nature, effecting quiet contemplation, and a connection with the divine, as opposed to choosing the ale house, the pleasures of the flesh and the profane temptations of the city.

In terms of this collection, the example is a reminder that women's interest in sport is nothing new. Before the middle of the nineteenth century sport meant blood and field sports of a variety of kinds, and it was only with greater codification, and

Female Archers, 1799

rulemaking, after 1850, that modern sport was born. Thereafter, blood sports decreased, human games became less violent, and the idea of 'fair play' became more widespread. These processes were slow and uneven. Sport was contested as part of the right of the common man – and woman – to enjoy themselves when work was done. The various forms of "Olimpick," "Ho-Limpyc," "Olympian," and "Olympiad" festivals were part of a wider engagement with the philosophies and practices of the ancient Pan-Hellenic Olympic games. For instance, from 1612 to 1642, Robert Dover reinvented the folk Cotswold Games as annual 'Olimpick' celebrations of sport and, to an extent, culture. Women were integral to the events, and this was contentious because James I had defended the right of respectable leisure, after worship on a Sunday particularly, in *The Book of Sports,* formally known as the Declaration for Sports, in May 1618. In 1633 it was reaffirmed by Charles I in the face of increased Puritan influence, especially against Catholic gentry. Dover's heritage was Catholic, and his games included archery, dancing, leaping, hare coursing, and shin kicking.

Women participated and benefitted from many industries around early modern sport and leisure such as ale, and guest houses, the food and drink industries, and in clothing manufacture. A woodcut from the time clearly shows women as integral to the festivities.

The connection of bodily practices with spiritual and ethical values continued. Much of this involved the celebration of human interaction with nature and, by extension, the divine principles that crafted a harmonious environment. However, this could be disrupted by man-made conflicts such as the English Civil Wars, and prohibition remained in place until Charles II was restored to the throne in 1660.

Sport could be a career as well as an enthusiasm. As the career of swimmer, entrepreneur and theatre performer Agnes Beckwith indicated, there could be several forms of 'penny entrepreneurialism' across a lifetime. Born in 1861 in Lambeth, London, Agnes' father's occupation was listed as 'Swimming Professor' in the census. Aged 14, Agnes would swim five miles in an hour and nine minutes from London Bridge to Greenwich, as well as performing 'ornamental swimming' in glass tanks in music halls and theatres and declaring her occupation in the 1881 census as swimmer. She also attempted much longer, 20-mile, open water swims and appeared at the 'Aq' the London Aquarium in front of paying crowds, not all of whom could swim themselves. So, in many ways Agnes was a typical pioneer, in seeking to become the first, or the best, or preferably both. Certainly, her youth, and what the press of the time called rational dress, which enabled her to swim unfettered by swathes of fabric,

Lady Florence Dixie c.1880

made her appearances topical and timely, just at a time when women were seeking to become more assertive physically by wearing bloomers to ride cycles, and for greater freedom of movement. Women boxers, equestrians, pedestrians, rowers, and swimmers could define their own careers by setting feats such as this and seeking to earn a fortune, large or small.

In contrast, Scottish aristocratic equestrian, Lady Florence Dixie, born in 1855, could deliver her rakish husband Beau, an 'heir and a spare' son before leaving for Patagonia. She wrote *Across Patagonia* (1880) as the only female of the party, and while her second son was less than two years old. She presented Darwin with a copy on her return, and as field correspondent of the *Morning Post*, covered the First Boer War while travelling with Beau. An intrepid equestrian, she later came to condemn blood sports as cruel. By then, her feminist sympathies had caused her to become non-playing President of the British Ladies Football Club, from 1894 onwards, insisting the players train and compete in recognisable football gear. Along with stories for children and writing for adults, fiction, and non-fiction, we can see that she was a woman who embraced modernity, at the same time as remaining an imperialist by political inclination. Versatile, ambitious, and unconventional, both Beckwith, who died in South Africa, and Dixie were also internationalists.

Croquet was a Victorian craze that enabled men and women to socialise together in their finest dress, and from this, lawn tennis became even more popular with both men and women. The first great female all-rounder of the modern era, Merseyside's Charlotte 'Lottie' Dod, born in 1871, also shared an international outlook, but would excel in several sports in transnational tournaments, ensuing her global fame from an early age. She won the Wimbledon Ladies' Singles Championship five times, firstly, at the age of fifteen in 1887 and again in 1888, 1891, 1892 and 1893.

Wearing a fetching cricket cap and with ankle-length skirts, the image of a young Dod would remain in the minds of the public, and she was dubbed the 'little wonder,' even as she later became an Olympic silver medallist in archery in 1908, with her brother Willy, taking

Charlotte "Lottie" Dod, 1891

Australia vs England, 2nd Women's Test Match, Sydney, 1935

the gold in the men's event. In the meantime, she climbed, cycled, and skated in Europe, and became an England hockey and a golf international, also winning the 1904 British Ladies Amateur Championship. She almost won a triple crown of national championships but came second in the 1910 archery Grand National, after leading on day one. Serving in World War I as a nurse, she also sang, played the piano and the banjo. She was able to attend Wimbledon into her 80s, dying while listening on the radio to the tournament, in June 1960.

By the 1880s, women were leading women's team sports, notably the All-England Women's Hockey Association, formed in 1884. Cricket has a long history too, with the White Heather Club formed in 1887, and a team of professionals formed briefly in 1890, until they made so much money that the male professional who fronted the enterprise absconded with the takings three years later. Like women's early football matches in 1881, between teams calling themselves England and Scotland, this was evidence of new freedoms, not least in dress.

By 1896 the modern Olympics had been established, and the first edition was held in Athens. By 1900, in the Paris Olympics, women took part in croquet, tennis, golf, sailing, equestrian and ballooning competitions, held in conjunction with a World Fair over five months. No wonder that some competitors died without knowing they were Olympic pioneers. The 1904 St Louis Olympics were more of an exhibition than a sporting tournament, and the London Olympics of 1908 innovated practices that remain today, such as the Marathon distance being 26 miles 385 yards, rather than 40 kilometres, after Queen Alexandra requested that the race start on the lawn of Windsor Castle, so the children could watch from the window of their nursery and finish in front of the royal box at the Olympic stadium. Madge Syers won an individual gold medal in the new Olympic event of figure skating, and earned a gold with her husband, Edgar, in the pairs.

By 1912, Australian swimmers Sarah Frances, or 'Fanny', Durack born in 1889 and her close friend Wilhelmina, or Mina, Wylie, born in 1891, revolutionised their sport internationally. While breaststroke was considered less of an exhausting stroke for both sexes, and particularly women, Australian crawl, as the freestyle stroke both Sydney women perfected, outperformed the side-stroke of the British and

EARLY SPORTS PIONEERS

Fanny Durack, Mina Wylie and Jennie Fletcher 1912 Olympic Games, Stockholm.

German competitors at the 1912 Stockholm Olympic Games. Having had to fund themselves, and their chaperones, over to Stockholm, Durack became the first Australian woman to win a gold medal in a swimming event, and Wylie came in second. From 1912 to 1920 she held the world 100-metre freestyle record and added to this many other national and regional titles. In subsequent Olympic Games women's freestyle swimming used the crawl technique perfected by the Australians and it became the preferred choice of stroke for competitors, as it was athletic performance, rather than a wish to perform a more moderate stroke, which dominated the pool.

Another swimmer, known as 'America's Best Girl', inspired more than 60,000 women to achieve Red Cross swimming certificates and was a celebrity known around the world in the 1920s. Gertrude Ederle competed at the 1924 Paris Olympics at the age of 18. A favourite to win all three of her events, she was part of the world record-setting 4x100m freestyle relay team which took home the gold. She also won bronze medals for the women's 100-metre freestyle and women's 400-metre freestyle, contributing to the United States' table-topping 99-medal haul.

In 1925, she turned professional and became the first woman to swim the 22-mile course from Battery Park, New York to Sandy Hook, New Jersey. She completed the swim in 7 hours and 11 minutes, a new record which would not be beaten for eight decades. In 1926, wearing a modern two-piece swimming suit and special goggles she designed herself, she took to the English Channel from Cape Gris-Nez in France using freestyle, rather than the typical breaststroke others had used to attempt the feat. Despite challenging conditions, and egged on by her family and journalists in two accompanying boats, Gertrude completed the swim in 14 hours and 34 minutes. In doing so, she smashed the previous men's record of 16 hours, 33 minutes and became an overnight international sensation. She told the press: "People said women couldn't swim the Channel, but I proved

Gertrude Ederle, swimming the Channel

Sophie Pierce-Evans, aviator

they could." Upon her return to the US, she received a ticker-tape parade where more than 2 million people celebrated her achievement, and was congratulated by President Calvin Coolidge at the White House.

During World War I women used skills learned from their sporting careers as part of the war effort. Women who had organised swimming club galas were judged to be capable and became matrons on nursing wards due to their leadership skillset. The young Sophie Pierce-Evans, (later known as Mary, Lady Heath), who had been a good tennis and hockey player at school and had trained at the Royal College of Science for Ireland, rode dispatch and developed a passion for aviation, as well as competing in Olympic-standard track and field athletics.

Tasmanian-born Ethel Locke King, who, with her husband Hugh, had established the world's first motor racing circuit at Brooklands in Surrey in 1907 entirely at their own expense, turned over her house there to become a Red Cross hospital from 1915-1919. She also operated a Voluntary Aid Detachment in Surrey in a dozen hospitals, mainly in houses belonging to her husband. For her work during the war, she was appointed **Dame Commander of the Order of the British Empire (DBE)** in 1918.

Many of the women who went into munitions factories, played football to raise money for injured soldiers, including those suffering PTSD, as did many of the nurses who sought to minister to the wounded, and surprisingly, this was popular with the women who worked in the Lyons coffee houses which were then as ubiquitous as the chains of coffee shops we expect to see on high streets today.

After the end of World War I, sport looked backwards and forwards. Women's football was banned in 1921 from the grounds of the Football Association, as the all-male organisation considered the game 'quite unsuitable' for females. The ban was in place for almost fifty years. Gradually, though, the Olympic schedule expanded to provide more events for women including women's track and field athletics from 1928. That was the year that all women in Britain attained the vote and, since then, women have been campaigning on a range of issues to gain equality not only on the sporting field, but across society. These and many other women pioneers, are examples of those whose courage, physical strength, and determination in the public arena of sport, played a part in challenging social attitudes about 'the weaker sex.'

Norway's Sonja Henie (1912-1969) was perhaps the most

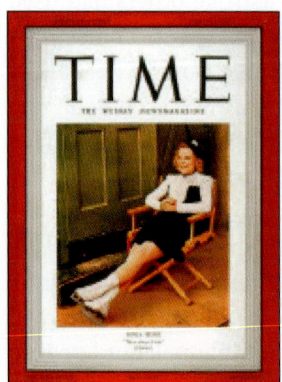

Sonja Henie, 1939, *TIME*

'Babe' Didrikson, 1947, NPG, Smithsonian

astute self-publicist of her generation. From 1927 to 1939 Henie dominated figure skating, winning ten consecutive world titles and individual gold medals, at three Olympic Games in St. Moritz, Switzerland (1928), Lake Placid (1932), and at Garmisch-Partenkirchen in Bavaria (1936). Turning professional that year, Henie became, for a time, one of the highest-paid actresses in Hollywood movies with the successful release of the film *One in A Million*. High-profile athletes were not just beneficiaries of social conditions of the time but also created their own markets, and her sales of branded skating costumes and footwear earned a fortune in their own right.

If 'Lottie' Dod was the first great female all-rounder, Mildred Ella 'Babe' Didrikson Zaharias (1911-1956) was the second — an American athlete who excelled in golf, basketball, baseball, track, and field. She won two gold medals in track and field at the 1932 Summer Olympics, before turning to professional golf and winning 10 LPGA major championships. Of Norwegian descent and born in Texas, first coming to attention as a track and field athlete, she was also an excellent basketball player with the Golden Cyclones. She set four world records, winning two gold medals and a silver in 1932, her fame helped by the Olympics being on home soil in Los Angeles.

Ilona Elek c.1936

After becoming a celebrity professional golfer in the 1930s and 1940s, playing in the PGA championship alongside men, she initially failed to make the cut, but she was able to make the cut in later events, the only woman to do so. She also pioneered women's golf competitions.

Hungarian-born Ilona Elek was of Jewish heritage, so her first Olympic win in fencing in 1936 caused a sensation. Elek defeated a German with a Jewish father, Helene Mayer. The bronze medal went to Ellen Preis, an Austrian Jew. Although the 1940 and 1944 Olympic Games were cancelled, Elek retained her title in 1948 in London. She then won the silver medal in 1952, having been in contention for gold.

Blankers-Koen in the women's 200m, 1948 London Olympics

Her dominance in the world championships was almost complete from 1934-1954, with a few second places that belied her command. Elek was later awarded the Olympic Order, having won more international fencing titles than any other woman.

Fanny Blankers-Koen (1918-2004) was a Dutch Olympic champion and world record-setter who was declared the 'Female Athlete of the Century' by the International Amateur Athletics Federation in 1999. Nicknamed 'the Flying Housewife' by the press, she overcame prejudice surrounding her gender, age and motherhood to triumph in a long and remarkable career. Aged 17, she set a national record for the 800m race in her first competition. The following year she made her debut at the 1936 Olympic Games in Berlin, where she competed in the high jump and 4x100m relay.

After international athletics competitions resumed in 1946, Blankers-Koen won five European titles over five years. At the 1948 London Olympic Games, Fanny entered three individual events, the maximum women were allowed to compete in at the time, and served on the Dutch relay team. She almost quit once she had won her first gold for the 100m race, but her husband convinced her to continue. She went on to win gold at the hurdles, and in the 200m sprint, she won by a 0.7-second margin, a victory that has not been equalled. In her final event, in the anchor leg of the 4x100m relay, she came from fourth place to win the race. She was the first woman to win four medals at any single Olympic Games, the first woman to win four gold medals, and was the most decorated athlete at the 1948 Games. Blankers-Koen triumphed in the face of critics who had presumed that, at 30, she was too old to succeed, or who had denounced her for being a mother who dared to continue competing. It was later revealed that she had been pregnant with her third child during the Games and the cliché of the advantage of youth over age had to be revised in the press.

Wilma Glodean Rudolph (1940–1994) was an American sprinter, who became a world-record-holding Olympic champion and international sports icon in track and field following her successes in the 1956 and 1960 Olympic Games. This was largely due to the Olympics being increasingly televised.

In 1956, Rudolph competed in the 200 metres and won a bronze medal in the 4x100m relay at the Summer Olympic Games in Melbourne, Australia. She won three gold medals, in the 100 and 200-metre individual track and field sprints and the 4x100m relay at the 1960 Summer Olympics in Rome, Italy. Rudolph was acclaimed the 'fastest woman in the world,' and the first American woman to win three gold medals in a single Olympic Games. She was one of the most visible black female sporting icons of the twentieth century.

Wilma Rudolph wins the 100-metre sprint
at the 1960 Rome Olympics.

Jean Williams

Professor Jean Williams is a leading historian of sport, having published six monographs and several articles relating to women and gender relations. Jean was an average, but enthusiastic, footballer, tennis player, and swimmer having also recorded one of the slowest times possible for the completion of the London Marathon. Working extensively with the Galleries, Libraries, Archives and Museums sector (GLAM), she co-curates, writes, and advises on making the hidden histories of sport, particularly of marginalised groups, more publicly available. Williams has also consulted on walks of fame, halls of fame, the installation of statuary, and plaques at key sites internationally.

Cathy Freeman lighting the Olympic cauldron at Sydney Olympic Games, in 2000.

WOMEN IN SPORT: POST-WAR TO TODAY

Jean Williams

London 1948 was the last Olympic Games where literature, art, sculpture, architecture, etchings and musical compositions were awarded medals. Thereafter, sport became the main focus rather than culture and the arts. Before World War II, the Olympics had already been radically politicised at the 1936 Berlin edition, which were so overlaid with propaganda and symbolism that they might be considered a postmodern event with any sporting values lost under Nazi misinformation.

Technological innovation was to be important in 1948, including photo finishes and BBC outside broadcasts. A sense of time, space and place changed as simultaneous multi-media records of events became increasingly the norm. Radio, television and film presented the second London Olympics of 1948 as one of the first big post-war opportunities for sporting communion. However, this was not necessarily a national moment, as most of the half a million TV viewers lived within eighty miles of London. For the British press and radio, Olympic competition was a small sign that the war was over and things were slowly improving, although there was still rationing and a wide sense of austerity. Cinema and radio were still more important to most people than television. Although less than 5% of the adult population had a television set in their homes (it has been estimated at about 70,000 in total) Olympic outside broadcasts provided one of the milestones of post-war TV transmission, following the Victory Parade in 1946 and the Royal Wedding of Princess Elizabeth and Prince Phillip in 1947. This was a particular 'media moment' in British sport where a competitor might see their first television set shortly before appearing on the screen, as Dorothy Tyler (née Odam), a high jump competitor, reported that she had done.

The shift towards Commonwealth and post-colonial relations following the 1947 partition of India and Pakistan radically changed perceptions of Black and South Asian communities in Britain. On 22 June 1948 HMS *Windrush* arrived carrying just under 500 people from Jamaica, the first large group of West Indian immigrants to Britain.

For women's sport, the London 1948 Olympics looked selectively backwards and forwards. Of the 4,100 athletes, 400 were women. Pong Sik Pak, a discus competitor would be the only woman in the Korean team. Alice Coachman took the gold in the high jump to become the first African American woman to win an event outright. But absent from the Games was Mrs Winifred Pritchard, who had won four races in the Royal Yacht Association trials but was prevented by IOC rules from representing her country as late as May 1948. In spite of women previously competing on water, she was informed that mixed sailing events would be 'introduced' in 1952. Beryl Preston had been the most recent female competitor at the 1936 Berlin Games, but Britain would not have a female yachting representative again until 1960 when Jean Mitchell took part in the Star class. Although a female kayaking discipline was introduced in 1948, canoeing or any event over 500 metres was considered too strenuous for women.

Of the five sports open to women in 1948, track and field athletics, gymnastics, fencing and kayaking were minority interests and only swimming a genuinely popular recreational activity. The disciplines available to female athletes within those sports were also limited and somewhat arbitrary. All of this was covered by new media outlets, such as a dedicated magazine *World Sports: International Sports Magazine,* which was established as the official publication of the British Olympic Association (BOA). The star spectators of the London Olympics of 1948 were Princess Elizabeth and her sister Margaret. From the age of 10, Elizabeth had been educated privately at home in preparation to become Queen, and she began to undertake public duties during World War II, serving in the Auxiliary Territorial Service. Following her marriage to Prince Philip in 1947, their first son Charles was born in November 1948. The editor of *World Sports* felt that when she came to the throne on the death of her father in 1952 that a 'New Elizabethan' age was born and the inexorable rise of women's sport would be part of her reign.

Both in her professional duties and in her personal life the Queen is known to be 'outdoorsy', and she has used mega events to connect with the public in ways that have made her personally popular. As well as riding ponies from a young age, both Princess Elizabeth and Margaret were keen field sports exponents, including shooting, salmon fishing and deer stalking. Elizabeth and Margaret had been taught to swim and dive at the Bath Club at the age of 10 and 8, respectively. Many pioneering firsts that were celebrated by a new form of monarchy began when the princesses were young. Elizabeth had become the first person to be awarded the Royal Life Saving Society's Junior Resuscitation Badge, at the age of 12. While young, she became the patron of many sporting bodies, including the Amateur Swimming Association. Both Elizabeth and Philip were also accomplished sailors and The Island Sailing Club in Cowes gave the Royal couple *Bluebottle*, a Dragon-class yacht, as a wedding present. It is no coincidence that their daughter, Anne, the Princess Royal, and her granddaughter, Zara Tindall, are both Olympian equestrians. Anne has led the British

Olympic Association, since the mid-1980s. The influence and patronage of the Queen in promoting sporting pursuits may well have encouraged more women to take part in sport nationally. Women amateurs became increasingly visible to the general public in a wider range of sports in the approach to the Rome Olympic Games of 1960.

The woman who would go on to be the most significant of the British female fencers would not win a medal at the London Games of 1948. Mary Glen Haig (née James, 1918) contested the foil at four Olympic Games from 1948 to 1960. She participated in the British Empire Games (later the Commonwealth Games) from 1950 to 1958. She won gold medals in the fencing competition in both 1950 and 1954, representing England, and won a bronze medal in the individual foil at the 1958 British Empire and Commonwealth Games in Cardiff, Wales. A hospital administrator by profession, she was already an important leader, as Chairman of the Central Council of Physical Recreation during the 1970s. Glen Haig would become the first woman representing the BOA at the International Olympic Committee, in 1982. As an IOC representative she worked closely with The Princess Royal and led the first edition of the Women's Islamic Games in February 1993 and ensured the smooth running of the competitions.

At the first Women's Islamic Games, 407 athletes in eight different sports took part from such countries as Azerbaijan, Turkmenistan, Tajikistan, Kyrgyzstan, Bahrain, Bangladesh, Pakistan, Malaysia, Syria and Iran. She was made Dame Commander for services to sport in 1993. The Central Council for Physical Recreation was an important funder of amateur athletes, and it was not until the advent of Lottery Funding, introduced by John Major in the late 1990s, that UK Sports funding for professional Olympic athletes changed national fortunes. Whereas UK Sport had only £5 million funding in 1996, by Sydney 2000, it had £54 million, and by 2012, £264 million.

There was the issue of national prestige in the 1950s, that Olympic Games made more important. Elizabeth II was a constitutional monarch and Head of the Commonwealth, at the 1954 British Empire and Commonwealth Games in

Mary Glen Haig with foil, 1955

Iranian women's youth football team 2013

Vancouver as well as the 1956 Melbourne Olympic Games and the 1958 British Empire and Commonwealth Games in Cardiff. Although the Olympic movement remained ambulatory, hosted at Helsinki in 1952, and Rome in 1960, the role of the British in promoting the Olympic Games would continue to be considerable.

The 1951 England and Australia Test match series perhaps attracted more popular comment than usual because, in men's cricket, the South African team were to visit the same year and the rivalry was not so intense. It helped that in Festival of Britain year, Australia's women cricketers were defending their Test victory of 1948–1949. With one win each and a draw, the series was as much a victory for diplomacy and was followed by a Test against New Zealand in 1954. Helped by increasing prosperity, women's Test cricket became contested with more frequency. England travelled to Australia and New Zealand in 1957–1958 and 1968–1969; Australia returned to England in 1963; New Zealand revisited in 1966. Having hosted the Australians in a game versus the Midlands, Eileen White was the overall lead co-ordinator of the 1954 visit by New Zealand and oversaw the second Test match, played at the County Ground, Worcester.

The issue of how widely British cricket recruits its team members is still contentious. Neville Cardus felt in 1951 that the Australian women's cricket team came from a wider social background than the English team: Mollie Dive held a BSc from Sydney University and worked as a research officer in the Commonwealth Scientific Organisation; Ruth Dow was a fifth-year medical student; the opening bat, Mary Allit was a farmer and horse trainer; wicket keeper, Gladys Philips a machinist; Betty Wilson, a clerk and Amy Hudson a factory supervisor.

Women's cricket was the first in a series of female sports to set up a world cup competition in 1973 (two years before the men's competition was created), with women's football and rugby union following suit in 1991. At the 1993 Cricket Women's World Cup, teams from the following nations contested the honours: Australia, Denmark, England, Holland, Ireland, India, New Zealand and the West Indies. These matches were hosted at prestigious grounds, which included the John Player Sports Ground in Nottingham, Charterhouse College, Eton College, the Bank of England Sports Ground at Roehampton and Wellington College, Berkshire.

Rachael Heyhoe Flint was a cricketer, businesswoman and entrepreneur. She played for England from 1960 to 1982, becoming captain in 1966 until 1978. In this time, she was unbeaten in six tests and won the inaugural women's world cup in 1973, which

England hosted. She also played in goal for the England women's hockey team in 1964. She was one of the first ten women to join the MCC, until then an all-male club, and a director of Wolverhampton Wanderers Football Club. Ennobled to the Lords as a Conservative peer in 2011, she took the title Baroness Heyhoe Flint. A number of fixtures were named in her honour after her death, aged 77, and she had the honour of having a gate named after her at the MCC, although a mooted statue has yet to be erected. In 2020, The Rachael Heyhoe Flint Trophy, an English women's cricket domestic competition, was also named in her honour.

The All England Women's Hockey Association (AEWHA) formed in 1894, had encouraged the tradition that annual international matches became the 'club and school' day out for the whole hockey family. Women's international hockey matches dated from 1896 and in 1921 a match held in Old Deer Park, Richmond was attended by 1,809 spectators. A 1933 match at Merton Abbey was followed by a move to The Oval in 1935, holding 10,000 spectators. But crowds continued to grow and Mary Russell Vick, widely known as MRV, played as an international at the Oval, where her father-in-law, Godfrey, went along to watch and asked why the games were not at Wembley. Godfrey rang the former owner and Chairman of Wembley, Sir Arthur Elvin, and the first Wembley international was held in 1951 in front of 30,000 spectators who were encouraged to use special trains to get to the stadium. The Queen attended as a special guest in 1981. There were crowds of up to 68,000 and the fixture lasted until 1992.

Although the Queen was a Patron of the AEWHA, it still came as something of a surprise when she attended for lunch in a match against Wales. She was struck by the 65,000 spectators and, although God Save the Queen had been sung before the match, a second impromptu version was sung by the mainly schoolgirl crowd with

Heyhoe Flint in bat, August 1973. Photo: *Evening Standard*

considerable enthusiasm, and this touched her before she departed. A hand signed Thank You letter from Elizabeth was hung proudly in the AEWHA offices.

There were important women sports journalists writing from the 1950s onwards. There was a regular feature in *World Sports* on women's sport, written for an extended period by former national squash champion between 1932 and 1934 and tennis player, Susan Noel. Swimming journalist Pat Besford also contributed regularly but there were also many generalist pieces where women featured in the newspapers and magazines. Carolyn Dingle's *Sports For Girls,* published by the *News Chronicle* in 1951 provided a perspective on the sports that young women followed. One survey of 4,238 young female adults between 11–18 years of age conducted in 1951 showed a response of 96% to the question 'Are you interested in sport?' with 3.2% answering that they were not and 0.8% replying in the 'Don't Know' category.

The Olympics changed immeasurably when Cold War rivalries intensified nationalism from Helsinki 1952 onwards. Predating the wider Paralympic movement, equestrian Lis Hartel of Denmark, made Olympic history in the most inspiring way in 1952. At the age of 23, Hartel had been almost entirely paralysed by polio. Through riding and a regime of clinical exercise, she had gradually regained the use of most of her muscles, although she did not recover the use of her lower legs. Aged 35, Hartel made her Olympic debut by being lifted onto and off her horse, 'Jubilee'. Nevertheless, she took the silver medal with a score of 850, just 10 points behind the gold medallist Henri St-Cyr, who rode Master Rufus for Sweden to victory. André Jousseaume of France on 'Harpagon' took the bronze medal. Hartel was helped by St-Cyr onto the podium to receive her honour, and the medallists received their awards in tears.

Lis Hartel 1952 Summer Olympics in Helsinki. Photo: IOC

In 1954, Diane Leather, was the first woman to break the 5-minute barrier for the mile distance, just less than a month after Roger Bannister broke the 4-minute mile record in 1954. Although she had won two important silver European championships in the 800-metres, in 1954 and 1958, against leading Soviet contenders, the distance would not be included until 1960 in Rome, when she was past her racing best. It would not be until 1967 that

Angela Buxton, tennis star

the International Amateur Athletics Federation recognised a distance of a mile as an official women's event. Again, Diane Leather was ahead of her time and would otherwise, most likely, have become an Olympic medallist.

Tennis player Angela Buxton was not allowed to join the Cumberland Club in London because of her Jewish background although she was able to affiliate to Queen's. Travelling to the United States to try to develop her career, Buxton and her mother were also prevented from using the Los Angeles Tennis Club and instead practised on public courts. Buxton progressed to the elite nevertheless and would lose in the 1956 singles final at Wimbledon to American Shirley Irvin. This would be her most successful year, as she won the Ladies' doubles trophy with African American Althea Gibson, after the pair had also taken the French doubles title. Entrepreneur Simon Marks, co-owner of the Marks and Spencer chain of stores, who was also of Jewish heritage, allowed Buxton to use his private court to practise.

Both Gibson and Buxton had suffered discrimination that had hampered their tennis careers. This drew them together as doubles partners and friends for life. Gibson won the 1956, 1957 and 1958 Wimbledon doubles titles with Buxton, Darlene Hard and Maria Bueno. Bueno was a Brazilian world-class player, and she, along with Gibson and Buxton began to diversify Wimbledon winners, and Grand Slam title holders in women's tennis. But success could be short-lived, and precarious.

In the track and field athletics events at the Rome Olympics of 1960, America's Wilma Rudolph would take the 100-metres ahead of Dorothy Hyman for Britain and Giuseppina Leone for Italy. In the 200-metres, Rudolph took the second of her gold medals, ahead of Jutta Heine of the Unified Team of Germany and 19-year-old Hyman. Rudolph would lead the USA's 4x100 metres relay team to victory for her third gold medal, ahead of squads from Germany and Poland. Breaking three world records in the process, Rudolph was dubbed 'The Black Gazelle' by the European press for her speed, beauty and grace. The intersection of gender and ethnicity was implicit in what was meant to be a complimentary nickname, but which placed the African American athlete as exotic and 'other'.

Inspired by Polly Fairclough, who boxed in the late Victorian and Edwardian era, Barbara Buttrick was born in Cottingham, Yorkshire, England in 1930. A shorthand typist by profession, she also had the nickname 'The Mighty Atom of the Ring', and at less than five feet, weighed 98 lbs, becoming the world's unbeaten flyweight and bantamweight champion from 1950 to 1960. The National Fairground and Circus Archive at the University of Sheffield, holds a collection showing how she started her boxing career in 1948, touring Europe with carnivals as a bantamweight in the fairground booths with Professor Bosco and Sam McKeowen. She and other boxing pioneers, like Jane Couch, would campaign for women to have full boxing licenses, which Couch achieved in 1998. They made the way for later stars like Nicola Adams to win Olympic gold medals when the sport was added to the Olympic programme in 2012, before Adams progressed to professional boxing and later appeared with partner Katya Jones as the first same-sex couple on *Strictly Come Dancing*.

The Olympic Games could not keep up the pretence of amateur sport beyond 1984, when it was clear that state sponsored amateurs from various countries were actually professional athletes in all but name. By 1988, the Olympic Games had gone 'Open' to all elite athletes and had aspirations to become a world championship of sorts, although world cups were by now established. The British team was becoming more diverse. On 20 June 1984, the Royal Shakespeare Company (RSC) premiered *Golden Girls*, by playwright Louise Page at their smaller theatre, the Other Place, in Stratford-upon-Avon. Published in March 1985, *Golden Girls* featured a cast of three Black British and two white female aspiring Olympic track and field athletes. The plot followed the selection process, whereby one of the five principal characters would be left out of a squad of four, who would go on to compete as the British women's 4 × 100 metres relay team at a fictional forthcoming Athens Olympic Games. The overarching paradigm of the piece was the high personal cost of female ambition, and it was a critical success, moving to London's Barbican shortly after its debut. The drama also highlighted how important Black, Asian and ethnic minority women would be to Britain's Olympic history by the opening night of the play. Track and Field stars like Fatima Whitbread, Denise Lewis, and Tessa Sanderson would become household names, and Lewis would go on to present extensively on television after her 2000 gold medal win in the heptathlon. A £1 million sports hall was named in her honour at her old school in Wolverhampton.

Fatima Whitbread, throwing the javelin

The governance of world sport was also becoming more diverse and inclusive. Nawal El Moutawakel made history in 1984 when she became the first Moroccan, African and Muslim woman to win an Olympic gold medal. Nawal's iconic Olympic performance was watched live in her hometown of Casablanca in the early hours of the morning and locals poured onto the streets to celebrate. Her Olympic success earned her instant recognition in her country and the King of Morocco decreed that all girls born on the date of her victory were to be named in her honour.

In 1995, Nawal El Moutawakel became

Denise Lewis, 2000 Sydney Olympics

a council member of the International Association of Athletics Federations, and two years later, she became the first Muslim woman ever to be elected to the International Olympic Committee (IOC). A member of the IOC Women and Sports Commission, the IOC Marketing Commission and the IOC International Relations Commission, in 2004 she was appointed Chair of the IOC Evaluation Commission for the 2012 Olympic Games. In January 2010, she was appointed Chair of the IOC's Co-ordination Commission for Rio and in July 2012 she was elected a Vice-President of the International Olympic Committee – the first woman from a Muslim and Arab nation ever to be elected.

The FIFA Women's World Cup, first held in China in 1991, moved in 1995 to Sweden, the USA in 1999, and 2003, before returning to China in 2007. This reflected changing international sporting relations where Brazil, India, and China became more important as host countries in the 21st century. A more globalised audience could follow events such as these due to the rise of the internet in the 1990s, and, after the millennium, the spread of social media. Social media would be particularly significant for women's sports because the world media scape was also changing.

Rupert Murdoch's move to own several tabloid newspapers in the UK, and on to television in the USA has been dubbed the 'Murdochisation' of the media. The tabloid values of misogyny, drama, populist and sensational stories tended to marginalise women's sport, even from the back pages of these publications. Whereas there had been a range of women journalists working in sport, the Murdoch era homogenised sports writing as a 'male' domain. Although this was a backward step, it was widely influential, so that even the BBC Sports Personality of the Year had no female nominees in 2011, the year before the third London Olympic Games, a historic first in world sport.

The head of BBC sport, Barbara Slater, had presided over the London 2012 Olympics and Paralympics as the largest television event in British broadcasting history, but had previously relied upon print broadcasting journalists to shortlist sportsmen and women, and journalists for publications like *The Sun*, and *The Daily Mail* were included as judges.

Women athletes have cultivated their social media feeds as ways of developing their off-pitch endorsements and sponsors. Gymnast Simone Biles, and pro wrestlers [Natalie] Eva Marie, Paige and Natalya Neidhart are amongst the most popular. World Cup winner and Olympic football star Alex Morgan has 9.3 million Instagram followers, 4 million Twitter followers, and 3.5 Facebook followers, indicating a range of different social media users. Tennis star Sania Mirza from India has 9 million Twitter followers, 14 million Facebook followers, and 6.2 million Instagram followers, reflecting a different demographic than Serena Williams, who has 12.2 million Instagram followers, 10.9 million Twitter followers, and 5.9 million Facebook users. But visibility is important and previous stars who have retired, like Ultimate Fighting Championship competitor, Ronda Rousey, have fewer followers now than in the past.

The fight for equal pay has been a slow process. In tennis, previously, the disparity in the number of sets, with five contested by men as opposed to three sets for women, was used as an excuse to maintain the gender pay gap. The claim being, that men play best in five set matches, and women play best in three set matches. The argument was that men were entitled to a greater pay packet because they played more sets and provided a longer period of entertainment. Wimbledon was the last of the Grand Slam tournaments, along with the French Open, to move to equal pay for both genders in 2007.

In the US, a collective bargaining agreement was agreed in 2022 after a long dispute. Although often called equal pay for the men's and women's teams, it hid the fact that the women had been paid less for winning world cups than the men's national team had been paid for not doing as well. The reason for this is the disparity in the overall prize money for men's world cups, which was $791 million in 2018 in Russia, up from $576 million in 2014. The Women's World Cup in 2019 had a total prize of $30 million. The gap between the prize money is actually growing, with the women able to take home $4million for winning the tournament. This is a tenth of what the male winners take home. Pay equality for the US team follows similar pledges by major national football teams, including Brazil, Australia, Norway, New Zealand and all four UK teams. But few women players earn enough money as a professional footballer to sustain themselves.

However, although the Olympic Games and world sport are now more diverse, it is important to understand how there is a strong continuity in the patriarchal governance of the most significant sporting organisations. A case in point is [Mokgadi] Caster Semenya, widely known as Caster Semenya, a South African middle-distance runner and winner of two Olympic gold medals, in London 2012, and Rio de Janeiro in 2016, and three World Championships (2009, 2011 and 2017) in the women's 800 metres. She held both gold medals in the 2018 Gold Coast Commonwealth Games

Eva Marie, WrestleMania 32 Axxess in 2016

WOMEN IN SPORT: POST-WAR TO TODAY

Caster Semenya at 2012 London Olympics

for the 800m and the 1500m. She is a multiple African Games and African Championships gold medallist. Since 2019, Semenya has had to contend with assertions made by World Athletics that she required gender verification tests to run as a woman. New rules specifically targeting the distances that Semenya ran were introduced in April 2018, and this mean that she had to try and run in 200 metres or 5000 metres. Attempting these distances, she did not qualify for the 2021 Olympics, and legal battles over the World Athletics ruling on testosterone meant that she could not compete in the 2019 World Athletics Championships. Many commentators view the World Athletics ruling by a white European-male led elite, led by President Sebastian Coe, as discriminating against women from the global south. The IOC, now almost 130 years old, has never had a female President. Nor has FIFA, the world governing body of football, formed in 1904. Changes in the governance of sport are long overdue and much needed.

In spite of these structural forces, women and girls have found considerable self-determination and agency in relation to sport, and some, such as LGBTQ+ football players Megan Rapinoe, and Marta, have used elite sport as a platform for greater gender equity. Marta has been named FIFA World Player of the Year six times, five consecutively, from 2006 to 2010, and most recently in 2018. With 17 goals, Marta holds the record for most goals scored in the FIFA World Cup tournament, women's or men's. She was the first footballer, (male or female), to score at five World Cup editions, which was matched by Christine Sinclair in 2019, and also the first female footballer to score at five consecutive Olympic Games. As more women become defined as individuals, rather than defined by gender, the future for sport looks increasingly bright. Even Marta's dogs have their own Instagram account.

This trajectory for women's sports to attract more high-level sponsorship will continue. A lot of financial brands who lost credibility in the 2008 banking crisis have moved into women's sports: Mastercard sponsor women's rugby, Barclays and Nationwide Building Society sponsor women's football. Pepsi and Coca Cola, as well as personal hygiene and cosmetics brands also sponsor a range of women's sport and these sponsorships are becoming increasingly lucrative. Fashion is another huge

Emma Raducanu

industry partner with British tennis star Emma Raducanu making her Met Ball debut in 2021, shortly after winning the US Open, wearing printed monochrome Chanel.

The rise of women's sports, and of women in the sports industry more widely, has been inexorable since 1945, but heavily contested. The recent decision to withdraw US and UK troops from Afghanistan, as it passed into Taliban control occasioned the need for the women's football team from that country to be smuggled out, along with their friends and family. That the Taliban perceive sport to be something that women should be prohibited from doing, under a regime of 'traditional' values, highlights the fact that gains made by women and girls to access a wider range of leisure activities, can be lost quite quickly.

Where the human rights of women are ignored or abused, who can blame women athletes, fearful of reprisals, for fleeing their homeland? Women's astonishing sporting achievements often challenge outdated notions of femininity in those nations which have yet to grant women equal rights. Gone are the stereotypes that women are not as strong or fast as men, as ultra-endurance athletes, like triathlete Chrissie Wellington, have shown. There is much then to celebrate in both team and individual disciplines, and increased diversity in our female sporting heroes.

Chrissie Wellington, leading in the Frankfurt Ironman race 2008

Fatima Diame, jumping for Spain. Photo: J. Fontan

Habiba Ghribi taking a silver (later gold) medal at London 2012. Photo: Citizen59

Bethany Hamilton surfing, 2016. Photo: Troy Williams

GREAT PARALYMPIANS

Gemma Lumsdaine

The Paralympic Games is now the pinnacle of disability sport, and it is almost every disabled athlete's dream to represent their country at a Paralympic Games and win a medal. Over the last 70 years the Paralympic movement has grown significantly, and this has helped to challenge perceptions around disability and create more opportunities for disabled people both on and off the field of play.

When thinking about the history of the Paralympics there is one name which stands out – Sir Ludwig Guttmann. German-born Guttmann understood the importance of sports participation for injured servicemen and women's physical and mental health, and regularly encouraged individuals to get active as part of their rehabilitation at Stoke Mandeville Hospital where he worked.

The growing significance of the role of sport within the rehabilitation process led to the first milestone in paralympic history, in 1948, when Guttmann organized a sporting event for 16 wheelchair users at the same time as the opening ceremony of the Olympic Games. This was the first-ever competition for wheelchair athletes and the first time both disabled and non-disabled people were competing simultaneously in sporting events, hence the term Paralympics, which stands for the 'Parallel Olympics'.

In 1960, one of Guttman's patients at Stoke Mandeville Hospital would soon put his philosophy about the significance of sport to the test. When the first Paralympic Games took place in Rome – the incredible Margaret Maughan was ready to compete.

Margaret Maughan (1928-2020) cemented her place in paralympic history when she became Great Britain's first ever Paralympic Gold Medallist. She competed in two events in Rome: firstly, the Women's Archery Columbia Open where she scored 484 points to secure Britain's first ever gold medal. The fact that the first of Team GB's medals there was won by a woman helped to raise the profile of women's sporting capabilities in general.

Maughan competing. Photo: wheelpower

Maughan went on to win the Women's S5 50-metre backstroke race, principally because she was the only competitor to complete the race that initial year.

After experiencing success in Archery and Swimming at the 1960 Rome Paralympics, she continued to work hard and develop her sporting abilities in a number of different sports including Dartchery (a combination of darts and archery) and Lawn Bowls. Once again, she excelled at these and gained multiple Paralympic medals over a number of years. During her sports career, Maughan competed in five Paralympic Games, winning four golds and two silvers in an impressive range of four different sports.

Even after Maughan had retired from competing in sport she continued to champion disability sport and promote the positive effect that sport can have on disabled people. Maughan finally got the recognition she deserved in 2012 when she was given the honour of lighting the flame at the opening of the London 2012 Paralympic Games. This was a fitting tribute to mark her pioneering contribution to the Paralympic movement over four decades.

Another extraordinary paralympian swimmer who followed Maughan is American Trischa Zorn (1964-). Blind from birth, she competed in paralympic swimming (S12, SB12, and SM12 disability categories). She is the most successful athlete in the history of the Paralympic Games, having won 55 medals (41 gold, 9 silver, and 5 bronze), and was inducted into the Paralympic Hall of Fame in 2012. She studied at the University of Nebraska and now teaches children with special needs. She advocates the inclusionary teaching model, which lets special needs students integrate with their classmates and have richer learning experiences. She now works with the Indiana Pro Bono Commission in Indianapolis, USA.

Grey-Tompson in Sydney, 2012.
Photo: www.tanni.co.uk

In 1988, another powerhouse within disability sport came to prominence – the inspirational Tanni Grey-Thomson DBE (1969-), who was born with spina bifida. Grey-Thompson's sporting prowess is legendary. Her career in wheelchair racing spanned over sixteen years and she participated in five Paralympic Games. Within that time she has broken 30 world records and has won an incredible 15 paralympic medals. Grey-Thompson's results prove how talented, determined and tenacious she is. These characteristics don't just describe her on the field, they encapsulate the kind of person she is off the field too, leveraging her public profile to advocate for the disabled community.

Through her roles on many charity boards and as an independent crossbench peer in the House of Lords, since 2010, she has fought tirelessly to improve provision and opportunities for people with a disability, particularly with regard to accessibility of services. As well as focusing on disability rights, Grey-Thompson has also spent a large amount of time on improving Duty of Care in Sport. One of her key priorities has been looking at the support athletes receive when transitioning out of sport.

Recently, Grey-Thompson has been appointed Chair of Sport Wales which is a big step forward in terms of representation for women in leadership and disability. Named a BBC Personality of the Year three times, in 2019, she was justly given the BBC Sports Personality of the Year Lifetime Achievement Award.

In terms of inspiring others, Sarah Storey (1977-) has to be in the vanguard. She is Britain's most decorated and successful Paralympian. A former swimmer, she is now a world record-setting para-cyclist and has competed at the very top of both sports. Overcoming many personal and physical challenges, she is an icon of the Paralympics as well as a stunning example of a female athlete breaking down barriers.

Storey became adept at several sports from a young age, including swimming. She competed at her first Paralympic Games in Barcelona in 1992, aged 14, where she won six medals including two golds. In the following Paralympics, she took home another five medals including three golds, becoming the only Paralympian to win five gold medals before she turned 19. She competed in a further two Paralympic Games in 2000 and 2004 where she won further swimming medals. Overall, Storey's tally of medals from swimming includes five paralympic golds, eight silvers and three bronze medals as well as five world titles.

She took up cycling in 2005 and by the end of her first year in the sport, Storey had broken a world record in para-cycling and won three golds at the European Championships. With her sights set on competing in another Paralympic Games, she took her first two silver medals at the

Sarah Storey with medal haul, 2012

Storey competing as a cyclist

Para-cycling Road World Championships in 2006, and her first world title in the Individual Pursuit at the Paracycling Track World Championships the following year. At the Beijing Paralympics in 2008, Storey met the weight of high expectations and won two gold medals at her inaugural Games as a cyclist. She competed at a further three Paralympic Games and took a further ten gold medals, and at 44 years old, competed at the Tokyo 2020 Paralympics in 2021, where she won gold again three times.

Like American skier Diane Golden (1963-2001) who challenged stereotypes and persuaded the US Ski Association to allow disabled skiers to compete against non-disabled skiers, in her cycling career Storey has destroyed expectations about what athletes with disabilities can achieve.

Shortly after her first paralympic cycling performances in 2008, Storey competed in the National Track Championships where she won the Individual Pursuit race against non-disabled competitors. She has since claimed national titles in multiple events. In 2010 she became the first para-cyclist to compete for England at the Commonwealth Games, again riding against non-para cyclists.

In racquet sports, Mary Vergeer (1981-), a Dutch wheelchair tennis player, achieved an impressive four Paralympic singles tennis gold medals, three Paralympics double tennis gold medals, 48 Grand Slam tournaments, 23 Wheelchair Tennis Masters' Championships and seven Paralympics titles. For almost 15 years, from 1999, Vergeer was the world number one wheelchair tennis player, retiring undefeated in singles matches having won 148 singles titles.

In Asia too, the appeal of the Paralympics has been growing. In the 2008 Summer Paralympics in Beijing, under the slogan 'One World, One Dream', almost four thousand athletes from 146 countries took part, the largest number of nations ever to compete.

Alison Yu Chui Yee (1984-) from Hong Kong, who had to have her left leg amputated as a child due to bone cancer, was one of the competitors. Switching from swimming to wheelchair fencing as a teen, she won four gold medals at the 2004 Summer Paralympics, in both the individual and

Wheelchair fencer, Yu Chui Yee

GREAT PARALYMPIANS

Christiansen competing at 2012 Olympics

team events of épée and foil. Although team matches were cancelled at the 2008 Summer Paralympics, she achieved both a gold medal and a silver medal in the individual events. Yu Chui Yee has gone on from competing, to host a radio show and co-found a Fencing Academy too.

Sophie Christiansen CBE (1987-) is a Grade 1 Para Dressage Rider who has been involved in the Paralympics since Athens 2004 where she won a bronze medal at just 16 years old. From then onwards, there's been no stopping Christiansen. She has participated in four Paralympics (Athens, 2004, Beijing 2008, London 2012 and Rio 2016) and has won a total of eight golds, one silver and a bronze.

It isn't just her medal haul that impresses, but the fact that Christiansen challenges perceptions around disability. Not only is she a dedicated athlete, but she has achieved success academically gaining a first-class MA in Mathematics from the University of London, currently working as a Software Developer. Christiansen is also a disability activist and focused on encouraging the next generation of Para Riders. She has established her own club, which other riders with disabilities can join, and where they can learn from the best.

Paralympic athletes have gained visibility on TV screens around the world and are now accorded respect and recognition for their sporting abilities as athletes, no longer seen just as athletes with a disability. While there is still a need to challenge outdated notions and stereotypes of disabled people in society and to fight for disability rights in general, paralympians lead the way in demonstrating that it is possible to overcome daunting obstacles and achieve lasting success on the world stage.

Gemma Lumsdaine

Gemma Lumsdaine is a member of the GB Wheelchair Rugby Talent Squad which helps to prepare athletes to make the step to the Paralympic Squad. Gemma is also in the Scottish Disability Sport Athlete Academy.

Prior to wheelchair rugby, she played wheelchair basketball at a national level. She also coaches wheelchair sports for Dundee Dragons Wheelchair Sports Club and won the COVA Young Coach of the Year in 2018. Lumsdaine sits on the Scottish Women and Girls in Sport Advisory Board and has been a member of the Scottish Disability Sport Young People's Panel. She was also named as one of the the Shaw Trust Disability Power 100 in 2021.

Nicola Adams *(left)* in the ring with Isabel Millan. Photo: *Morning Star*

50 WOMEN IN SPORT

PIONEERS AND LEGENDS

Three young women swimmers with their medals
c.1920s. Photo: Library of Congress

TONI STONE

Toni Stone (1921-1996) was a trailblazing American baseball player. The first woman to play professional baseball in a men's league, she overcame racism and sexism to expand opportunities for women in her sport.

Stone was born in July, 1921 in West Virginia and named Marcenia Lyle Stone. As a child she thrived in many sports, but after her family moved to Minnesota when she was 10 years old, Stone started focussing on baseball. She began playing in the Clavers Catholic Church team in the Catholic Midget League, to the disapproval of her parents. In her mid-teens she started playing for the all-male, semi-professional team, the Twin Cities Colored Giants. The team was also a barnstorming team which toured the Midwest and Canada. It seems that Stone soon dropped out of high school to focus on playing baseball.

Although Major League Baseball was integrated by baseball heroes like Jackie Robinson in the 1940s, the women's game remained unofficially segregated throughout the decade. Nevertheless, the migration of Black male players from the all-Black Negro Leagues to the major leagues would provide the opportunity for Stone to become the first woman to play in the Negro Leagues. After moving to California in the 1940s, Stone started going by 'Toni' Stone and worked odd jobs while playing for a local

TONI STONE

American Legion team and waiting for chances to arise. She finally got her start at professional baseball in 1949, when she played for the San Franscisco Sea Lions, part of the West Coast Negro Baseball League.

From the Sea Lions, Toni moved on to the New Orleans Creoles and the New Orleans Black Pelicans, where she played second base. Then, in 1953, she was signed to the Indianapolis Clowns, taking over second base from Hank Aaron, who went on to become one of the greatest Major League players of all time. Toni played there for one season. Although the Clowns' owners denied accusations that they had taken Stone on to garner publicity, her presence did attract attention and high attendance figures. But she was also a good player. Over two years she recorded a batting average of .243 and allegedly returned a ball thrown by legendary pitcher Satchel Paige.

Toni played the next season with the Kansas City Monarchs, after which she retired in 1954. Throughout her career she faced sexism, not only from the press but from the players, and was not allowed in the players' locker rooms. Yet her perseverance in the face of such treatment undoubtedly opened doors for other women. She was replaced as second base of the Indianapolis Clowns by another woman, Connie Morgan, and the Clowns added pitcher Mamie 'Peanut' Johnson to the roster in the same year.

These women followed Toni as the second and third women ever to play professional baseball.

Although she lived the rest of her life quietly, working as a nurse and caring for her husband until he died in the 1980s, her hometown of Saint Paul, Minnesota, celebrated her in 1990 by declaring 6 March 'Toni Stone Day.' Toni was introduced to the Baseball Hall of Fame in 1991 and the International Women's Sports Hall of Fame in 1993.

She died in 1996 and a play based on her career titled *Tomboy Stone* by Roger Nieboer was staged at the Great American History Theater. In 2019, another play titled *Toni Stone* written by Lydia Diamond premiered Off-Broadway based on Martha Ackmann's biography, *Curveball: The Remarkable Story of Toni Stone.*

Stone batting. Photo: localwiki.org/oakland

Photo: Fred Palumbo

ALTHEA GIBSON

Althea Gibson (1927-2003) was a trailblazing African American tennis player who broke down barriers for future Black tennis players. She was born to sharecropper parents in segregated South Carolina, but when she was 3 years old, her family moved to Harlem, New York, the heart of Black America. Here she learned paddle tennis, which she played in the Harlem streets, becoming a local champion. She caught the attention of jazz musician Buddy Walker and local tennis teacher Fred Johnson, who introduced her to tennis and helped her gain entry to tournaments run by the American Tennis Association (ATA), the Black version of the whites-only US Lawn Tennis Association (USTA). She won her first local tournament in 1941, and from 1947 she won the ATA's women's singles championship ten years in a row.

Her tennis skills earned her a scholarship to Florida Agricultural and Mechanical University in 1949, the same year she became the first African American woman to play in the USTA's National Indoor Championships, where she reached the quarter finals. Despite her achievements, tennis was still a segregated sport and Gibson was barred from many of the world's most prestigious competitions until, in 1950, four-time US

National Champion Alice Marble publicly condemned Gibson's exclusion from the sport. Althea played at the US National Championships that year, the first African American player ever to do so. She also became the first Black player to compete at Wimbledon in 1951.

By 1955 Gibson had reached national and international renown, embarking on a six-month tour of southeast Asia with three white players sponsored by the State Department. Then, in 1956 she gained her first two Grand Slam victories at the French Open, as women's singles champion and doubles champion. Her doubles partner was Angela Buxton, a Jewish player who had also faced discrimination on the tour, and who became Gibson's lifelong friend. The following year, Gibson won Wimbledon and finally gained victory at the US Open. She became only the second African American to receive a ticker-tape parade down Broadway, appeared on the front covers of *Time* and *Sports Illustrated*, and was announced as the *Associated Press*'s Female Athlete of the Year, the first African American woman to earn the title.

Between 1956 and 1958, Gibson won eleven Grand Slam titles, including five singles titles, five doubles titles and a mixed doubles title. In 1958 she attempted to ascend to professional level, touring with the Harlem Globetrotters, playing in exhibition matches and competing in smaller tournaments. Ahead of the start of the Open Era in 1968, this was not a lucrative option and Gibson retired from tennis shortly afterwards. After releasing an album and acting in a John Wayne film in 1959, and publishing a memoir in 1960, Gibson turned her attention to golf. She became the first Black woman to join the Ladies Professional Golf Association tour in 1964.

Althea Gibson is congratulated by Darlene Hard after winning the 1957 Wimbledon Women's Singles Championship

Althea Gibson's career engendered many firsts and saw her reach the top of the women's game, yet she faced much discrimination and struggled to garner recognition from the tennis community. Although she was inducted into the International Tennis Hall of Fame in 1971, she suffered financially throughout her later life and was not celebrated by USTA until the unveiling of the Althea Gibson Sculpture Garden at Flushing Meadows, the home of the US Open, in 2019. She died in relative obscurity in September 2003. She had been married twice, and had no children. Despite the lack of praise from the tennis establishment, she has been hailed by the likes of Billie Jean King and Serena Williams as a hero and pioneer for the game of tennis.

BARBARA BUTTRICK

Barbara Buttrick (1929-) was born in Cottingham, East Riding, in Yorkshire. She is a former boxer and Women's World Boxing Champion who fought against prejudice and sexism to achieve legendary status in her sport.

Buttrick first became inspired to try boxing after reading about an early women's boxing pioneer, Polly Burns. She started training as a teenager and by 18 had moved to London, being coached by her future husband Leonard Smith, while working as a typist. She began her career in 1948, touring with fairs and carnivals as a sideshow booth act in which she would challenge women from the audience to try and beat her. She became known as "The Mighty Atom of the Ring" for her ferocity despite her 4ft 11 inch stature.

Her participation in boxing matches, including with men, provoked a great deal of criticism in the British press, culminating in calls for a boycott of her exhibition match against a man at the Kilburn Empire in 1949. By the early 1950s she had moved with her husband to the United States, training at Miami's famous 5th Street Gym, where she met future boxing icon Muhammad Ali. Although she started her career in the US in the carnival circuit, she soon turned professional and participated in the first women's

boxing matches ever held in a number of states.

Throughout the 1950s she was the unbeaten flyweight and bantamweight champion, winning the first-ever Women's World Boxing Championship by beating Phyllis Kugler in 1957.

During her career, Buttrick competed in over 1,000 exhibition matches, including fighting many matches against men, and claims to have broken three noses. In her professional career, she won 30 matches, drawing one and losing only one against Joanna Hagen, who was significantly taller and heavier than her. She took part in her final match while four months pregnant with her first child.

After retiring from boxing, Buttrick continued to be a leader in her sport. She helped found and was president of the Women's International Boxing Federation in the 1990s, and was inducted into the International Women's Boxing Hall of Fame in 2014.

She has recently been praised as a pioneer by the boxer Nicola Adams, who became the first British woman to win a women's boxing gold medal at the London 2012 Olympics. (see p. 76)

A play inspired by her achievements was performed as part of Hull's 2017 UK City of Culture festivities. It was entitled *Delicate Flowers* and written by Mark Rees. Buttrick has also appeared in a number of documentaries about legendary women boxers.

Buttrick herself has reflected in interviews on how her efforts to participate in boxing were also a fight against sexism, and has expressed satisfaction that women's boxing is far more accepted and accessible today, progress which she helped to facilitate.

LARISA LATYNINA

Larisa Latynina (1934-) is a former artistic gymnast who received the most Olympic gold medals of any woman in history. Until 2012, she had earned the most medals of any athlete, male or female, and is recognised today as one of the greatest gymnasts of all time. She helped catapult the Soviet gymnastic team to international success and renown.

She was born in Kherson, a city in southern Ukraine. Her father was killed in the Battle of Stalingrad and she was raised by her mother. Initially interested in ballet, she moved away from dance and became focussed on gymnastics in her early teens (although she has said she incorporated a balletic style into her gymnastics routines). She made her international debut, aged 19, at the 1954 Rome World Championships, where she contributed to the Soviet Union's team all-around victory.

Latynina attended her first Olympic Games in 1956 in Melbourne, where she became a sensation. Triumphing in the all-around event, vault, floor exercise and as part of the team event, she also won silver on the uneven bars and bronze at the team apparatus. From then, she dominated the sport for eight years, taking home

LARISA LATYNINA

five gold medals at the 1957 European Championships and five at the 1958 World Championships. At the 1960 Rome Games, she won gold in the all-around event, the floor exercise and the team event, and also took home two silver medals and a bronze. Remarkably, Latynina was pregnant at the 1960 Games, although she had not confided this to anyone for fear of being stopped from competing. She went on to have a son, and was married three times. She appeared at her final Olympic Games in Tokyo in 1964, capping her achievements by becoming the only woman ever to win a medal for the all-around event at three consecutive Olympic Games, and only one of three women ever to win gold for the same event three times, for the floor exercise.

Over the course of her career, she became the world's most decorated Olympian, with 18 medals, a feat not surpassed for 48 years. She also earned fourteen medals at the World Championships, including nine gold medals, and fourteen medals at the European Championships. While still competing, she completed a graduate programme at the Kiev State Institute of Physical Education.

After retiring from competing in 1966, Latynina turned to coaching, guiding the Soviet women's gymnastics team to victory in the team event at the Olympics in 1968, 1972 and 1976. She was involved in the planning of the 1980 Moscow Olympic Games. She remains a sporting hero in the former Soviet Union; the Larisa Latynina School of Artistic Gymnastics was named in her honour in Obninsk, Russia, in 2007. She was inducted into the International Women's Sports Hall of Fame 1985. In a 2012 interview she attributed her success to her strong focus and desire to win.

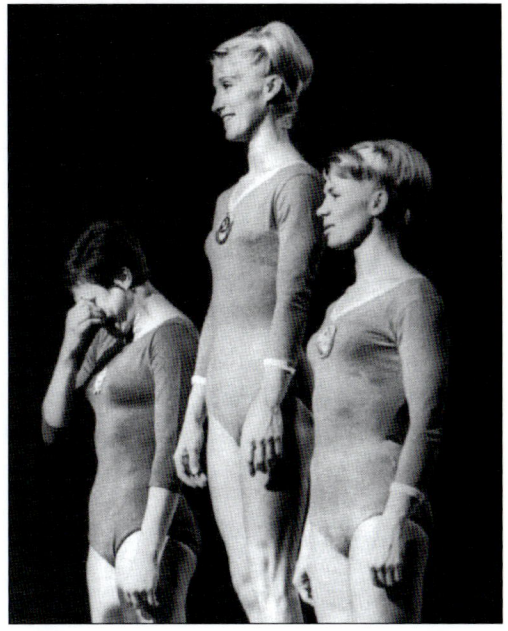

Photo: Fred Palumbo

KRYSTYNA CHOJNOWSKA-LISKIEWICZ

Krystyna Chojnowska-Liskiewicz (1936-2021) was a Polish sailor who completed the first solo circumnavigation of the globe by a woman.

She was born in Warsaw in Poland. After World War II, her family moved to Ostróda, where Chojnowska-Liskiewicz first became interested in boats and learned to sail. She studied shipbuilding engineering at the Gdańsk University of Technology, where she met her husband Waclaw, who would later oversee the construction of the yacht for Krystyna's famous voyage. As well as working in shipbuilding, Chojnowska-Liskiewicz continued to sail, undertaking a voyage from Poland to Scotland with an all-female crew, and a journey to the Gulf of Bothnia with just one other crewmate. This experience proved vital when, in 1975, the Polish Sailing Association launched a competition to choose the first woman to sail around the world, to coincide with the United Nation's International Women's Year: they selected Chojnowska-Liskiewicz as their candidate.

Preparations including the building of Chojnowska-Liskiewicz's 32-foot yacht *Mazurek*, took several months. On 10 March 1976, she began her voyage from Las Palmas in the Canary Islands; this first attempt was thwarted by the failure of the yacht's auto-steering system, and she was forced to return to Las Palmas. Undeterred, she set out again on what would be her successful voyage on 28 March 1976. She began by crossing the Atlantic, passing through the Panama Canal, then crossed the Pacific and went on to Australia, where she remained for several months and was reunited with her husband. After this she travelled across the Indian Ocean, arriving in Cape Town in early 1978. From there, she set out on her final leg, arriving back in Las Palmas on 21 April 1978. She had travelled over 28,500 nautical miles, over 401 days of sailing.

Chojnowska-Liskiewicz faced remarkable challenges on her journey. As well as treacherous conditions and the failure of technology and damage to her yacht, she was also hospitalised for a kidney condition, apparently had her boat searched for drugs in Fiji, and once temporarily lost her boat when its anchor broke and it drifted away. She was often accompanied by pods of dolphins on her voyage.

While in Cape Town, she learned that she was in close competition with another woman who was attempting to sail the globe, Naomi James. James completed her journey 39 days after Chojnowska-Liskiewicz. These two women set the stage for the achievements of Australian Kay Cottee, who completed the first nonstop singlehanded loop of the world in 1988, and Dame Ellen MacArthur, the English sailor who broke the world record for the fastest circumnavigation of the globe in 2005, among other yachtswomen.

Chojnowska-Liskiewicz had garnered global media attention on her voyage and was welcomed back to Poland to mass acclaim. She was awarded the Commander's Cross of the Order of Polonia Restituta and was declared Gdansk's Citizen of the Year in 1978. She published a book detailing her voyage in 1979. According to the Polish Sailing Association she helped to popularise sailing in her native country.

She died in 2021, aged 84.

Krystyna Chojnowska-Liskiewicz on the Conrad 32 sloop, *Mazurek*

Junko Tabei, 1985 Photo: Jaan Künnap

JUNKO TABEI

Junko Tabei (1939-2016; née Ishibashi) was a Japanese mountain climber who challenged gender restrictions and stereotypes in Japan to become the first woman in the world to climb Mount Everest.

Tabei was only 4 foot 9 inches tall and was reportedly weak as a child. Nevertheless, after a school trip to some nearby mountains, Junko fell in love with climbing, aged 10. Although her family could not afford for her to pursue her hobby seriously in her childhood, she joined a men's climbing club after graduating from the Showa Women's University in 1962. She was met with suspicion and derision by some men in the group, who accused her of only participating in order to find a husband. However, Tabei became a proficient and well-known mountain climber and had reached the summit of Japan's highest mountains by the mid-1960s. She did also meet her future husband, mountaineer Masanobu Tabei, on an excursion on Mount Tanigawa. He supported her and helped raise their children when her hobby evolved into a more serious undertaking.

In 1969, Tabei founded a women-only climbing club, the Joshi-Tohan club, which carried the slogan "Let's go on an overseas expedition by ourselves." This is exactly what the club did in 1972, when they became only the second group ever to reach the

Mt Everest, 2016. Photo: Wang Lama Humla

summit of Annapurna III in Nepal, via a new route. They already had their sights set on higher peaks, having applied to put the club on the waiting list to climb Everest in 1971. They were accepted for the climb in 1975. However, the fifteen members of the club (including working women and mothers) faced a struggle to generate sponsorship for the expedition. Tabei recalled contacting potential sponsors only to be told to focus on childrearing instead.

Fiinally, some last-minute sponsors emerged (after the women had contributed financially themselves), and the Joshi-Tohan club made it to the base camp of Everest. After commencing the climb, the group were hit by an avalanche. Tabei was completely buried and had to be rescued by nearby Sherpas. Although she could not walk for several days, she was determined to continue. More challenges were ahead, as altitude sickness meant that Tabei was the only woman able to complete the climb. As she approached the summit, she encountered an icy ridge that she had not expected, having read the accounts of previous climbers. She crawled across this dangerous section and, twelve days after she was buried in an avalanche, at the age of 35 and as a mother of two, Junko Tabei made history as the first woman to reach the summit of the world's tallest mountain, accompanied by Sherpa guide Ang Tsering.

Tabei became famous instantly, but downplayed her achievement, stating that she was 'the 36th person to climb Everest' and eschewing corporate sponsors. Nevertheless, she continued to be a trailblazer in the world of climbing, becoming the first woman to climb the highest mountain on all seven continents by 1992.

She returned to education to study ecology after becoming concerned about the destructive effects of climber traffic on Mount Everest, and headed the Himalayan Adventure Trust of Japan. She continued climbing into her later life despite a diagnosis of stomach cancer in 2012, and even led an expedition of young people, who had been affected by the Fukushima nuclear disaster, to climb Mount Fuji in 2016.

She died that year aged 77.

On Communism (Ismail Samani) Peak in 1985. From left: Alfred Lõhmus, Jaan Künnap, Kalev Muru, Junko Tabei and Ilmar Priimets. In front: Nobuko Yanagisawa and Mayuri Yasuhara. Photo: Jaan Künnap

Billie Jean King in Iowa, 2016. Photo: Gage Skidmore

BILLIE JEAN KING

Billie Jean King (1943-) is a former Grand Slam tennis champion, gender equality advocate and an LGBTQ+ icon.

    Billie Jean Moffitt was born in Long Beach, California, to an athletic family. Her father had been close to becoming an NBA player, her mother was a keen swimmer and her brother Randy Moffitt was a Major League Baseball pitcher. Billie Jean herself started her sporting career playing basketball and then baseball, before being introduced to tennis in the fifth grade. She practised on Long Beach's public tennis courts and earned the money to buy her first racket. She started competing as a teenager in the 1950s, winning her age bracket at the Southern California championship. The former US Open winner Alice Marble became her coach in 1959 and King won her first Grand Slam at Wimbledon in 1961 as part of a doubles team. Her and her partner, Karen Hantze Susman, were the youngest pair ever to win the title.

    She attended California State University in Los Angeles from 1961-64, where she met Larry King, whom she married in 1965. A year later, King won her first singles Grand Slam at Wimbledon. This victory heralded a new phase in King's career, and she became No. 1 in the singles rankings for the first time. The following year she won the singles, doubles and mixed doubles titles at Wimbledon and the US Open and was

Billy Jean King & Bobby Riggs 1973

named the Associated Press's Female Athlete of the Year. By 1980 Billie had won an astounding 39 Grand Slam titles: 12 singles titles, 16 women's doubles and 11 mixed doubles titles.

Having turned professional, she became the first woman to earn over $100,000 in prize money in a single year. However, she was unhappy with the disparity in prize money between the men's and the women's game, declaring after her US Open victory in 1972 that she would not play the following year if the prizes were not equal. Her campaigning led to the creation of the Virginia Slims Circuit tour in the early 1970s, the first women's professional tour. In 1973, following her efforts, the US Open became the first major competition to offer equal prize money. In the same year King helped found and became the first president of the Women's Tennis Association.

Former singles champion Bobby Riggs had claimed that the women's game was inferior to men's and had set out to prove it, beating No. 1 women's player (and King's rival) Margaret Court in 1973. That same year he challenged King and they met in what was dubbed 'The Battle of the Sexes.' 29-year-old King beat 59-year-old Riggs in straight sets and won the $100,000 prize, watched by a record audience of 50 million. Her victory is seen as a milestone in the fight for equality in women's sport.

After being publicly outed in 1981, King became an advocate for gay rights and in 1991 won the Arthur Ashe Award for Courage. She retired as a player in 1984 and became the first woman commissioner in professional sports with the World Team Tennis League. She captained the US Fed Cup team to victory for many years. The tournament was renamed the Billie Jean King Cup in 2020 in her honour. Among dozens of other accolades, she has been inducted into the International Women's Sports Hall of Fame, the International Tennis Hall of Fame and the National Women's Hall of Fame, and was awarded the Presidential Medal of Freedom by Barack Obama in 2009. She was the subject of the 2017 feature film, *The Battle of the Sexes*, and has published multiple memoirs. She is recognised as one of the best players of all time, and as a hero in the fight for women's equality in tennis and for sports in general.

JAYNE TORVILL

Jayne Torvill (1957-) is a former ice dancer and Olympic champion who, as half of the world-famous pair 'Torvill and Dean,' revolutionised the sport of ice dancing.

Torvill was born in Nottingham, the daughter of a bicycle repairman and a machinist. She started skating at an early age and by 14 had won her first competition, the British National Pairs championship, along with her then-partner Michael Hutchinson in 1971. She started dancing with Christopher Dean in 1975. This partnership would go on to be one of the greatest in ice dancing history, and they had their first triumph in the British Northern Ice Dance championship in 1976.

'Torvill and Dean' gained further success and acclaim by winning the British Ice Dance championship in 1978, the first of six consecutive wins. As amateur ice dancers, they had to work to support their passion, Torvill as an insurance clerk and Dean as a policeman. They performed at the 1980 Olympic Games at Lake Placid and came in fifth place. Soon afterwards, they quit their jobs to dedicate their time to training, supported by a grant from Nottingham City Council. This would be a turning point in their career. They won their first gold in the European Championships and the World Championships in 1981. The pair would be World Champions for a further three consecutive years.

In 1984 they performed at their second Olympic Games, in Sarajevo. Going against the tradition of dancing to a musical medley, the pair performed their dance set to

Maurice Ravel's 'Boléro'. They gained an unprecedented perfect score of 6.0 for artistic impression and won a gold medal, watched by 24 million people in Britain alone. That year Torvill was awarded the BBC Sports Personality of the Year award along with Dean, the first time the prize had been given to two people.

The pair turned professional in 1985 and won the World Professional Championships five times. They toured around the world and worked with the Duchesnays, another famous ice dancing pair. After a rule change surrounding the participation of professionals, Torvill and Dean returned to the Olympics in Lillehammer in 1994, earning a bronze medal. The pair retired in 1998 but remained prominent in the ice dancing world (and continued to promote the sport to new audiences) by becoming judges on ITV's *Dancing on Ice* in 2006.

Torvill was awarded an MBE in 1981, an OBE in 2000 as well as receiving the Freedom of the City of Nottingham in 1983. She remains one of the most recognisable ambassadors for ice dancing in the world.

In 1990 she married sound engineer Phil Christensen and they have adopted two children: a son, Kieran and a daughter, Jessica. Torvill has spoken publicly about her struggles with asthma and with trying to conceive in her forties.

Dancing on Ice tour in Manchester, England, 2010. Photo: Rach

LUAN JUJIE

Luan Jujie (1958-) is a Chinese-Canadian fencer who was the first Chinese winner of an Olympic fencing medal. Having competed in her final Olympics at the age of 50, she defied expectations about longevity in sport by competing at the top of her game for decades.

Born in Nanjing, China, Luan was an enthusiastic athlete from an early age, adept at running and badminton before she was selected to do trials for fencing in her teens. She was soon competing at international level and came to widespread prominence for her performance at the 1977 World Junior Championships, where she battled to second place under extraordinary circumstances. During her first match with a Russian competitor, her opponent's foil snapped and Luan was stabbed through her foil arm. Quickly attended to by medics, Luan went on to fight for over two hours to win the match despite her continuing bleeding. She became an instant hero in China for her fortitude.

Her legendary status in China was confirmed in 1984, when she became the nation's first-ever winner of an Olympic gold medal for fencing at the Los Angeles Olympic

Games. She won numerous Chinese national titles and was a popular national figure. She competed for China for a final time at the Seoul Olympic Games in 1988 before retiring that year.

However, her career was not yet over. Luan had fallen in love with the city of Edmonton, Canada, and moved there in 1989, gaining Canadian citizenship in 1994. She maintained a coaching career before an unexpected return to competition. Aged 42, and having had three children, she represented Canada for the first time at the 2000 Sydney Olympic Games. After her performance there, Luan had assumed her competitive career was over, but when China was announced as the hosts of the 2008 Olympics, she felt compelled to try to gain qualification at the historic tournament, which would hold special significance for her. She climbed from the bottom of the rankings to achieve qualification for the Beijing Games. She was representing Canada at 50 years old, 24 years after her Olympic debut, competing in the country where she was born. Although she did not advance far in the competition, her presence garnered international interest due to her age, her nationality and her heroic reputation in China.

Luan still coaches fencing in Edmonton, alongside two of her children who are also professional fencers. In 2008 she rejected the idea that the age gap between her and other competitors was a problem for her at the Olympics, saying she merely felt like an athlete. A film about her was released in 2013.

Luan in competition. Photo: Team Canada

JACKIE JOYNER-KERSEE

Jackie Joyner-Kersee (1962–) is an American former Olympic champion and one of the greatest track-and-field athletes of all time .

Born Jacqueline Joyner, her grandmother said that Joyner-Kersee was named after then-First Lady Jacqueline Kennedy because, her grandmother believed, she would go on to be 'the First Lady of something.' Joyner-Kersee grew up in East St. Louis, Illinois, one of four children in a family which struggled with poverty and alcoholism. They were also an athletic family; her father had been a keen athlete and her brother Al won a gold medal in the triple jump at the 1984 Olympic Games, the same day Joyner-Kersee won her first Olympic medal.

Joyner-Kersee excelled in sports at school and won the National Junior Pentathlon championships four years in a row. Her talents earned her a full scholarship to University of California, Los Angeles, where she played basketball as well as competing in track and field from 1980-1985. It was here that she started training for the pentathlon with Bob Kersee, whom she later married. She participated in her first

Olympics while at college, in the 1984 Los Angeles Olympic Games, where she won silver in the inaugural women's heptathlon event. Remarkably, she was a world class 100m and 200m runner as well.

Joyner-Kersee gained prominence by setting a world record at the 1986 Goodwill Games in Moscow, where she became the first woman to gain a score of over 7,000 in the heptathlon. Two years later, at the 1988 Seoul Olympic Games, she beat her own record and won the gold in heptathlon and the long jump. In 1992, she crowned her achievements by becoming the first woman to win the Olympic title for heptathlon in two consecutive Games, and won bronze at long jump.

Appearing at her final Games in 1996 in Atlanta, she earned another bronze at the long jump despite injury, having withdrawn from the heptathlon. *Sports Illustrated* named her the 'Greatest Female Athlete of the 20th Century', ahead of her idol the great all-rounder Mildred 'Babe' Zaharias. As well as her Olympic medals, she also won four World Championship gold medals. Remarkably, she attained all these sporting achievements despite suffering from severe asthma which affected her at several competitions throughout her career.

After her athletic victories, Joyner-Kersee turned to basketball, signing for the Richmond Rage team in 1996. She then tried to qualify once more for the Olympic long jump event in 2000, before officially retiring the following year.

She established the Jackie Joyner-Kersee Youth Center Foundation in 1988 with the aim of helping at-risk children in education and sport, an organisation which exists to this day.

In 2007, she co-founded Athletes For Hope alongside other prominent sportspeople such as Muhummad Ali, which encourages athletes to contribute to charitable causes. She was inducted into the American Track and Field Hall of Fame in 2004.

She remains a world record-holder for heptathlon for her 1988 Olympics score of 7,291 points.

Joyner-Kersee is the author of both *A Kind of Grace* (1997), her autobiography, and *A Woman's Place is Everywhere*. She is now considered one of the most inspiring motivational speakers in sports.

1988 US Olympic Trials. Joyner-Kersee performing the Long Jump

Doha Stadium, Qatar, 2012. Photo: Mohan

NAWAL EL MOUTAWAKEL

Nawal El Moutawakel (1962–) is a Moroccan former hurdler and Olympic champion who broke down barriers for women in sport in Africa and Islamic nations.

Nawal was supported by her family in her decision to start taking part in athletics in her mid-teens. She settled on 400m hurdles and started competing. She won her first title at the Arab Championships in 1981 and her first African Championships title in 1982, where she also came first in the 100m hurdles. A breakthrough came when she reached the World Championships in Helsinki in 1983, the same year she took home a gold medal in the Mediterranean Games. After winning an athletics scholarship, she enrolled at Iowa State University to study Physical Education and Physiotherapy in 1984. With more access and better coaching, she won several National Collegiate Athletic Association titles. This was all a build-up to her 1984 Olympic Games debut.

At the 1984 Games in Los Angeles, Nawal was the only woman in the Moroccan Olympic delegation. Her event, the 400m hurdles, was included for women for the first time. Nawal was not a favourite to win. Nevertheless, she prevailed, achieving victory in 54.61 seconds, setting the first Olympic record for the event.

She was the first woman from an Arab or Islamic country, and the first Moroccan ever to win an Olympic gold medal. She became an instant symbol of hope and liberation for women in sport and her victory is credited with creating opportunities for girls to participate in sports in Morocco. King Hassan II declared that all girls born on the day of her victory would be named in her honour.

Nawal retired from competing aged 25, only three years after her Olympic victory. She had been beset by problems with her knee and had faced several tragedies, from the passing of her father shortly before the Olympics, to the deaths of her university coaches and teammates in a plane crash in 1985. But Nawal continues to work towards equality in sports and promoting sports in Morocco. She is the organiser of the Courir pour le Plaisir, an annual fun-run in Casablanca, Morocco, that attracts up to 30,000 women. She served as Minister of Youth and Sports in Morocco from 2007 until 2009.

She has also held important roles in the international sporting community. Nawal was the first Muslim woman to become a member of the International Olympic Committee in 1998, and became its Vice President in 2012. She headed the Evaluation Commission for the 2012 and 2016 Olympic Games, and in 2017 was awarded Brazil's highest honour for foreign nationals for her work towards the 2016 Rio Olympics.

Nawal el Moutawakel, 1984 Olympic Games, Los Angeles.

NATALIA MOLCHANOVA

Natalia Molchanova (1962-2015) was a Russian professional free diver and former competitive swimmer who was widely regarded as the world's greatest free diver.

Molchanova's dominance over her sport was particularly remarkable because she came to it later in her life. Although she had been a competitive swimmer when she was younger, she did not train for nearly 20 years after having children. She started free diving after a divorce, aged 40. Within one year she had set a Russian record and within the next decade she would be recognised as the best free diver in the world, the 'queen' of her sport.

Molchanova set 41 world records and won 23 gold medals for free diving, including 20 individual golds. She still holds the record for the longest time a woman has held her breath for her performance in the static apnea discipline, at 9 minutes and 2 seconds. Her winning time in the same event at the 2007 Freediving World Championships beat the male champion's time. While she dominated the disciplines in the pool, she favoured free diving in the sea.

She was the first woman to break the 100m diver barrier in 2013. She dove through the Blue Hole arch near Dahab, Egypt, a depth of 71 meters, which was a record for a dive without the use of fins. Molchanova was relentless in her pushing of the limits to what she could achieve. When, in 2012, American Ashley Chapman broke one of her records, Molchanova re-set the record 72 hours later, on her 50th birthday. She utilised 'attention deconcentration,' akin to meditation, to minimise the mental and physical resistance that impedes the ability to dive so deep.

Molchanova acted as an ambassador for her sport, starting a free diving school in Moscow and lecturing at the Russian State University of Physical Culture, Sport and Tourism. With her son Alexey, who is also a world record-setting free diver, she started a free diving apparel company. She was hailed as a sporting legend in Russia and was revered by free divers around the world.

As part of her efforts to popularise the sport, Molchanova taught lessons in free diving. During one such session near Formentera, Spain, in 2015, she made a dive without a safety diver to spot her. She never resurfaced. Following a search effort, she was presumed dead, perhaps carried away by an underwater current. The mystery of her disappearance, considering how accomplished she was at free diving, captured the world's attention. Her son Alexey suggested that his mother would have been pleased that her final resting place was the ocean – the place she had loved the most.

Molchanova said of free diving that it's '…a way to understand who we are. When we go down, if we don't think, we understand we are whole. We are one with [the] world.'

Natalia Molchanova, 2005. Photo: AFP

Lisa Leslie, 2010. Photo: Angela George

LISA LESLIE

Lisa Leslie (1972-) is a former professional basketball player who helped shape the Women's National Basketball Association (WNBA) game from the very beginning. She was the first person to dunk in the WNBA, the first to reach 6,000 points, and is one of only two women to have won four Olympic gold medals in basketball.

Leslie was born in Compton, Los Angeles, one of four children. She grew up in a single-parent family as her father left early in her life. Her mother supported the family by running a trucking business. Already 6 foot tall by middle school (she eventually reached 6 ft 5), Leslie was at first hesitant about playing basketball until she was persuaded by some classmates. Despite being left-handed, when she started playing she trained as right-handed, meaning she later had the advantage of being ambidextrous. Leslie's height and talent quickly catapulted her to national attention. By the time she joined high school, she had already attracted numerous college scholarship offers, and her team at Morningside High School won two state championships.

Leslie decided to attend the local University of Southern California on a full

At the 2008 Summer Olympic Games

sports scholarship from 1990-1994. She was a phenomenon in college basketball, garnering a 20.1 point average, gaining All-American status in 1993, 1994 and 1995, and being named National Player of the Year in 1994. She graduated with a Bachelor's Degree in Communications.

After leaving college, Leslie played a season in Italy as there was no professional team for women in the US at the time. Then, in 1996 the WNBA was formed, and Leslie was signed to the LA Sparks for its inaugural season. She spent the rest of her career with the team, reaching two WNBA championship finals. She was its leader in points and was named Most Valuable Player three times.

She started her international career when she made the US team in 1995, winning her first Olympic gold the following year. During the next fourteen years, Lisa won four Olympic gold medals and two World Championship gold medals. She won her final Olympic gold at Beijing in 2008, the same year after she gave birth to her first child, Lauren.

Leslie worked as a model throughout her basketball career. She returned to college and gained an MBA in 2009. She has also served as a sports commentator, and is now a co-owner of her former team, the LA Sparks. She published an autobiography in 2008, titled *Don't Let the Lipstick Fool You*.

She coaches the BIG3 league team Triplets, one of the few women to coach a men's professional basketball team and led them to win the BIG3 championship in 2019.

She has been praised for her lasting impact on women's basketball and was inducted into the Women's Basketball Hall of Fame in 2015.

She is married and has two children.

Cathy Freeman at AusAid 2008. Photo: Jason Pini

CATHY FREEMAN

Cathy Freeman (1973-) is an iconic former middle-distance runner. She became the first Indigenous Australian person to win an Olympic medal in 1996 and the second to win a gold medal, which she did in iconic fashion at the 2000 Sydney Olympics, becoming a symbol of Australian reconciliation with its Indigenous peoples.

Freeman's mother is from the Kuku Yalanji people of north Queensland and was born within the Indigenous community of Palm Island while her father is from the Burri Gubba people of central Queensland. Freeman's family was key to her early success when she took up athletics from a young age: her stepfather was her first coach. She won her first gold medal at a school athletics championship at the age of 8 and went on to achieve national success at the junior level.

In 1990, aged 17, Freeman became the first Australian Aboriginal person to win a gold medal at the Commonwealth Games as part of the 4x100m relay team. Her victory rocketed her to national attention and she was named Young Australian of the Year. After two years of strong competition at the World Junior Championships, where she won a silver medal for the 200m in 1992, Freeman was selected to make her Olympic debut at the 1992 Barcelona Games.

But it was in the 1994 athletics season that Freeman made her breakthrough success, earning gold medals in the 200m and 400m races and a silver as part of the 4x100m relay. She also won praise and generated much discussion for completing her victory lap after the 200m final, draped in the Aboriginal flag as well as the Australian flag, despite unofficial flags being banned at the Olympic Games. Her identity as an Aboriginal Australian athlete was particularly pertinent two years later at the 1996 Atlanta Olympics when she became the first Aboriginal Australian to win an Olympic medal by taking silver in the 400m final. From there, she maintained her position at the top of athletics, winning her first World Championship title in the 400m race in 1997 and, after a break from competition, repeated this success in 1999.

Freeman had already become an Australian sporting hero by the time of the nation's hosting of the second home Games, the 2000 Sydney Olympics. She lit the Olympic cauldron during the Opening Ceremony of the Games. In an electric final for which she sported a full-length bodysuit, Freeman stormed to victory in front of a home crowd. She was the second Aboriginal Australian to win an Olympic gold medal and the first for a track event, and she was the winner of Australia's 100th medal. She celebrated as she had in 1994 by wearing both the Aboriginal and Australian flags for her victory lap, which was heralded by many as an important moment of reconciliation in Australia's history. This was the peak of Freeman's career, and after briefly returning to a competition podium as part of Australia's gold medal-winning 4x400m relay team at the 2002 Commonwealth Games, she retired in 2003.

Freeman's career, while beset by the usual difficulties athletes face such as injury, as well as family tragedies, was also remarkable for her having to overcome the barriers faced by Indigenous Australians. She has been heralded as an inspiration by other Indigenous athletes such as the Australian Open tennis champion Ash Barty, who is a descendant of the Ngaragu people through her great-grandmother.

Since retiring, Freeman set up the Cathy Freeman Foundation, to support Indigenous youth in their education. She was named Australian of the Year in 1998 and the Laureus World Sportswoman of the Year in 2001, earning the Arthur Ashe Award for Courage the same year.

For the TV series *Going Bush* (2006), with actor Deborah Mailman, Freeman went on a road trip and visited Indigenous communities in the Australian outback. A few years later, in the SBS TV program *Who Do You Think You Are?* (2008), she discovered that her mother's heritage was Chinese and English, as well as Aboriginal.

After her victory in the 400m final of the Sydney Olympics

At Lancaster House. Photo: Amplified 2010

ELLEN MACARTHUR

Dame Ellen MacArthur (1976-) is a former competitive sailor and campaigner known around the world for her successful 2005 attempt to break the record for the fastest solo trip around the globe.

MacArthur developed her interest in sailing from a young age, reading books about the sport and saving her dinner money for years to buy her very own boat. She started competing in her teens. At the age of 18 she completed her first voyage around Great Britain in her boat *Iduna*. In 1998 she competed in the Route du Rhum transatlantic solo race and won the Yachting Journalists' Association's Yachtsman of the Year Award for her performance, the youngest person ever to win this honour. In 2001 she caught the nation's attention by coming second in the Vendée Globe, a solo around-the-world race in which she was also the youngest person ever to complete the voyage, at 24, and the fastest woman. The following year she won the Route du Rhum for the first time, breaking the monohull record for the event by completing the journey from France

Arriving in Falmouth, 2005. Photo: Rod Allday

to Guadeloupe in 13 days and 13 hours.

In 2004, MacArthur embarked on her most daring expedition yet: her attempt to break the record for the fastest time anyone has sailed around the world solo. She set out from Falmouth on 28 November 2004 on her 75ft boat, the *B&Q/Castorama*. During her journey, she faced not only challenging weather conditions and difficulties associated with being at sea, but went off her food at one point, encountered whales and icebergs, and could only sleep in 20-minute intervals for the entire voyage. She communicated with her family and supporters via email and documented her voyage in a diary that was later published. She arrived back in Falmouth on 7 February 2005, having completed the 27,000-nautical mile journey in 71 days 14 hr 18 min 33 sec, breaking the previous record set by Francis Joyon by 1 day 8 hr 35 min 49 sec. She was met by a flotilla upon her return to the UK as well as universal acclaim and the announcement that she was to be made a Dame Commander of the British Empire, possibly the youngest woman ever to receive the honour. In 2008 she received the Legion d'Honneur from President Nicolas Sarkozy.

Dame Ellen MacArthur is now an environmental campaigner and launched the Ellen MacArthur Foundation in 2010 which advocates for a 'circular economy.' Since then she has worked with businesses, schools and the government to develop a framework for an economy that is restorative and regenerative by design. She became involved in this area having relied on finite resources during her voyages.

She has published three autobiographies about her life and achievements.

Photo: Mark Lloyd DPPI/BT Team Ellen

SERENA WILLIAMS

Serena Williams (1981-) is an American tennis player widely considered to be the greatest player of all time. Along with her sister Venus she revolutionised the women's game and she holds the highest number of Grand Slam singles titles of any player in the Open Era.

Born in Michigan, her family moved to Compton, California, where she and Venus started playing tennis on public courts from a young age, coached by their father, Richard. The family then moved to Florida so the sisters could receive professional tennis training. Although their incipient careers were disrupted when their father decided to withdraw them from the training academy and decrease the number of tournaments they played in, Serena turned pro at the age of 14 in 1995, a year after her sister. Four years later, she won her first Grand Slam singles title at the US Open, becoming only the second African American woman to do so, after Althea Gibson. The following year, she won her first Wimbledon title and Olympic gold medal in the doubles, partnered, naturally, with her sister Venus.

It was in 2002 that the Williams sisters began to dominate the sport. That year, Serena won the singles titles at the French Open, Wimbledon and the US Open, defeating Venus in the final of each and in the process gaining the No. 1 ranking from her sister for the first time. The following year she won her first Australian Open singles title, completing the Career Grand Slam and, holding all four Grand Slam titles simultaneously, the 'Serena Slam.' After injury hampered her in 2004, Serena returned to form in 2005 and went on to win a further 17 Grand Slam singles titles in the following 12 years.

Williams completed the 'Career Golden Slam' by winning a gold medal in the singles event at the London Olympics in 2012 – the only player, male or female, to have done so in both singles and doubles. Overall, she has achieved 39 Grand Slam titles: 23 singles, 14 doubles (all with Venus) and 2 mixed doubles. She has also won five WTA Championship titles. Her list of achievements, though, goes beyond her unprecedented title tally. She is also the highest-earning female tennis player of all time in terms of prize money.

She achieved her final Grand Slam victory, at the Australian Open in 2017, while she was two months pregnant, and returned to the top of her game following her daughter's birth and after suffering a pulmonary embolism and postpartum depression. She reached the finals of the US Open and Wimbledon in 2018 and again in 2019, demonstrating that a woman could play world-class tennis after becoming a mother.

Serena and her sister Venus faced racism throughout their careers, with the pair boycotting the Indian Wells Masters tournament from 2002-2014 due to abuse they faced there. She has rejected conventional ideas about age in tennis, playing at the top of her game in her late 30s and not looking to retire after she turned 40 in 2021.

Williams was declared the Associated Press's Sportsperson of the Year in 2015 and its Female Athlete of the Decade for the 2010s. She continues to play tennis as well as pursuing other ventures in fashion and philanthropy.

St. Moritz 2003 World Championships. Photo: Hans Bezard

JANICA KOSTELIĆ

Janica Kostelić (1982-) is a Croatian former professional Alpine skier who is the most decorated female Olympic skier of all time.

Kostelić was born in Zagreb, Croatia, then part of Yugoslavia. She first tried skiing at the age of 3, and was training by the time she was 8. She was coached by her father along with her brother. Croatia did not have many training facilities for skiing, and the family was poor, but they transported Kostelić to competitions across Europe themselves, often sleeping in tents or in the car. She started reaping success from these efforts in 1996-1997, when she won all the 22 events she entered. She had her Olympic debut at the 1998 Nagano Games, where she came eighth in the combined event.

In the 1998-1999 World Cup season, Kostelić gained international attention by winning her first World Cup slalom event. Despite injury interrupting her training, she continued to improve and in 2001 won her first World Cup overall title.

Then, in 2002, she stunned the world with her performance at the Salt Lake City Winter Olympic Games. She won gold in the combined event, the slalom and the giant slalom, and a silver medal at the Super-G. She was the first woman to win four medals for Alpine skiing at a single Games, and the first person from Croatia to win a medal at the Winter Games. Kostelić's achievements at Salt Lake City are all the more astonishing as they followed a tumultuous year in which she had undergone three knee surgeries and was still recovering.

The 'Croatian Sensation' continued to dominate the sport following her Olympic success, winning a further two World Cup titles in 2003 and 2006. At the 2006 Winter Olympics in Turin, Kostelić added to her Olympic tally with another gold medal in the combined event and another silver at the Super-G. Over the course of her career she also won five gold medals at the World Championships.

She was lauded as a national hero in Croatia, earning the title of Croatia's Best Female Athlete six times. She was the first Croatian sportsperson ever to be featured on a Croatian postage stamp. She won the Laureus Sportswoman of the Year title in 2006, the first skier to win the award.

Kostelić suffered multiple injuries and underwent many surgeries which caused her pain throughout her career. She took a hiatus after the 2006 Olympics and announced her retirement the following year, at the age of 25. She has since served as a state secretary for Science, Education and Sport in the Croatian government.

Janica Kostelić, St.Moritz 2003 World Championships, Gold Medailles, Slalom.
Photo: Hans Bezard

NICOLA ADAMS

Nicola Adams OBE, (1982-) the first woman to win an Olympic gold medal at London 2012. The British former professional flyweight boxer, nicknamed 'Babyface', holds two Olympic gold medals (London 2012 and Rio 2016), became a World Champion and has won several other amateur championships, including Commonwealth and European Games' titles.

Adams was born in Leeds, West Yorkshire, and grew up in a family keen on boxing, citing Muhammad Ali, Sugar Ray Leonard and Sugar Ray Robinson as her idols. She witnessed domestic violence at home and her parents split up when she was 11 years old. She began training, aged 12, at Burmantofts amateur club in Leeds where she was the only girl. While at the Church of England High School at Agnes Steward, she fought and won her first match at the age of 13, but she faced a lack of opponents. She went on to study at Hopwood College. In 1998 a landmark legal ruling opened the door to women's boxing and Adams began to fight competitively in 2001, representing England for the first time in a battle with an Irish boxer that same year. Two years later, she was crowned English Amateur Boxing Champion and retained the title for the next three championships.

In 2007, she garnered a silver medal in the European Championships in Denmark. In 2009, she fell down the stairs and injured her back, which left her bedridden

for three months and out of the sport for a year. Following her recovery, she won the first-ever GB Women's Amateur Boxing Championship, held at the Echo Arena Liverpool, in 2010. She was runner-up in the Women's World Championships three times (2008, 2010, 2012). Due to a lack of funds to pursue her boxing career, she worked as a builder and did some TV extra work in soap operas like *Coronation Street, Emmerdale,* and *EastEnders* at the same time as training. In 2011, she won gold in the European Championships and was finally awarded some funding to train.

Adams was one of the thirty-six female fighters to compete at London Summer Olympics 2012, when women's boxing made its debut, after the International Olympic Committee's executive board had ruled in 2009 that boxing should no longer be a male-only event at the Games. She created history after becoming the first woman to bag an Olympic Gold medal in the women's boxing, beating Chinese Cancan Ren in the final. She then received the Joe Bromley Award for outstanding services to boxing. Openly bisexual, she was also named as the most influential LGBT person in Britain by *The Independent*.

At the 2014 Commonwealth Games in Glasgow, she knocked out Michaela Walsh to win another gold medal in the women's flyweight division. She surprised many when she successfully defended her Olympic title, winning a second gold medal at the 2016 Rio Olympic Games, after beating Sarah Ourahmoune in the final, becoming the first British boxer in 92 years to retain an Olympic title.

Adams turned professional on 23rd January, 2017, signing with promoter Frank Warren. She won her professional debut match after defeating Argentina's Virginia Carcamo 40-36 and went on to win two further matches that year becoming World Boxing Champion. In 2018, she beat Argentina's Soledad del Valle Frias and Mexico's Isabel Millan, retaining her title. Her match against Mexico's Maria Salinas, which took place at the Royal Abert Hall in September 2019, ended in a draw but the rematch caused injury in the form of a torn pupil.

She retired a few months later, writing in the *Yorkshire Post*: "I'm immensely honoured to have represented our country... I've been advised that any further impact to my eye would most likely lead to irreparable damage and permanent vision loss."

A documentary film about her life entitled *Lioness,* written and directed by Helena Coan, aired in 2021 and a Barbie Doll in her honour has been made in a new release of more diverse, inspirational dolls for girls.

Megan Rapinoe, Victory Tour 2019 in St Paul, Minnesota. Photo: Lorie Shaull

MEGAN RAPINOE

Megan Rapinoe (1985-) is an iconic soccer player who has helped the US national team to two World Cup titles and two Olympic medals. She is an activist who has stood up for LGBT+ people and minorities facing racism and violence in the US, and has sued for and won equal pay for women in soccer.

Rapinoe started playing soccer from an early age along with many other sports, and says she started to feel like a tomboy in her early teens. She credits the US women's team's triumph in the 1999 World Cup tournament with inspiring her to pursue her passion for soccer. She started playing as a junior at the national level with her twin sister, Rachael. Both sisters gained sports scholarships to attend the University of Portland, where Megan competed in the FIFA U-19 Women's World Cup in 2004, in which the US team finished third.

After college, Rapinoe embarked on a professional soccer career in the US, starting with the Chicago Red Stars and then the Philadelphia Independence team. In 2011 she moved to Australia to play for Sydney FC, before returning to play for the Seattle Sounders. She played in the UEFA Women's Champions League after signing with

Olympique Lyonnais in 2013. Since 2013 she has played for Seattle Reign FC, where she has served as a midfielder and a forward and has been recognised as a Reign FC Legend.

It is in her international career that Rapinoe has won most glory as a player. While she made her international debut with the US women's side in 2006, it was not until 2011 that she played in a major international tournament, the 2011 FIFA Women's World Cup. Although the USA lost in a dramatic final against Japan, Rapinoe won praise for her breathtaking assists, made late on in the matches. The next year, Rapinoe helped her team to achieve a gold medal at the London 2012 Olympics. In 2015, she contributed two goals and one assist to the national team's effort to win the World Cup, and she was shortlisted for the Golden Ball award. In 2019, as co-captain of the national team, she led the US to its fourth Women's World Cup title. She was awarded the Golden Ball award for best player and the Golden Boot award for highest scorer, despite injury having stopped her from appearing in the semi-final match. She won the Ballon d'Or Féminin and was declared Sportsperson of the Year by *Sports Illustrated*. At the 2020 Tokyo Olympics in 2021, the US team earned a bronze medal.

As well as her remarkable sporting achievements, Rapinoe has earned renown for her activism, which she has said is inextricable from her soccer career. She came out publicly in 2012, ahead of the London Olympics, and has been proud and outspoken ever since, appearing with her fiancée Sue Bird on the cover of ESPN's *The Body Issue*, the first same-sex couple to do so. In 2016 she was the first prominent white athlete to take the knee during the national anthem in solidarity with Colin Kaepernick, who was heavily censured for his protest against racial violence and discrimination. Rapinoe herself faced a torrent of criticism and felt that she was being left off the roster more often in the season following her protest.

Despite being one of the most well-known and successful soccer players in the United States today, Rapinoe has been paid significantly less than her male counterparts both nationally and internationally. Since 2016 she has been involved in legal efforts to force US soccer authorities to remunerate men and women players equally. As a result of her and others' efforts, in 2022 the US Soccer Federation reached a $24 million settlement, agreeing backpay and ensuring that male and female players on the national teams will be paid equally going forward. She is the first soccer player to receive the Presidential Medal of Freedom.

Rapinoe speaking about Equal Pay Day, 2021, at The White House

Football Against Poverty Match, 2014.
Photo: Ludovic Peron

MARTA

Marta Vieira da Silva (1986-), known by the mononym Marta, is a Brazilian football player who is one of the best-known and most successful players of all time.

Marta was born and grew up in Dois Riachos, a poor municipality in Western Brazil. She was raised by her mother, who worked on plantations to support her after her father left the family. Marta grew up playing street football, sometimes joining boys in their games, but was often jeered and harassed for her interest in the sport. It had been illegal for women to play football in Brazil until just seven years before Marta's birth, and the effects of this prohibition are still felt in the country today both in the lack of facilities available for women's football and in attitudes towards the women who play. Yet Marta's skill was undeniable, and she was signed up for Vasco da Gama, a team in Rio de Janeiro, when she was 14 years old, after taking a three-day bus journey to try out for the team.

Two years later, Marta made her international debut for the Brazilian U19 team at the 2002 FIFA U19 Women's World Championship in Canada. The following year she made her senior debut at the World Cup in the United States, where she scored three goals. Her performance attracted the attention of a Swedish team, Umeå IK, which she joined in 2004. She was the first Brazilian woman to play professionally in Europe and helped lead the side to victory in the Union of European Football Associations (UEFA) Cup competition the year she arrived. Umeå IK won the Swedish domestic league title four years in a row while Marta was a player there.

In 2009 Marta transferred to Los Angeles Sol, a Women's Professional Soccer (WPS) league team, and was named the Most Valuable Player that year. When Sol folded, she moved to Gold Pride in Santa Clara, California, leading them to a WPS title and earning another Most Valuable Player award. When she moved to the Western New York Flash team in 2011, they too won a WPS championship. She returned to Sweden to play from 2012-2014 but returned to the US in 2017 to join her current team, Orlando Pride.

While Marta is remarkable for her record of leading club teams to title victories, it is her international career that has won her worldwide acclaim. After her 2003 debut, Marta has played in a further four World Cup tournaments. Winning both the Golden Ball and the Golden Boot awards for her performance at the 2007 World Cup in China, Marta has since become the highest scoring player, male or female, in the history of the FIFA World Cup tournaments, scoring 17 goals across five tournaments. She led the Brazil side to silver medals at the 2004 and 2008 Olympic Games and in 2021 in Tokyo, she became the only female footballer to have scored a goal at five consecutive Games. She has won FIFA's World Player of the Year award six times, including five times consecutively between 2006-2010.

From the beginning of her career, Marta faced sexism, harassment and homophobia, and was hampered by structural limits to the women's game. Several of the teams she played for folded because of a lack of money/investment, and while she is one of the best-paid women players, her pay is far below that of top players in the professional men's game.

She has been a passionate advocate for women in football, and after Brazil's 2019 loss to France in the final-16 round of the World Cup tournament, she implored women around the world to carry on her and her generation's legacy in football.

She is now a UN Women's Goodwill Ambassador for women and girls in sport and continues to play for Orlando Pride.

She became engaged to her Pride teammate Toni Pressley in 2021.

Marta interviewed by Anna Brolin of TV4 after a UWCL match with Paris-Saint-Germain, 2013.
Photo: Anders Henrikson

Rachael Blackmore Champion Irish Conditional Jockey, 2017

RACHAEL BLACKMORE

Rachael Blackmore (1989-) is a history-making Irish jockey who has (literally) leapt over barriers to women in her sport.

Blackmore was born in County Tipperary, the daughter of a farmer and a teacher. She started riding from a young age and took part in pony club meets, hunting and pony races throughout her childhood. She initially wanted to become a vet but switched to study Equine Science at the University of Limerick, continuing to compete throughout her studies. Her first victory as an amateur came in 2011, when she won the Tipperary Ladies' Handicap Hurdle on the horse Stowaway Pearl. She went on to 11 point-to-point winners and several other winners in her amateur career.

Turning professional in 2015, Blackmore's progress was steady. She won her first race that year on the horse Most Honourable. For the 2016-2017 season, she became the first woman to win the Champion Conditional Riders' Title after garnering 32 winners. In 2018, she made her first appearance at the Grand National and the following year she had her first winner at the Cheltenham Festival on A Plus Tard in the Chase Brothers Novices' Handicap Chase. That week she won another race at Cheltenham, claiming her first Grade 1 victory with Minella Indo in Albert Bartlett Novices' Hurdle. With 90 winners, she ended the season runner-up in the Irish Champion Jockey competition.

In 2020, prior to the outbreak of the Covid-19 pandemic, Blackmore had a promising start to the season, winning the Close Brothers Mares' Hurdle race at the Cheltenham Festival on Honeysuckle. But it was upon her return to the sport following the easing of pandemic restrictions that she made history. At the 2021 Cheltenham festival, she garnered two firsts: as the first female jockey with a winner in the Champion Hurdle and as the first woman to win the trophy as the leading jockey of the Festival. A few weeks later, Blackmore topped this achievement, riding Manilla Times to victory and becoming the first female jockey ever to win the Grand National, the world's most famous steeplechase, which women had previously not been allowed to compete in until 1977.

Commenting on her achievement after the race, Blackmore minimised the impact of her win on women in her sport, saying, "I don't feel male or female right now. I don't even feel human... It's unbelievable." Blackmore has shrugged off the responsibility as the first woman to achieve so many firsts in the world of horse racing, instead highlighting how they were the culmination of her lifelong dreams and hard work. She has overcome the falls and injuries which are constant dangers attendant with her sport and has become a celebrated figure beyond the world of horse racing.

She was named the 2021 RTÉ Sports Person of the Year and won the BBC World Sport Star of the Year award at the 2021 BBC Sports Personality of the Year ceremony. In March 2022, Blackmore rode into the history books, when her horse Honeysuckle became the first mare to win two Cheltenham Festival Champion Hurdle titles.

Rachael Blackmore winning top jockey race at Cheltenham, 2021

SAINA NEHWAL

Saina Nehwal (1990-) is a trailblazing Indian badminton player. The winner of India's first Olympic medal for badminton, Nehwal has been credited with popularising badminton in a cricket-obsessed country.

Nehwal is the daughter of two former badminton players; her mother had played at state level for Haryana. When she was 8 years old her family moved states from Haryana to Hyderabad. To cope with the language barrier, Nehwal started playing badminton aged 9. Five years later she became the junior national badminton champion and started her ascent to the international level. In 2006 she won her first international competition, the Philippines Open. In 2008 she became the first Indian Badminton World Federation (BWF) World Junior Champion and was named Most Promising Player of the Year by the Badminton World Federation. The same year, she made her Olympic debut in Beijing and reached the quarterfinals, defeating the world no. 5 player in the process and becoming the first Indian woman to advance to this level of the competition.

From 2009 onwards, Nehwal began earning more international titles, starting with victory at the Indonesia Open. The following year she defended this title and won the India Open, the Singapore Open and won her first Commonwealth Games gold medal. Her success was all building towards her participation in the London 2012 Olympic Games, where, entering the competition seeded fourth, she went on to take home the bronze medal. She was the first Indian badminton player, male or female, to achieve medal success in badminton at the Olympics, and she was celebrated in India for her achievement.

In the 2014 Uber Cup, she captained the Indian team and remained undefeated, helping India to win a bronze medal. In the following years, Nehwal won the Australian Open twice as well as the Indian Open and the China Open, before finally reaching no. 1 in the world rankings in 2015. Also in that year, she won a silver medal at the World Championships and reached the final of the All England competition. 2018 marked another stellar year for Nehwal when she won her second Commonwealth women's singles gold medal as well as a bronze at the Asian Games. She married fellow badminton player, Parupalli Kashyap, too, that year.

Overall, Nehwal has acquired twenty-five international women's singles titles including eleven Superseries titles. She is the only Indian player to have won a medal at every BWF major. She also helped her team to a Commonwealth Games gold medal in the mixed team event in 2018. She has been celebrated in India and was awarded the Khel Ratna Award and the Arjuna Award, India's highest sporting honours, as well as receiving the country's Padma Bhushan civilian honour in 2016. Despite being beset by injuries in her later career, Nehwal is still an active and prominent badminton player.

She has won the Indian National Championship four times. Her incredible winning record at the World Championships came to an end when she was finally beaten by Mia Blichfeldt in 2019.

She published an autobiography, *Playing to Win; My Life On and Off Court,* in 2012 and a film based on her life titled *Saina* was released in 2021 starring Parineeti Chopra.

She is also a keen philanthropist and is involved in a sports academy in Hisar.

LAURA KENNY

Dame Laura Kenny (1992-, née Trott) is a British track cyclist and the most successful British female Olympian of all time.

Kenny was born prematurely with a collapsed lung. After recovering from this near-fatal birth, Kenny suffered from asthma in her childhood and was advised to take up sport to help her breathing. She started cycling when her mother took the whole family on weekly visits to an outdoor cycle track. At first resistant to the sport, by the age of 8, Kenny started winning cycling competitions, and prize money. She rose to prominence after winning the omnium gold medal at the UCI Junior Track Cycling World Championships in 2010, aged 18. The following year, she stormed to success on the world stage at senior level, winning her first UCI Track World Championship title and World Cup title as part of the team pursuit as well as two European Championship titles for the omnium and team events. In 2012, Kenny built on this success with more glory in the team pursuit at the World Championships and World Cup, as well as her first individual titles at these competitions, for the omnium race.

All this was in preparation for the London 2012 Olympics, where Kenny raced to victory in the omnium race as well as in the team pursuit, helping Team GB to its

Rio Olympics 2016. Photo: Sander van Ginkel

most successful Games medal haul since 1908. In the years that followed, Kenny garnered further success on the track, including recovering dramatically from a kidney infection to win gold in the 25km points race at the 2014 Commonwealth Games.

In road racing, she came first at the National Road Championships in 2014. Then, at the 2016 Rio Olympic Games, Kenny repeated her achievements of London 2012 when she won gold in the omnium race and team pursuit.

That same year, Kenny married fellow Team GB cyclist and Britain's most decorated Olympian, Jason Kenny, and gave birth to their son in 2017. She returned to cycling in 2018, earning a clutch of gold medals at the European Championships and the World Cup as well as a silver in the team pursuit at the World Championships. She continued her success in 2019 but was upset late in the year by a shoulder injury, followed shortly by a broken arm, which threatened her chances in her third Olympic Games. The postponement of the Tokyo 2020 Games to 2021 was something of a godsend for Kenny, allowing her to return to form in time to compete, becoming Britain's most successful female Olympian and tying with dressage rider Charlotte Dujardin for the woman with the most Olympic medals. She won gold with Katie Archibald in the first-ever Olympic women's Madison event, as well as silver in the team pursuit. To add to her record of firsts, she became the first British woman to win a gold medal at three separate Olympics as well as the most successful woman in the history of track cycling. In honour of her astounding achievements, Kenny was selected as the flag bearer for Team GB at the Closing Ceremony of the Games.

Kenny was appointed a Dame Commander of the British Empire on the same day as her husband received a knighthood in 2022. While her husband retired from cycling that year, Laura Kenny has her sights set on more Olympic glory at Paris 2024.

Matrix Fitness Series Closed Circuit. Photo: Eugene Everson

FU YUANHUI

Fu Yuanhui (1996-) is a remarkable figure in competitive swimming. A national record-holder, world champion and Olympic medallist, she has earned worldwide acclaim for her outspokenness with regards to the difficulties female athletes face.

Fu began swimming from a young age as her father thought it would improve her childhood asthma. By the age of 15, Fu had earned two medals at the Junior World Championships in 2011: a silver in the 100m backstroke and a bronze in the 200m freestyle. The following year she made her Olympic debut at the 2012 London Olympic Games and finished eighth overall.

Fu built on her early achievements by winning a silver in the women's 50m backstroke at the 2013 World Championships. She then topped that win by taking gold at the World Championships in the same race in 2015, where she also contributed to China's gold medal for the 4x100m medley relay. In 2014 she also won two golds at the Asian Games in Korea and a gold for backstroke in the Swimming World Cup.

It was at the 2016 Olympic Games in Rio where Fu won global fame as well as her first Olympic medal. She tied for bronze in the 100m backstroke race, the first Chinese swimmer to win an Olympic medal for backstroke, and caught the internet's attention for her jubilant reaction when told of her success.

The same week, Fu suffered a disappointing performance in the women's 4x100m medley relay. Emerging from the pool after the race clutching her stomach, Fu was asked whether she was in pain. She responded matter-of-factly that she had started her period the day before, so was feeling particularly weak and tired. Fu's candour and lack of shame won plaudits around the world: menstruation is rarely discussed openly by female athletes and is a taboo topic in China, where very few women use tampons, so Fu's unflinching honesty was particularly unusual and refreshing.

Against a backdrop of strict discipline and high expectations imposed on Chinese athletes which made many of her teammates more taciturn, Fu's openness, as well as her enthusiasm, gained her many fans.

"Only ghosts know what I have endured in the past three months. Sometimes I thought I was going to die. The training sessions for the Olympics are a fate worse than death," she said at one point. She had previously also complained about the tightness of the women's swimming costumes and has joked about the difficulty in meeting romantic partners while training.

Her funny faces, geekiness and personality have made her a social media star on blog site Weibo where she has 3.5 million followers. Her lovable antics, such as waddling like a penguin, have delighted viewers around the world. She was one of the most popular Chinese athletes of the 2010s and was named on *Forbes*' 30 Under 30 list for Asia in 2017. After her moment in the international spotlight, Fu went on to win a further World Championship silver medal for the 50m backstroke in 2018, and another silver at the Asian Games.

Her ability to let her personality shine through and express her emotions after a gruelling heat has led the way for other competitors and helped to humanise the world of women's sport.

Victory in the 4x100m relay, Kazan 2015.
Photo: Oleg Bkhambri

SIMONE BILES

Simone Biles (1997-) is an American artistic gymnast who has been widely hailed as the best female gymnast of all time. With 32 World Championship medals including nineteen golds, seven Olympic medals and having four gymnastics moves named after her, Biles has made a monumental mark on her sport despite numerous challenges.

She was born to Shanon Biles, in Ohio, one of four siblings who were put into foster care until 2000, when her maternal grandfather and his wife adopted her and her younger sister. Biles grew up in Spring, Texas and was inspired to become a gymnast during a day-care visit to a gym. After trying to imitate the moves of the women she saw training, a coach approached her family and she started training, aged 6. She began competing at elite level, aged 14, and came third in the all-around event, first in the vault event and on the balance beam at American Classics in Houston. From the next year onwards she chose to be home-schooled so that she could focus on her training.

In 2013, competing at a senior level, Biles won gold in the all-around event at the World Artistic Gymnastics Championships, the first African American woman to do so. She also won gold in the floor exercise. Over the next three years she became the first gymnast to win three consecutive all-around World Championship titles and started to garner wider acclaim for her performance of routines of a high level of difficulty. Then, in 2016 she reached new levels of achievement and renown when she won four gold medals at the Rio Games, in the individual all-around event, the floor event, vault event and as part of Team USA in the team all-around event. She also won bronze on the balance beam. She was celebrated at home and abroad and was named Female Athlete of the Year by the Associated Press.

After a hiatus, Biles returned to the World Championships in 2018 with panache, taking gold in four events. Her technical virtuosity was in evidence the following year when she was the first American gymnast to win all five events at the World Championships, becoming the most decorated gymnast of all time. As well as her tumultuous early life and multiple struggles with injury and illness (including powering through a kidney stone diagnosis to help the US women to a team gold at the World Championships in 2018) Biles spoke out publicly, revealing that she was a victim of sexual abuse perpetrated by US Gymnastics' team doctor Larry Nasser. She and other victims were awarded the 2018 Arthur Ashe Award for Courage for speaking out about the abuse and the subsequent coverup.

At the delayed 2020 Tokyo Olympic Games, Biles withdrew from most events suffering from 'the twisties,' a condition which affects the spatial awareness of gymnasts who undertake complex and technically advanced moves. By making way for another team member, she gave her team a better chance of securing a medal and she received praise for prioritising her mental well-being. She continued to train privately and returned for the balance beam event, winning a bronze medal.

Her autobiography *Courage to Soar: A Body in Motion, A Life in Balance*, written with Michelle Burford, became a New York Times bestseller in 2016. She was awarded the Presidential Medal of Freedom in 2022.

Competing at 2016 Rio Olympics. Photo: Fernando Frazão/Agência Brasil

Women's Hockey Varsity match, Nottingham Trent University, 2015

50 WOMEN IN SPORT

WOMEN IN SPORT IN THEIR OWN WORDS

CHEMMY ALCOTT

Chimene Alcott, known as Chemmy (1982-) is a popular British Ski racer and sports presenter. Born in Hove, England, Alcott was named after Sophia Loren's character in the 1961 film *El Cid*. She started skiing as a child and became a member of the British Junior Alpine team in 1994 travelling to New Zealand to train in the winter. In 1995 she was named *Sunday Times* Junior Sportswoman of the Year. She was Senior British National Champion seven times between 1999 and 2009, and Overall British Ladies Champion eight times and was inducted into the London Youth Games Hall of Fame in 2011.

In 2008, Alcott climbed Mount Kilimanjaro along with fellow ski racers Julia Mancuso and Laurenne Ross, and Alcott's then boyfriend Mark Weaver. The climb raised US$30,000 for the charity Right to Play.

In 2012, Alcott competed in ITV's *Dancing on Ice* alongside professional skater Sean Rice. They finished 5th place in the competition.

Alcott now presents the BBC's *Ski Sunday* programme and is part of the BBC team covering the Winter Olympics. She is married with two children and has a large following on social media.

HOW DID YOU GET INTO SPORT?

I got into the sport very young. I was 18 months old and I was definitely the product of a ski-mad family. Both parents were very athletic. My dad was a rugby player and my mum was a swimmer, so I would say genetically I got his glutes and her lungs. I was made to be a mountain goat. I also have two older brothers, and my eldest brother was very talented at skiing. When he started he was spotted by a French ski school. He was already racing by the time I was born, I thought he was really cool, so I kind of just followed him into the sport. I did my first race at 3 years old, and then I won the World Children's Olympics at 11.

WHO ENCOURAGED YOU?

My mother inspired me growing up. Everyone used to say, "Oh, you've got such a pushy mum. She's making you do all this." But actually, it all was driven by me. I just hid behind her so that I could become more popular.

My athlete inspiration definitely was an Italian ski racer called Alberto Tumba, who was not only incredibly talented, but he was very good at projecting a huge personality. He had women draped all over him and so many stories and excitement surrounding him, it kind of transcended the sport. I thought that was really exciting until I met him as a young athlete and he passed me his telephone number, which kind of popped that bubble of idolisation for me.

WHEN DID YOU KNOW YOU WANTED TO PURSUE A CAREER IN SPORT?

When I was 11, I went to the World Children's Olympics and I actually won. I was standing on the podium and there were Union Jacks waving and our national anthem was playing. So I came back from that and I used to wake my dad up at 5:45am in the morning and he would get on his bike and we'd run around the park. He was mostly being pulled by our big Great Dane. But that's really when I was like, "Right, this is the sport for me." I used to play tennis a lot as well, but I would never have cut it as a tennis player because I wasn't mentally strong enough to battle the athlete on the other side of the net. Whereas skiing, you actually have incredible relationships and friendships with your peers, because there's so much danger involved in skiing downhills at 80, 90 miles an hour. The respect you build for someone who's faster than you is huge.

WHAT WERE THE MAIN CHALLENGES THAT YOU FACED IN YOUR CAREER?

Injury is the biggest challenge then fear of failure. I found this comfortable platform of performance. I was underperforming, giving 80%; it was good enough to be the best in Britain, and it was okay on the world stage. But I knew I was holding something back, keeping that 20% in my back pocket to self-validate when I wasn't winning.

In a sport like skiing, there's such a fine line between success and disaster. Many times I crossed that line and then suffered multiple injuries. There is a dark moment on the back of an injury where you don't know if you'll make it back to the sport you love. Every time I got an injury, it's because I had the confidence to push myself out of my comfort zone and find that growth mindset. All my scars, my broken bones, all my metal work, helped me do that.

Funding was challenging too because after my first big crash in 2010, when I had a compounded tib-fib and the bones broke through my ski boots, UK sports decided to pull my funding straight away, although I was ranked 8th in the world at the time. They didn't believe I could come back. Having to go out there and self-raise money to keep your Olympic dreams alive was really challenging. But in hindsight, I gained a huge amount of skill doing that and making people believe in me. Having the confidence to walk into rooms and say, "You can be part of my story because I'm going to be back."

TELL US ABOUT A PARTICULAR CHOICE THAT WAS GOOD AND ONE YOU REGRET.

The best choice I made was in Sölden. Just being able to be free in the start gate, free of expectations, and letting myself use the pressure in a positive way as opposed to an

Skiing at Lake Louise, Canada. Photo: Chris Carmichael

inhibiting way. I had this wild run. It was really messy. It wasn't my best skiing, but it was really fast and loose and I remember going into the finish area and I was leading for so long I was ecstatic. Then my coaches came down and they'd always believed that I could do it, whereas for me it was a shock. It was like I'd been wearing a heavy cloak my whole life and I took it off because I realised that if I made that choice to give 100% then I could achieve what I dreamed of.

Fear is great. I think that's a really important thing to talk about. A lot of people say, "Look, I'm scared", and I'm like, "Well, that's great". You feel that because you care about the outcome. You should have that fear bubble. You can push yourself through it, and then it's healthy because you're showing yourself that you can manage anything. You can have all these hurdles and challenges in front of you, but you know that they will make you a better version of yourself. When you mentor athletes, you can see they're absolutely petrified, but they won't tell you that because they think it's them being vulnerable, especially the boys. But actually, it's really important to feel that.

TELL US HOW YOU DEVELOPED AS A COMPETITOR?

I was very strong as a junior. I podiumed twice in the Youth Olympics. But I had this mental block bubbling below the surface that took me until that run that I talked about in Sölden, to overcome. And then I came 11th. I was 14th in my first Olympics and then in 2006 I was 11th in the downhill. That was an incredible run. And all my family were at the finish of that run, and I was in third place until the last split. I was ranked 150 in the world at the time, so I was really happy with eleventh place.

I did four Olympic Games. I wanted to keep going. I remember at the end of my last Olympics, the BBC were in the finisher expecting my retirement announcement. I was so happy and I'd put so much on the line. I'd broken my legs three times in the four years preceding the Olympics. I'd only skied four minutes before I got into the start gate of my last Olympic Games. I was on such a racing adrenaline high. But I was like, no, I'm not retiring. Then at the World Cup after the Olympics, I crashed and when I went to see my surgeon, he said to me that if I crashed with the metal work I have in my leg that he'd put in a year before, then they would have to take my leg away from my knee down. That was a wake up call. I love skiing, I love ski racing. That's why I still work in the industry presenting *Ski Sunday*. But I probably would have kept going, had someone not put the rest of my life on the line by saying, "Look, this is what you're jeopardising. Let's play all the cards now."

WHAT WAS A PARTICULAR CHOICE THAT WAS GOOD AND ONE YOU REGRET?

I try not to regret anything. It would be easy to sit here and say, I regret all the injuries that I had, but those are the moments where I had the confidence to push myself, to take risks. I regret that I didn't find that freedom, that personal growth, that I wasn't able to handle the expectation put on me, or that I put on myself, earlier on in my career. So probably my regret is that I didn't make that decision earlier when I was healthy and young.

WHAT ARE YOU MOST PROUD OF?

I'm proud that I can use my experience as an athlete in a positive light. I put my body, my health and my life on the line to win medals for a lot of years, but I didn't achieve that dream. Through adversity, you learn how to grow. That makes the transition into the real world easier because sport is a very selfish existence. It's all about you. How can I be stronger, faster? Even into motherhood now, those skills that I learned to overcome adversity, I put into my life now, and it makes me far more grateful.

TELL US ABOUT A FAVOURITE SPORTING MOMENT, YOUR OWN OR SOMEONE ELSE'S.

Alpine skier Dave Riding, who I've known since he was about 15, won his first World Cup this winter in January in Kitsville. No ski racers have ever won a World Cup before. I've won a run, but he won the whole World Cup, and it was an incredible performance. I was very fortunate to be there for *Ski Sunday* when there weren't any crowds. It was an amazing moment to watch, and I was incredibly emotional.

It was fantastic to see someone from Britain who had grown up on a dry ski slope, showing the Austrians that we can be the very best. It shows that British grit does exist and you don't have to have all the money and facilities that everyone else has. He was the oldest World Cup winner, and it was a great story, that has inspired a huge number of younger athletes to get involved. When you win this race, you get a gondola named after you, and it's a big ceremony with a gondola unveiling. So we're going out to film that too.

IF YOU HAD TO GIVE YOUR YOUNGER SELF SOME ADVICE NOW, WHAT WOULD IT BE?

Passion, perseverance and positivity, if you had those as strategies, you can overcome anything. And risk-taking has to be part of your development. We live in this world where we're so scared of failure that we don't take risks. You learn far more from risks than you do from achievements. I always say that I never lose. Either I win or I learn. That's something that I wish my younger self had had the confidence to live by.

WHAT WOULD YOU LIKE TO SEE CHANGE FOR WOMEN IN SPORT?

I'd like to see women be allowed to be more self-confident and expressive with their determination. A lot of young male athletes get a pat on the back and you give them respect when they say "I want to be the best," whereas girls are thought to be arrogant and unattractive if they say the same thing. If we could be more vocal about the ambitions that we have as women, we can achieve far greater things, in a more supportive community.

WHAT DO YOU THINK ABOUT MEDIA COVERAGE OF WOMEN IN SPORT?

The big aim of mine when I retired was to try and get more female sport on TV. We're slowly getting there. We've seen historic viewing figures for cricket matches, the World Cup last year for football matches. I think it is improving. I think the level of the athletes is really helping to show that it's a very attractive thing to watch.

Photo: Chris Kirkham

You've got to show that sports supersedes winning or losing. It's about all these imperative life skills, then you create sporting passion in young girls and then they grow up to be the fans that we need to support the elite level. But I think it's slowly getting there. Slowly is the biggest word I can say there, because it would be great if it was quicker, but brands are starting to recognise it, brands are supporting both men's and women's sport equally, and I think that's really important getting that message out there, that it's an attractive thing, it's an inspirational thing to watch.

WHAT IS SPORTS PRESENTING LIKE AS A CAREER?

Sometimes it's quite challenging. The last two Olympics, I was fortunate to work alongside Claire Balding and we have a lot of female experts in winter sport. Every Olympics we get comments like, "Oh, this is the *Loose Women* brigade again". It's like, "No, we are elite sports people who have the best voice to talk to you about sports and it's gender irrelevant". You do have to battle that. We used fashion this Olympics to get the messaging across to women who weren't into sport. I did this campaign where I wore only recycled clothing or rented clothing. And I know people were following my journey for that. And then they would listen to me speak about how important sport was to me in the world, and then some do get into sport.

HOW CAN WE ENCOURAGE MORE WOMEN AND GIRLS TO PARTICIPATE IN SPORT?

I think it's changing the messaging. It's about life skills. It's about social skills. It's about pushing yourself out of your comfort zone. It's about health, mental health, physical health, resilience, picking yourself up when you get knocked down, which is completely synonymous with life. If you think about a young lady going to pass her driving test, they get completely out of their comfort zone. They get inhibited by fear. They're blocked. They don't know how to handle it. If you've participated in sport beforehand, these are all emotions that you know how to handle and how to break down because you feel them on a weekly basis.

IS IT MORE DIFFICULT FOR WOMEN THAN MEN WORKING IN YOUR INDUSTRY?

I'm probably not the person to speak to about this because I have always used being a female to gain sponsors, gain traction, gain brand images and opportunity, and put that back into my scheme. I used to get judged quite a lot when I was younger because my agent told me that I had to look a certain way. I wasn't allowed to cut my hair or dye my hair when I was younger. It was all controlled because if I changed how I looked, then I would have been less marketable. I know that I got sponsors sometimes because of how I looked, so I will really be honest and say that I used being a woman to help me advance in my sporting career. I went the other way.

It was this big egotistical sport with men who are pushing themselves down the mountain. Yes, there were women doing it, but the women doing it all shaved their heads and walked like men, and they didn't have the confidence to be a woman. My generation of athletes, we said, "You know what? Getting up in the morning, putting a mascara on doesn't mean you can't ski 80 miles an hour." I was very lucky that Lindsay Vonn and Julia Mancusa, these great American athletes, they did that, and we could all do it together. And it showed that you could be much more confident in who you were, and you didn't have to be a certain type to do well at it.

WHAT ARE YOUR HOPES FOR THE FUTURE?

This trajectory we're on now with women's empowerment and using sport as a positive message is getting there. Changes are being made. There are all these incredible female role models that teenage girls can follow. The more we get the messages out there to support people, whether it's on social media or through books, the better. It's so important. I just think the movement is in the right place. We now need to inject some steroids into it.

Photo: Mansoor Ahmed

CAT CARR

(Sarah) Catherine Carr was born in Bernardsville, New Jersey, USA in 1989. She studied at Bernards High School and Holy Family University where she played for the Tigers' basketball team. Carr is the Tigers' all-time leading scorer with 1,995 career points, averaging 16 points per game. She accumulated numerous honours during her four years at Holy Family as a four-time All-Central Atlantic Collegiate Conference (CACC) honoree, named Rookie of the Year, and Player of the Year. Carr received All-Region honours three times and capped her career with WBCA All-America accolades in her senior season. Holy Family appeared in the CACC Tournament all four years of Carr's career and raised the championship banner in 2008.

Moving to the UK, she started at Northumbria, and then competed in the WBBL with the Sevenoaks Suns, twice becoming the league's Most Valued Player and winning eight trophies with the club. Carr is the league's all-time scorer in points and rebounds – the only player to pass the 1000 mark in the WBBL Championship – and also ranks second in assists having been a consistently dominant performer. She was twice named WBBL Player of the Year. She retired in 2022 and intends to return to the US to spend more time with fiancé, basketball player and author Alex Owumi, and her family.

WHAT WAS YOUR FIRST EXPERIENCE IN SPORT?

At a young age I got into sports relatively quickly. My parents signed me up for basketball, soccer. I did dance growing up. I was involved in a lot of different sports, and I didn't really narrow into solely basketball until I went to university. At first, I was really into soccer and then I slowly transitioned into enjoying basketball more and realising that's what I really wanted to do.

WHO WERE YOUR INFLUENCES AND ROLE MODELS GROWING UP?

My dad for a large part. He was my coach growing up. I would say my older brother Nick as well. My number is 22 because of him, so I feel like they were the main two that I looked up to and wanted to kind of aspire to be like. Especially in the sports world. And then my peers as well growing up, fellow teammates. When it came to basketball, I would say Sheryl Swoopes inspired me to be dominant; she was pretty dominant in the basketball world during the time that I was growing up.

WOULD YOU SAY THAT YOU WERE VERY EXPOSED TO WOMEN'S BASKETBALL, BEFORE YOU BECAME A PROFESSIONAL BASKETBALL PLAYER YOURSELF?

Yeah, I think I was, but I also think that that league has grown so much now. Obviously, the exposure and the promotion that they get now is much better than when I was younger. The first WNBA game I went to was probably not until I was in high school, so I think I was aware of it, but we're more aware of it now and appreciate the league a lot more now than I did when I was younger.

DO YOU THINK THAT IS THE CASE FOR PEOPLE WHO MIGHT HAVE AN INTEREST IN MEN'S BASKETBALL AND ARE NOW STARTING TO GET AN INTEREST IN WOMEN'S BASKETBALL?

Absolutely, I think that the league has grown. There's still a lot of discrepancies between the men and women, but the league has had significant growth, especially in the universities. It's March Madness right now in the States which is the biggest tournament for men and women, and I think that they have also gained a lot more exposure throughout the years of just being able to showcase women's talent.

WHEN DID YOU KNOW THAT YOU WANTED TO PURSUE A CAREER IN SPORT?

I think once I was in university. In the States it's from 18 to 22. I realised that I wanted to continue playing after university; it was in the back of my head, "This is something that I enjoy and I'm very passionate about and if I can do it as a living, why not?"

TELL US ABOUT A PARTICULAR CHOICE THAT WAS GOOD FOR YOU AND ONE THAT YOU REGRET.

One that I think was hard for me was there's a big recruiting process when it comes to going to university and I think at that time I didn't know much about how to talk to coaches, what the procedure was like. We were pretty successful at Holy Family University, and I've had lifelong friends from that. Another one that I might regret is not going to another country to play. When I ended up at Sevenoaks, I wanted to get my feet back under me. I didn't really look to go elsewhere but I love it here. I really do. It's like my second home. I've met really amazing people and met my fiancé here so there's a lot of good things that have come from being in the UK.

WHAT ARE THE MAIN CHALLENGES THAT YOU FACED IN YOUR CAREER?

Luckily, knock on wood, I haven't had any significant injuries that have really set me back but I think basketball is a very mental game and sometimes you find yourself in slumps. It's really taught me how to get out of those and also has taught me to deal with failure. I was a sore loser growing up and very competitive and would lash out and do things that were immature. I was just so wrapped up in the idea of needing to win everything. Now I think that I've grown as a woman and I've realised that when you do lose, when you do take setbacks, that's part of life and that's going to happen.

WHAT DOES A TYPICAL DAY OF TRAINING LOOK LIKE FOR YOU?

A typical day of training would be getting up, doing a little morning routine. I also have my own business, it's called Happily Whole and it's a fitness/wellness business, so sometimes I'll have a couple clients that I need to check in with or do some workouts with them. Then I'll take myself to the gym for some weight training with my teammates. Then I'll come home, get a good meal in, work on my business, and then we'll go to practice. We usually train at night, so we'll go do that and then I'll come home, wind down and go to bed.

HOW HAVE YOU DEVELOPED AS A COMPETITOR?

I think that I have changed my energy from being so competitive that I want to win everything to being competitive in the sense that I want to go out on the floor and give it my all every time. And sometimes that won't equal winning, and that doesn't mean that I didn't do everything that I could to win. There's going to be days where the ball doesn't go into the basket. There's going to be days that you struggle and have bad games, but your effort and consistency can always be there. Just make sure that you show up for yourself in those moments of being frustrated. I think my competitive nature has developed from a negative to being about what do we need to do to be better and how can we challenge ourselves every day.

HOW DO YOU MAINTAIN YOUR MOTIVATION?

When you love what you do, showing up for yourself is not that hard. As I've gotten older, my drive is less about going to the gym and working out for five hours. I've had to modify the way that I approach the game. I take care of my body better. When I was in university, I couldn't care less what I was eating or about sleep or water. I've adjusted in that sense. I think that my motivation now comes from the love of the game and knowing that it's not going to be here forever, and I really do have to soak it up while I can. Whenever I go home in the summer, I've been saying that this is my last year for probably the last three years since I've turned 30.

WHAT ARE YOU MOST PROUD OF IN YOUR CAREER?

I was inducted into my high school Hall of Fame five or six years ago, and then I was also inducted into my University Hall of Fame maybe three years ago, and those honours are really near and dear to my heart because for somebody to think that highly of you and to really appreciate the craft that you have is special. Obviously, we've won at Sevenoaks, we've won a bunch of championships, so I'm proud of those as well. Also winning Player of the Year in the UK in the last year, the second time that I've won it. The older you get, the more basketball requires of your body and I transitioned into being a vegan two years ago. I started focusing on my body, prior to the pandemic, which really inspired me to take fitness, nutrition and mental health very seriously. I think last year was a test for me in the sense of it being my first full year of being vegan and seeing how my body reacted to that. I think that on my team I am required to do a lot. So I think that, just the older I get, the more precious those moments are of being like, 'you still got it, you still got a little left in your tank to keep going'.

TELL ME ABOUT YOUR FAVOURITE SPORTING MOMENT, YOUR OWN OR SOMEBODY ELSE'S

One of my favourite sporting moments is back in 2000, we won the trophy in Glasgow, and we were the underdogs. Nobody thought we were gonna win and it was super special because we only had maybe six or seven players. It was a tough feat. At my university we went undefeated for the whole season; that was special to me. Those two are near and dear.

IF YOU COULD GIVE YOUR YOUNGER SELF SOME ADVICE NOW, WHAT WOULD IT BE?

It would be to always find the positives in every situation, because losing or being injured or any of those things, it's going to pass. When I was younger, I was very hard on myself, but I was also hard on others, so I think that I would tell myself to be more positive and to encourage others as much as I can.

WHAT THINGS WOULD YOU LIKE TO SEE CHANGE FOR WOMEN IN YOUR SPORT?

I think recognition appreciation, promotion, support, especially in the UK. Obviously it has developed since I've been here, but really it comes down to the financial support because that is key to be able to develop women's basketball more. I think in our league we have a couple of teams that have some money, but then we have other teams that don't have a lot of money and I think that's where you see the disparity between the bottom level teams to the top teams. In the States, you don't have to go very far to find a good basketball programme or a court to go play on. In the UK, there's not a lot of outside courts, and if there's inside courts, you're battling over those with badminton, and all these different sports. It's still a minority sport here where people are more focused on football and netball. It's hard to take steps forward.

WHAT DO YOU THINK ABOUT THE MEDIA COVERAGE OF WOMEN IN YOUR SPORT?

It's obviously gotten much better. When we are paired up with the men's league, it does promote us better, but it's definitely grown, and I think that's the beauty of social media; each club can have their own social media and do their own promotion, but the league generally could do more on social media. One of the positives that came out of the pandemic is that every team was required to stream their games because especially people like me – my people in the States want to watch the game. This year it's very good on YouTube. That has helped our league as well.

IS IT MORE DIFFICULT FOR WOMEN TO MAKE A LIVING THAN MEN WORKING IN YOUR SPORT?

Yes, very much so. Even the women that play in the WNBA, a lot of them go overseas to make more money because they're not making much money in the WNBA, so it's a weird dynamic: popular in the States, but less so in UK. The WNBA are redoing all these packages for women to have maternity leave and all these things too.

Photo: Chris Cox

WHAT'S NEXT FOR YOU?

I plan on getting married in October, so that's what my main focus is right now, planning that and getting that all together, which isn't the easiest being across the pond, but it's also because my fiancé isn't here. He played basketball here, but he retired a couple years ago so he's at home. I plan on having some kids soon. And then I just want to really dive into my business, Happily Whole. It basically encompasses women really doing their self-care and putting themselves first. It's about nutrition and finding the best way to fuel your body and make yourself feel good, making sure that we're moving and exercising because it's important and then also the accountability aspect and really just diving into self-love and making sure that you know you're taking care of yourself. It's really about a lifestyle change. Rather than doing these fad diets or all these types of things, so I think that's what I want to do.

Note: Carr announced her retirement from basketball a few months after this interview.

Carr takes a shot. Photo: JS Sports Photography

Photo: IPC/World Para Swimming

ELLIE CHALLIS

Ellie Challis (2004-) is a British Paralympic swimmer, now living in Manchester. Challis grew up in Clacton, Essex and attended Tendring Technology College. When she was 16 months old, she contracted meningitis, which resulted in the above knee amputation of her legs and a below elbow amputation of her arms.

In 2017 she broke the British SB2 50m Breaststroke record that had stood since 1992. Her debut in the British Para Swimming International 2018, saw her claim gold in both the MC 50m Breaststroke and MC 150m Medley events. In 2019, she became the world record holder for SB2 50m Breaststroke in Glasgow. Next, Challis secured bronze in the S3 50m Backstroke in London. In the 2022 World Para Swimming Championships, Challis won SB2 50m Breaststroke gold (her first world title), S3 50m Backstroke silver, S3 50m Freestyle silver and S3 100m Freestyle silver.

Her favourite subject at school is Physical Education, and she also enjoys trampolining and snowboarding.

WHAT WAS YOUR FIRST EXPERIENCE IN SPORT?

I think my first experience was watching a lot of sport. My dad was always into football so we went to football matches. I went to watch the Olympics in London in 2012. I always did sport in primary school. Obviously, as you go through school, you try out loads of different sports. I got into swimming in quite a weird way. I was in Pizza Hut and someone recognised me from a newspaper, and said they were trying to get in touch with my family. My dad had already been trying to teach me to swim for two years, so he took me twice a week for two years and we were getting there. But then I found this disability swim club that was only 20 minutes from where I lived. I got involved with that and it just took off from there.

WHO ENCOURAGED YOU IN YOUR SPORTING CAREER?

My dad took me to everything. He still does, and he's moved me to Manchester now so I can train with Team GB, and that's obviously helped a lot. You've got people like Ellie Simmonds. I watched Richard Whitehead in London and just people like that really who I've always seen on the TV.

WHEN DID YOU KNOW THAT YOU WANTED TO PURSUE A CAREER IN SPORT?

I always wanted to do running. I didn't like deep water so I didn't want to do swimming! I was on blades until about 11 full-time. I went from seven in the morning till bedtime and I loved it. I was doing running club in primary school. But then I had an operation, which is usual for people that have had meningitis, where we have to get our bone shaved down because our bones will grow and poke through our skin. After the operation I just never really got back on my legs again. At the same time I started going to national swimming championships and then I did my first international meet in 2017. At the age of 15, I had my breakthrough competition. I got my international classification, and I won a world record, two European records and several British records in four days and then I got selected as a wild card for Worlds, so it all moved pretty quickly from 2016 till today, hasn't really stopped since. After experiencing World Championships, I was like, "This is what I wanna do!" Being in London, having my family come, and just being able to race in my own classification for the first time was such a good experience. Then Tokyo was even better.

DO YOU STILL TRY OTHER SPORTS AS WELL AS SWIMMING?

I'm doing snowboarding a bit, but mainly swimming. I got invited away when I was about 12, with a charity. I tried to sit-snowboard but I was too light and I couldn't move it myself, so then I did sit-skiing. I really enjoyed the sit-ski because it was so fast and a lot of fun, but I just wanted to try something that I could do myself and I had control of because in a sit-ski, you just sit and the person behind you has control of you. I found a charity called GS UK. They put me in touch with another guy that has made this snowboard for himself and now he helps others. His name is Darren Swift and he taught me how to snowboard. It's completely different from a swimming pool, which is why I like it.

TELL US ABOUT A PARTICULAR CHOICE THAT WAS GOOD AND ONE THAT YOU REGRET.

I'm a social person and we have quite a sociable team, so I love going away with everyone. With my roommate Louise, we had the best time. We're on the same schedule of when we want to sleep, when we want to go for food. It just works. There's no awkwardness. So that was one of the best decisions ever made even though I didn't make it. One of the worst? I think the area I lived in didn't really give me too much of the opportunity to develop my swimming sooner. Swimming comes from such a young age. Now there's so many people like me that have learned at an earlier age. But we didn't know it was possible. If I'd had the opportunity to have learnt sooner, I definitely would have. I only learned to swim, because we had holidays in Spain and my dad didn't want me to be a 15-year-old whose dad had to be with her all the time. They wanted me to be independent, and it kind of just took off. I don't regret any of the choices I made.

WHAT ARE THE MAIN CHALLENGES THAT YOU FACED IN YOUR CAREER SO FAR?

In para sports, the classification system is 1 to 14. One to 10 is physical, and the lower you are, the more disabled you are. And then 11 to 13 is visual and then 14 is intellectual. Ellie Simmons is a 6 and that's probably the lowest class I ever saw swim.

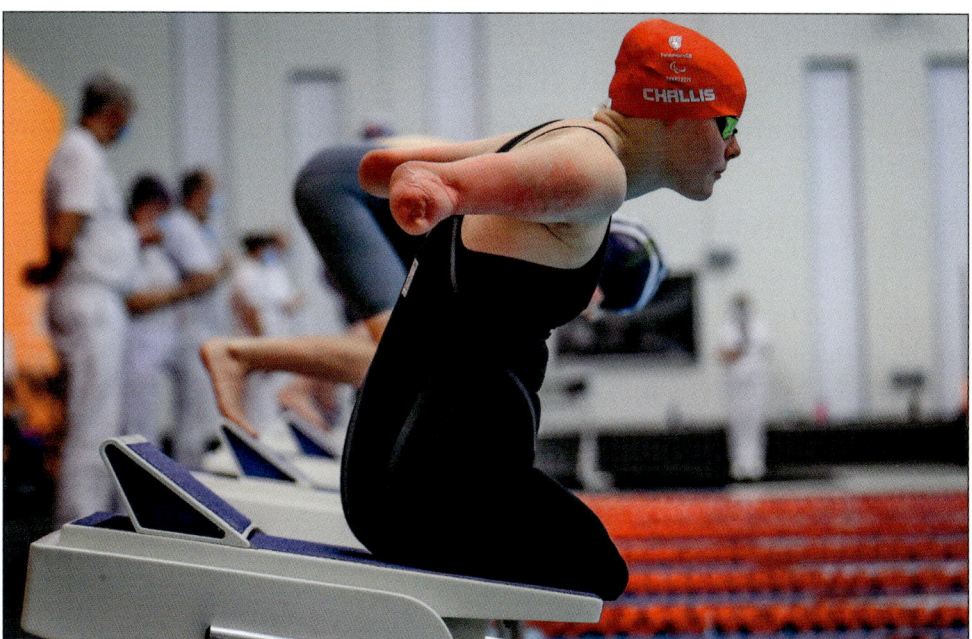

Photo: Georgie Kerr/BritishSwimming

I'm a class 3, so it's never really been shown on TV. Now we are more visible, it will help other children learn to swim. I just never saw it growing up so I think that's one of the biggest challenges. But I was lucky enough to be involved with some charities and I saw someone swim and that's when it clicked for me.

TELL US HOW YOU DEVELOPED AS A COMPETITOR.

I think I was very young when this all started, so I didn't really know what I was doing. When I got selected as a wild card for Worlds, I didn't even know it was trials for Worlds. I was just swimming, and I knew that international people were there and that was it. Going into Worlds at 15 and the youngest person on the team, I really didn't know what I was doing, though I enjoyed it so much and over the past couple years since, definitely as I got older, I've learned more about the swimming instead of just doing what someone said. So that's definitely helped. Also, moving up to Manchester is one of the best things I've ever done because having the coaches here is great and all the people around you to just help out with it. As I've grown older, I've learned more. Now I'm kind of doing what I need to do.

WHAT DOES A TYPICAL DAY OF TRAINING LOOK LIKE FOR YOU?

On Monday, I train twice and gym, but most days I just train once, so between an hour and a half to two hours a day, six days a week. Seven sessions a week and two gym sessions a week. It's a lot. My sleep schedule doesn't match up with my swimming. I'm still the normal teenager that doesn't like to go to bed and then wakes up at like 6:00am and somehow gets out of bed.

DO YOU TRAIN BY YOURSELF OR WITH OTHER PEOPLE?

There are about seven of us at the centre, but we all have a range of classifications. We've got two S7s, an S14 and S6, and some others.

HOW DO YOU MAINTAIN YOUR MOTIVATION?

I don't know to be honest, I just swim. I think it helps to have other people around you doing the same thing. When I was club swimming and I was trying to go to World Championships and Olympic Games, other people there had different goals. Now we're all aiming for Olympic Games and Worlds. We all just push each other. I know everyone there and we're all getting a lot closer now. Now we're not being locked down so we can actually see each other properly without masks and socialise outside of swimming. I think just being around people that want the same thing motivates me.

WHAT ARE YOU MOST PROUD OF?

Probably my silver at Tokyo. As I walked into the call room, I saw that one of the boys who had had to isolate because he was a close contact of someone with Covid got a bronze so I was very happy when I walked in for my main event. Then I watched my roommate Louise get silver and I was obviously very happy for her. I shouted out really loud and everyone looked at me! For me to go out and get silver at the same time, it's a great experience, but to be able to do it with your roommate and your best friend just makes it twice as good. It was such a great feeling when we got back to our flat, it was nice that it carried on for a bit longer.

TELL US ABOUT YOUR FAVOURITE SPORTING MOMENT, YOUR OWN OR SOMEONE ELSE'S.

Probably winning the silver with Louise at Tokyo. It's got to be one of our happiest couple of hours. Because you never know on the day, it could be like one of the best days ever, but it also could be one of the worst days ever and end really badly. If I'd won silver and she hadn't done, then the atmosphere wouldn't have been as good, but to do it at the same time as each other was just amazing.

WHAT THINGS WOULD YOU LIKE TO SEE CHANGE FOR WOMEN IN YOUR SPORT?

I think there's a need for more support when you get to the age when you're changing physically and you start your period. In swimming it is a very awkward situation because you don't know who to ask and obviously some people start menstruating at the age of 10. Some are 16. You have to wear a swimsuit and get in the water next to the guys and it's an embarrassing situation. Some people don't know how to deal with it.

I've grown up most of my life with a single dad. I was like, "Who do I ask?" But I'm lucky enough to have an older sister, so that was good; it's nice to have some support. When you're on your period, it can really affect how you exercise. It affects me a lot, I don't swim well that week. I'm open about it with my coaches so they don't push me too much. I also tend to get injured when I'm on my period. If that happens, it can affect you for weeks afterwards which shouldn't have to happen.

WHAT DO YOU THINK ABOUT THE MEDIA COVERAGE OF WOMEN IN YOUR SPORT?

We don't get much coverage, and for the lower classes it's even worse. The higher classes like for Ellie Simmonds's race were shown a lot. It was nice at Tokyo to know that everyone could watch it, but the TV coverage switched from swimming to basketball when it got to my race! All my family had to rush to get on a computer, go online and find the race. For people to see someone with such a disability be able to swim, would help them no matter what their disability is, or whether they have a disability or not.

IS THERE ANY PARTICULAR ORGANISATION THAT HAS SUPPORTED YOU?

Meningitis Now and Meningitis Research have been a big part of my life. And Limb Power, which is a charity which offers activity days. You get to try out loads of sport and that's when I first saw someone like me swim. We tried wheelchair tennis, sitting volleyball, archery. They had all different sorts of bikes. There was rock climbing, there was every athletic thing you could do. I've always been a big part of them, and I'm going to their event after Worlds, not as a child this time, which is weird because I've gone as a child since I was tiny. They involve the siblings as well, all my siblings were always involved in trying all these different sports. Meningitis Now and Meningitis Research have always been supportive of my family from the beginning, just helping us find out everything from since I was ill at 16 months old. And now I'm more involved with them, I hope to do more such as helping children with swimming.

WHAT'S NEXT?

I was supposed to be in Berlin, but I got Covid. Coming up next, we have a training camp in Lanzarote. I haven't been to a warm weather camp yet. I've been on the team for three years and most of that was during Covid. That's going to be a very good team experience and training camp, and then we have Worlds in June which will end my season. I'll be in five events! I've always only had two events in my classification. Otherwise, I have to race up, which obviously puts me at a big disadvantage. This is the first time I'm going to race internationally and not have to race up a class, so every race I'm going into, I'm going to race with people at the same level as me.

I'm excited about it. I think it'll be a good event because it gives me an opportunity and I'm ranked well in all of them. It should be a fun competition.

Photo: Georgie Kerr/BritishSwimming

PAMELA COOKEY

Pamela Cookey (1984-) played a variety of sports as she grew up, but she was soon spotted as an extremely talented netballer and placed in the Milton Keynes TDP before heading to Millfield School for Sixth Form. She then studied at the University of Bath and graduated with a BSc in Business Administration.

Cookey was first called up for her country for the Manchester Commonwealth Games in 2002 at just 17 years of age, but she had to withdraw due to injury. She eventually made her senior debut with England in 2004 against Australia, and two years later won a bronze medal with the England team at the 2006 Commonwealth Games. She won a second Commonwealth Games bronze medal in 2010, and later that year won gold at the World Netball Series. One of her career highlights is overcoming the challenge of injury to captain her country in a test series whitewash in 2013 against Australia and she has played for England 114 times overall. In August 2015, she returned to UK soil with a bronze medal in hand following the Netball World Cup in Sydney.

Cookey is widely recognised as one of the world's best attacking players and since retiring from Netball has kept involved in the game with a role as Director of Netball at Severn Stars, and is a regular member of the Sky Sports commentary team and a Mintridge Netball ambassador.

HOW DID YOU GET INVOLVED IN SPORT IN THE FIRST PLACE?

It started from a young age. As I was growing up, I did netball, hockey, Taekwondo, I did ballet too for a little bit, but that didn't last very long. I was too competitive! And then when I went into secondary school, I had a games teacher, Mrs Shepherd, who was passionate about netball. She took us to my first international netball game, and I saw England play Australia. They got beaten quite heavily, and she turned to me and said, "Once you get better, you can play for England and help overturn that." And I was like, "Yes, definitely!" That's kind of where my passion for netball was ignited. I went through playing for school, then for a club where girls from different schools around Milton Keynes where I grew up were selected together to be in a women's league. We learned not just the physical aspects of netball, but then also the netball nous that the older ladies had. We thought we could run rings around them, but their smart play made us work really hard! So that was a good lesson early on.

WHO WERE YOUR ROLE MODELS GROWING UP?

I loved Denise Lewis. As a family we always used to watch the athletics on the TV and seeing her smash it and be so humble with it all but still pushing women's sport and pushing that level of competition, that really inspired me growing up. And then Muhammad Ali, in terms of how he combined his sport and faith. He never let his values waver, yet he was still pushing to be the best in the world. There were no airs and graces about it. My parents as well, they always believed in me and always gave me the opportunity to do different things so that I could develop. Later on, as I was growing up, the NBA was a real kind of shining showcase. I mean, Kobe Bryant was one of my big idols. Just watching him dominate on the court, but also do it with such flair as well. It was entertaining. It wasn't just basketball – it was making it a showcase.

When I was 15, I got selected for the England under-17 squad and we won the European Championships. In the following year I was still young enough and I was made captain, my first honour representing my country and leading such fabulous young women. And that year I met Lyn Gunson, she was an ex-New Zealand Silver Fern and was coaching, and she'd come over to England to set up a programme at Team Bath. She instilled that you're not just a netballer, you're not just a student, you're not just an athlete. You're a rounded person, and it was always about making sure the person was all that she could be, and if that was all good, then what happened on the court would look after itself. She was just a real role model in terms of making sure that you're ticking all the boxes and you're not just focused down one route, and she taught us some mad skills as well.

WHEN DID YOU KNOW THAT YOU WANTED TO MAKE A CAREER OUT OF SPORT?

It was quite early on, I think. My mum reminds me of an essay I wrote that said I wanted to be in the England national team before I reached university for netball or athletics. And so, from that age, I guess I would have been about 14. Netball is not a professional sport, or it wasn't back then, so I'd always had to balance both my sport and my education. My parents were always going, "If you're not doing well at school, you're not allowed to play," and I'm so grateful, because I think it kept me balanced.

WHAT IS YOUR PROUDEST SPORTING MOMENT? EITHER YOUR OWN OR SOMEBODY ELSE'S.

My proudest sporting moment would be receiving my 100th cap. It was at the Copper Box. I was captain of the senior squad then and we were playing Malawi, and being in front of all the supporters, the fans, my family, my friends, all those that have got me through, because I had had lots of challenges along the way. They'd got me through to that point, to get that 100. I received an England dress, and it was signed and there was a little message from all my previous captains. It was just a real special moment. It wasn't the end of my career, I played a little bit more after that, but it's just a nice part of my journey that I can really take note of.

IF YOU HAD TO GIVE YOUR YOUNGER SELF SOME ADVICE, WHAT WOULD IT BE?

It would be to just chill a little bit! You can only control what's in your control. I think at times when I was younger, I got so bogged down with so many different things that were going on, whereas if I had just focused on what I was doing and what I was able to influence, then I think it would have made my life a little bit less stressful.

SINCE YOUR SPORTING CAREER, YOU'VE GONE ON TO DO OTHER SPORTS RELATED THINGS, CAN YOU TELL US ABOUT THAT?

I've always juggled school and sport, and then work and sport. My degree is in Business Administration, so I've worked in the corporate field, for engineering companies, and balanced all of that with the elite sport. I've had three main injuries: I did my ACL twice when I was younger. I did my first one when I was 18 and my second one when I was 20, and then I kind of had a big period in between and then in 2015 I did my Achilles in. And so that was devastating. Because then I was captain of the national team, so it wasn't just about me, it was my teammates as well. We'd just beaten Australia 3-nil in a Test Series for the first time in history and we really felt like, going into the Commonwealth Games, this was our year. But I did my Achilles in, so although I would have loved to have been with the girls, I wasn't playing.

BBC asked me to come and commentate. That was my first step into the media field, and it was so hard because I wanted to be on that court. But at the same time, I knew I was making a different impact. In between that, I got the opportunity to be Director of Netball and General Manager at the Severn Stars new netball franchise. I helped set that up with Anita Navin and also ran that for two years, getting that all going. That was all the coaches, all the sponsorship, all the commercial side of things, all the support staff, video analysis, strength and conditioning, psychologists. Then game day: ticket sales and making sure that match day arena was all set up as it needed to be. That was my move into the business of netball, which was really a love for me.

WHAT FEEDBACK HAVE YOU HAD FROM PEOPLE SEEING YOU COMMENTATING ON SPORT?

Well, I didn't train to be in that field, so I found that quite a challenge. But then coming from a sporting background, I love a challenge, and I started trying to make connections with lots of different people. And so many people have helped me and given me feedback and fans have said some really lovely things. It's been a real learning curve. Now I'm lead coms, so they can see something in me and that I am adding value. Because that's the thing, I've never wanted to just be there for being there's sake. I want to be somewhere doing the best job that I can do and be adding value.

WHAT WOULD YOU LIKE TO SEE CHANGE IN TERMS OF THE WAY MEDIA APPROACHES WOMEN IN SPORT?

It's come such a long way. We're definitely not where it needs to be, but the fact that you're getting sponsors that are now seeing women's sport as an investible proposition is great. You've got more people talking about it, you've got more ads. You've got more people going to games and watching it. But at times it's still compared to men's sport, and we are not men. They are stronger than us, more powerful than us. That's just biology. But what we bring is that tactical bit, where it's more technical. It is a different game but it's still just as enjoyable and just as warranted. I talked about the NBA, people don't go there just to watch the 40 minutes of basketball, they go for the pre-game build up and they go for the half-time show. They go for all the razzmatazz of it. I think if we can do more of that in women's sport, you'd get more people coming to watch the games because it's a showcase, it's an event. You're going there to have a day out as well as watch the game.

WHAT COULD BE DONE TO IMPROVE EQUALITY IN WOMEN'S SPORTS?

I guess with netball, because we're predominantly a female sport, we don't have that challenge that other sports have as highly, but still, there isn't parity in the funding and payments, not for players and not for other jobs in the sports. How many women journalists do you see out there that are given the opportunity to concentrate 100% of their time on writing and promoting the sport and players? Like I said, I was juggling careers, juggling family commitments, and umpires, officials, all those people that make the game, they were doing it part-time, whereas in men's sport that's not the case. I keep coming back to that investment piece, if we invest in all the people across the board then that surely can only lift the game. We see it in the workplace now: if a man and a woman are doing the same job, it's their right to get equal pay, so it should be the same in the sports field as well! We're slowly turning that tide, but it's still only 4% of women's sport gets shown on TV compared to the men. That's ridiculous, isn't it? How can you expect not just young people, but the general older population as well to feel like it's important, if it's not being shown, or if it's not being talked about?

IN TERMS OF THE WAY THE MEDIA APPROACHES THE QUESTIONING OF SPORTS WOMEN, WHAT COULD BE DONE TO IMPROVE THIS?

The first thing for me is: what you'd say to a man, say to a woman. You see it where they phrase the question slightly differently for women, and you're like, "But why?" They're both athletes, they're both performing at this world stage, they're both top of their games. So why make it different? And I think also spending more time with the women athletes, then you get to build more rapport with them and then you can have those conversations and you can learn. Then the third thing for me is just put women in those positions, so it's women asking those questions and then you'll get a balanced view.

IS THERE A PARTICULAR ORGANISATION THAT HAS HELPED YOU IN YOUR SPORTING CAREER?

The Women's Sport Trust and the Women's Sport Collective. I think they've gone above and beyond to get those messages out there and champion female athletes. I've worked with them quite a bit now and they help individuals, but then also help the wider group. It's all about visibility and they support that. I'm an ambassador for a charity called The Mintridge Foundation, which is all about supporting young people.

We coach, mentor and bring awareness of their possibilities through telling our journeys. I think that's really key for inspiring that next generation. If we can be visible to them and we can go out into those communities and help them develop themselves to be not just athletes, but leaders, then I think that can only be a good thing. They do some really good work across the country to support those young people.

DO YOU THINK IT'S IMPORTANT TO MENTOR OTHER YOUNGER WOMEN?

I looked up to Denise and when I met Denise in person, I was like, 'Oh my God, it's Denise Lewis!' But she's so calm and down to earth, and so giving and genuine. I feel privileged and honoured if I can be a role model for someone else now. It's just great knowing that I've potentially had an impact on someone else, and they've been able to do more. When I speak to my mentees a year or two after, they're messaging me to say, "I've done this," and, "I've done that." And "Thank you for giving me that confidence." It was all them, they had it in them. It was just someone spending a little bit of time and getting them to realise how great they are. And then they can flourish. So if I can do that for them then oh, it's amazing.

WHAT ARE YOUR HOPES FOR THE FUTURE?

For women's sport, I'd like to see consistent coverage, the ability for players, coaches, umpires, officials, and other staff, for this to be their sole job, so that they can make a good living out of it and then that, in turn, can entertain the fans and get young people inspired by the sports. Then they will want to follow in those footsteps. For me personally, it's those opportunities to be able to promote my sport more, to be able to continue on this new journey I'm on with the media side of things and then develop professionally and personally. I hope that by growing women's sport as a whole, that also grows me, and I can have an impact on that.

ALICE DEARING

Alice Dearing is a 24-year-old swimmer from Birmingham, UK, who made her Olympic debut at the Tokyo 2020 Games, competing in the 10km marathon swimming event. She started competitive swimming aged 8, and steadily progressed through the county, regional and national stages before swimming at her first international competition when she was 16, at European Juniors for the 400, 800 and 1500m freestyle. In the same year she attempted open water swimming for the first time and became European Junior champion in the 5km race.

A year later, Alice qualified for her first senior international team aged 17 at the European Championships and has been on the British marathon/open water team ever since. Her further successes include a Bronze Medal at European Junior Open Water in the 7.5km distance aged 17 and her first global champion title in 2016 aged 19 at the World Junior Open Water championships in the 10km race. Since then, Alice has transitioned to the senior stage claiming numerous top ten finishes at world cup races and finishing fourth in the Olympic qualifying event in 2021 to earn her spot at her first Olympic Games.

Outside of her sport, Alice has graduated from Loughborough University with a postgraduate degree in Politics and English and a Masters degree in Social Media and Political Communication. All of this was managed alongside swimming and competing at the highest levels possible in her sport. Since her Masters graduation in 2021, Alice has made the decision to make swimming her full-time career.

Alice helped make history with Team GB at the Tokyo Games by being the first Black woman to swim for GB at an Olympics. She has sought to use her platform to encourage more people to learn to swim or swim more regularly. In addition to this she helped co-found the Black Swimming Association (BSA) an organisation dedicated to making swimming a more inclusive place, breaking the barriers for Black communities.

In her free time, Alice loves to play video games and is a huge fan of esports. After her swimming career, she has aspirations of working as a presenter either in the field of esports, sport or radio.

WHAT WAS YOUR FIRST EXPERIENCE IN SPORT?

My first experience in sport was at school. Playing on the gym apparatus – which I was always too fearful to climb to the top of – bean bag races, football on the playground and eventually when I was 8 taking up competitive swimming. I had learned to swim at roughly aged 4, and my mum put my brother and I into the local swim club for two sessions a week. Our enjoyment of this blossomed into an elite pathway for me and swim teaching and coaching for my brother.

WHO WERE YOUR INFLUENCES AND/OR ROLE MODELS?

My key influence has always been my mum. She was the one who initally put us into a swimming club, on a whim, to stop us from being bored at home. Since then, she has given me her unwavering support in the pursuit of my sporting career. Neither of us expected, nor chased the success of being an Olympian or competing on an international stage, it was about enjoyment and being the best I could be. When it got difficult, she would be there to encourage me to keep going and remind me of my talent as well as all of the hard work which I had put into the sport thus far. She would wake up at 4:30am to take me training and then pick me up at 7:30pm at the end of the day. We spent long weekends at swimming pools for competitions and galas, restless nights in hotel rooms and long car journeys around the country. Her support made my career possible and I am forever grateful for the time and commitment she gave to me.

WHEN DID YOU KNOW YOU WANTED TO PURSUE A CAREER IN SPORT?

This thought only occurred to me when I was 22, 14 years into competitive swimming. I have always been very realistic about the likelihood and reality of the small number of people who manage to make a lasting career in swimming. Because of this, I always valued education alongside my sport as I knew I needed something to 'fall back on' in case of failure, injury or falling out of love with swimming. My education has only recently finished, with my graduation from Loughborough University with a Masters in Social Media and Political Communication in December 2021. However, in the summer of 2019 (when I was 22) I realised that I had a real chance to qualify for the Olympics for Team GB. Competing at the games would make me the first black woman ever to do so for Team GB in swimming. I thought I may as well give it my best shot and if it doesn't happen at least I tried and failed instead of wondering 'what if'. In June 2021, I had my questions answered and qualified for the games. However, I was still a student which, meant – in my eyes – I was not yet a professional, full-time athlete. Whilst some would debate this status, to me it was a way of managing the two key areas of my life which had ruled my time for decades. Now, in 2022, I have made the decision to swim beyond my academic life, something I said that I would never do as I didn't see myself being able to earn enough money to afford it. I am very happy I have proved myself wrong and given myself the opportunity to swim competitively until I know I am finished, and not forced out by financial issues.

TELL US ABOUT A PARTICULAR CHOICE THAT WAS GOOD AND ONE YOU REGRET.

Good choice: A life-defining choice of mine was taking the opportunity to get a scholarship for swimming at the Royal Wolverhampton school in Wolverhampton, England. I was 12 years old and had a great opportunity to swim at an elite squad for children aged 11-18 and study at the school. It worked well as we would swim in the morning, go to school for the day and swim again after school. The days were long and hard but helped shape and form who I am today – in and out of the pool.

Regret: In terms of my career as a whole there is nothing I regret as I have currently ended up in an amazing place which I am working to maintain. The main regret I have dealt with recently was my under-performance at the Olympics… this, I know, was down to a tactical error. Not a lack of fitness or athletic ability. However, this

Dearing qualifies for Tokyo 2021

has only grown my desire to be better and hopefully get the opportunity to correct these mistakes in Paris 2024.

WHAT ARE THE MAIN CHALLENGES THAT YOU HAVE FACED IN YOUR CAREER?

I have mainly faced a lack of confidence and at some points struggled to enjoy the sport in its entirety. Finding self-belief and confidence in myself when training and racing has never really come easily to me and, honestly, I'm not sure why. But it is something which I have had to work on over the past few years and trust in my ability to be the best athlete I can be. The other challenge was understanding how to manage the harder, more demanding aspects of the sport and learn to enjoy them (as much as possible!) alongside the fun, easier areas to cope with. For example, I am currently training ten swims a week, three gym sessions and two core circuits. This equates to 15 training sessions a week, some of which are more fun and exciting than others. However, I have made a promise to myself to turn up to each session with an equally high commitment to try my hardest at whatever we are aiming to improve. The hard work is all worth it.

TELL US HOW YOU DEVELOPED AS A COMPETITOR.

Naturally, I have always been a competitive person and driven to be the best I can be in school and then eventually swimming. I don't think I have had a specific process of growing as a competitor, nor do I have a specific 'ritual' for competing. However, I know that with each race the development is still on-going.

WHAT DOES A TYPICAL DAY OF TRAINING LOOK LIKE?

A typical training day where I have a double swim is:
- Wake up at 05:50, eat breakfast, stretch, travel to training
- Swim 06:45-08:45
- Gym 09:00-09:45
- Travel home, eat a second breakfast, nap (key!), chill out, watch TV, eat lunch
- Swim 18:00-20:00
- Go home, eat dinner, play video games,
- Go to bed at about 22:00 and then sleep by 23:00

HOW DO YOU MAINTAIN YOUR MOTIVATION?

I never find this too difficult as I have so many cool things which motivate me to be better. Getting to travel the world and represent GB at the highest levels of competition in my sport, as well as the opportunities outside of the sport which I have been given.

WHAT ARE YOU MOST PROUD OF?

Two things: (1) Qualifying and competing at an Olympic Games and (2) Speaking out about the challenges which I have faced being a Black woman in swimming. These are not issues which I feel have held me back in anyway. However, they are issues which have prevented Black people and POC from joining clubs, going swimming or even learning to swim in the first place. Whilst I have swam competitively since I was 8 years old and of course always been a Black girl/woman, I did not feel comfortable having these discussions surrounding race in public or online. However, when I was about 22 years old, I felt ready to tell my story and hopefully inspire and educate people on how great swimming is, how it is a life skill and the great opportunities which it can open up. This led to me helping co-found the Black Swimming Association in March 2020, an organisation which is bridging the gap between POC and our communities and the aquatic sector. This involves ground-breaking research with the RLNI which is seeking to dispel the myths that surround Black peoples' inability to float effectively in water. And research into what Black people feel is stopping them from swimming or learning to swim. The BSA is also a great area of support for me with numerous people who are invested in my career and want to help me excel as best they can. I am proud of speaking out on these issues as it has led to my involvement with the BSA and the historical and cultural changes which it is seeking to achieve.

IF YOU COULD GIVE YOUR YOUNGER SELF SOME ADVICE NOW, WHAT WOULD IT BE?

Don't stress the small stuff, or the big stuff for that matter. You'll land on your feet and have the world of opportunities in front of you. Keep committed to your work ethic, rest where you can, enjoy the ride. You'll be thrown challenges both from people who like you and people who don't but you're strong enough and capable enough to manage it all. Also, give Kit [my late cat] hugs more often.

WHAT THINGS WOULD YOU LIKE TO SEE CHANGE FOR WOMEN IN YOUR SPORT?

I would like to see more inclusion of people from different races and social economic backgrounds across the board in my sport. At the moment, swimming is dominated by people from certain backgrounds but this does not always have to be the case. It is a great sport with ample opportunities and clubs for people of all ages, backgrounds and abilities to join in on. In my opinion this will only help the sport grow as the more people we have doing it, the more chance you'll have to find great athletes.

WHAT DO YOU THINK ABOUT THE MEDIA COVERAGE OF WOMEN IN YOUR SPORT?

I think it's the same or equal to men! The one thing about swimming is that overall it gets fairly low media coverage compared to larger spectator sports such as football and rugby. But in terms of gender disparity it is equal.

IS IT MORE DIFFICULT FOR WOMEN TO MAKE A LIVING THAN MEN WORKING IN YOUR SPORT?

No, thankfully swimming for both men and women is done side-by-side with men and women earning the same prize money and opportunities to be a star.

WHAT'S NEXT?

I am still training and competing at the moment, with the goal of qualifying for the 2022 Commonwealth Games in Birmingham and then continuing on to qualify and compete at the Paris Olympic Games. At this point I have not given much thought about what comes after my swimming career, but I feel there are other aspects of life which I will want to discover. The opportunities which I have been given, be it photoshoots, appearances, writing, or panel talks, have given me a great chance to make a fun and exciting career which will continue outside of elite sport.

TRACY EDWARDS

Tracy Edwards, MBE (1962–) is a British sailor. Born in Purley-on-Thames in Berkshire, she left home aged 16, and backpacked across Europe to Greece where she signed on as a stewardess on a yacht in Piraeus, which inspired her to take up sailing. To enter the Whitbread Round the World Yacht Race in 1989, she took out a loan against her home to buy a 58-foot yacht and refurbish it, renaming it *Maiden*. With her all-female crew, *Maiden* finished second in its class, winning two out of six individual legs of the race. Returning to England aboard the yacht, they garnered worldwide reknown. Edwards was subsequently awarded the Yachtsman of the Year Trophy and an MBE honour. She wrote about her experiences in a book titled *Maiden* with co-author Tim Madge.

Edwards then skippered the first all-female crew to attempt the non-stop round the world record which broke seven world records before being dismasted in the Southern Ocean. Subsequently, she created and managed the world's first ever professional mixed sex racing crew. Six women and six men broke some of the most difficult records in the world and was widely viewed as a game changer in record breaking. Edwards retired from sailing in 2001 to take care of her daughter and began working for the Child Exploitation and Online Protection Centre (her first real job at the age of 45) and gained a degree in Psychology. In 2019, Edwards and her crew were the subject of an

Oscar-nominated documentary film, *Maiden*, the story of the 1989/90 race. Since then they have restored the yacht and now tour the world raising funds and awareness for girls' education. www.themaidenfactor.org

WHAT WAS YOUR FIRST EXPERIENCE IN SPORT?

My first experience in sport was growing up in Wales and watching the rugby! I always loved watching sports but I hated taking part because I thought I was useless at everything and so avoided sports at school.

WHO WERE YOUR INFLUENCES AND/OR ROLE MODELS?

My mother is my role model and if I am half the person she was, I will be doing something right. Her strength and determination influence every challenge I take on.

WHO ENCOURAGED YOU?

My mother, my family and friends have always supported everything I have ever done. My brother once described me as an Exocet Missile that just needs a guidance system. In addition, HM King Hussein I of Jordan was the primary reason I started *Maiden* because he convinced me I could do it. He also supported me throughout.

WHEN DID YOU KNOW YOU WANTED TO PURSUE A CAREER IN SPORT?

I have never wanted to pursue a career in sport. I fell into sailing and it was more a way of life than a sport. When I was winning sportswomen awards it always surprised me as sailing/racing was just something I did. It was everything in my life and I could not conceive of doing anything else.

Aboard *Maiden* in Uruguay after the 1st leg of the round-the-world race.

TELL US ABOUT A PARTICULAR CHOICE WHICH WAS GOOD AND ONE YOU REGRET.

Deciding to put *Maiden* together as the first all-woman crew to sail around the world when we raced in the 1989/90 was the best decision I have ever made (apart from having my awesome daughter!) The worst was when I had to sack my 1st Mate just before the start of the race, instead of tackling our issues head on, so she could find another boat to compete on. I hated myself for that.

Wet and wild in the Southern Ocean. Photo: Libby Mudditt

WHAT ARE THE MAIN CHALLENGES THAT YOU HAVE FACED IN YOUR CAREER?

I would have to say that apart from finding funds for all my projects (which is beyond hard), having confidence in my own abilities is a constant work in progress.

TELL US HOW YOU DEVELOPED AS A COMPETITOR.

I didn't realise I was competitive until I first raced on a yacht in Sardinia in 1982. The boat I was cooking on, *White Quailo*, a 45ft Swan, took part in the Swan Worlds and I couldn't believe how competitive I was. This makes my family laugh as they all say I was competitive from the moment I was born! I did wonder why no-one would play board games with me.

WHAT DOES/DID A TYPICAL TRAINING DAY LOOK LIKE?

All of the racing I did was long-distance, so you need stamina. It's what enables women to compete on a level playing field against men in round-the-world races. Yes, men are much stronger than women but women have great stamina and we also last longer in life-threatening situations i.e.on life rafts and mountains! We did lots of cardiovascular and weight building and we also did lots of research into sleep patterns and nutrition in preparation for the race with *Maiden* which had never really been done before. Training on the water is also an absolute must as you have to work as a team.

HOW DO YOU MAINTAIN YOUR MOTIVATION?

I don't actually know how to give up. I don't know how that actually works. If I ever felt disheartened getting *Maiden* to the start line, I would think about the women who would come after us if we failed. Not only would they have the misogyny and sexism that we were dealing with, but they would also have our failure hanging around their necks like an Albatross.

WHAT ARE YOU MOST PROUD OF?

Apart from my daughter – winning the second leg on *Maiden* into Australia. People thought that is the leg we would die on and not only did we *not* die, we sailed *Maiden* at the extremes of what was possible, we came together as a team, we worked together and respected each other and we thrashed the opposition by 38 hours.

WHAT ARE YOU DOING NOW YOU HAVE STOPPED COMPETING PROFESSIONALLY?

In 2014 I found *Maiden* rotting in the Seychelles (I had sold her at the end of the race) and knew I could not let her die there. No woman left behind. All of the original crew got together and we did a Crowdfunder to raise the funds to buy her. We rescued her and brought her back to the UK where we did an 18-month restoration and in November 2018 she was 'relaunched' in London by HRH The Prince of Wales and HRH The Duchess of Cornwall. She then set sail on a three-year world tour to raise awareness for the 130 million girls that are currently not in education. We also founded a Foundation to raise funds for girls' education programmes in developing countries all over the world. When Covid hit, we had sailed 22,000 miles and visited 23 destinations in 13 countries.

TELL US ABOUT YOUR FAVOURITE SPORTING MOMENT – YOUR OWN OR SOMEONE ELSE'S.

Mine: Finishing the Whitbread Round the World Race in second place and sailing up the Solent to the finish line with a flotilla of 600 boats and 50,000 people waiting for us in Ocean Village with Tina Turner's 'Simply the Best' blaring on the speakers. It was at that moment we knew we had achieved something unexpected and unique. Someone else's: The Jonny Wilkinson drop goal in the final of the 2003 Rugby World Cup.

IF YOU COULD GIVE YOUR YOUNGER SELF SOME ADVICE NOW, WHAT WOULD IT BE?

Stop saying sorry to everyone for everything!

WHAT WOULD YOU LIKE TO SEE CHANGE FOR WOMEN IN YOUR SPORT?

I would like to see more women at the top in governing bodies and committees and more women commentators. Also, we need more women in coaching as many teenage girls say they dropped out of sailing because of male coaches.

WHAT DO YOU THINK ABOUT THE MEDIA COVERAGE OF WOMEN IN YOUR SPORT?

In the UK, is it fairly dismal – every time I watch one of the those 'what great things happened in a certain year' *Maiden* is never shown for 1990 it is always the Spice Girls shown as 'Girl Power'. Don't get me wrong, I love the Spice Girls but we were there too! Women in sailing are celebrated in France and New Zealand and represented better in the States.

IS IT MORE DIFFICULT FOR WOMEN TO MAKE A LIVING THAN MEN WORKING IN YOUR SPORT?

Yes. It is harder to get the experience to get up the ladder onto big boats which is where the money is. That is why we take apprentices on *Maiden* so they can increase their ocean miles and be mentored by our awesome skippers and crew. It is still hard to find women engineers and electricians but that is why we are now focusing on enthusing girls into STEM subjects at school.

IS THERE A PARTICULAR ORGANISATION THAT HAS SUPPORTED YOU IN YOUR SPORT?

Maiden has so many amazing supporters and now we have a fantastic sponsor, DP World which is funding our next world tour with *Maiden*.

WHAT'S NEXT?

www.themaidenfactor.org is what I am doing now.
See https://vimeo.com/677290588/5e00425af5

Maiden restored to her former glory at start of TMF World Tour 2019. Photo: Kurt Arrigo

MENNA FITZPATRICK

Menna Fitzpatrick (1998-) became Great Britain's most decorated Winter Paralympian after a fantastic performance at her debut Paralympic Games in PyeongChang, South Korea, in 2018. Born in Macclesfield, she learned to ski on holidays with her parents who were both keen skiers. In 2015-16, Fitzpatrick became the first British skier to win the overall women's vision impaired World Cup. Fitzpatrick later received the 2016 Evie Pinching Award, given to an athlete under-24 who is considered an emerging talent by the Ski Club of Great Britain.

The next year she garnered a bronze medal in giant slalom at her maiden World Championships in Tarvisio, Italy. Guided by Jennifer Kehoe, she took gold in the women's slalom vision impaired, silver in the giant slalom and super-combined, and bronze in the super-G at the Paralympic Games in PyeongChang, South Korea, in 2018. She also ended second in the overall World Cup standings.

At the 2019 World Championships in Sella Nevea, Italy, Fitzpatrick and Kehoe won five medals, including gold in the visually impaired downhill and the Super-G. She joined forces with guide Katie Guest in 2021 and the pair went on to win slalom gold and Super combined silver at the 2021 World Championships in Lillehammer, Norway.

HOW DID YOU GET INVOLVED IN SPORT?

My parents both learnt skiing at university and loved it. When I was old enough, at about 4, they decided that they wanted to teach us how to ski. They didn't know how it was going to work with the visual impairment, but I just stuck right behind my dad and basically copied whatever he did. I loved the mountains, the snow, the speed of skiing, everything. I wanted to go every year as a family holiday. And then at the age of 13, I loved it so much that I wanted to get into racing. It was actually my dad who started guiding me, until I got too big and fast for him, and then we had to find a new guide!

TELL US A BIT ABOUT HOW YOU SKI.

You don't rely on your senses like sight, so you have to really tune into your touch through the ski boots and through your skis, and really know your body and where it's at and where your position is over skis, so you can be ready to react to anything, because when you hit a bump that you can't see, it often throws you quite a lot. For me it's just relying on those feelings and those senses, as well as hearing the guide come through the comms and trying to do exactly what they're telling me to do. We've got a microphone that is two-way so they'll be telling you what's coming up ahead; the rhythm of the gates; whether the slope moves; whether it steepens or flattens; whether there is a lump – if they've

seen it; maybe a few technical cues as well. If they've looked behind and noticed that I'm not quite in the right position, they'll say, "OK hands forward," and I'll say back to the guide, "Yeah," or I'll say the commands back to them so they know at what point I am in the turn, so they can tell how far away I am from them.

WHO ENCOURAGED YOU?

It was mainly my parents who loved it, and I just wanted to get into it. When I was first starting to race, I was listening to the Sochi Paralympics in 2014 and I was like, "Right, I want to be at the next one." So I trained really hard and ended up going to PyeongChang in 2018.

HOW DID YOU DEVELOP AS A COMPETITOR?

When I was in the first year of racing, me and my dad went on a Crystal Ski Fest and Ben Hunt-Davis and Steve Redgrave were there, and Steve brought his rowing medal. I put that round my neck and I was like, "I definitely want my own." Being a determined little girl and being visually impaired since birth, my parents just taught me every time I fell down to get back up again and try it again. So, I think I had the determination coming through, and the persistence to try things over and over again.

WHAT ARE YOU MOST PROUD OF?

There are a few moments I couldn't really choose between. Winning the gold at the PyeongChang Games was absolutely amazing, and I still can't quite believe that that happened. But I would also say completing the downhill at the Beijing Games. Even though I only came fifth, I've really been battling with a fear of downhill. A few weeks earlier we were at the World Championships, and I was too terrified to even do the race, to even be in that starting gate. So, to battle through that, to then stand in the start gate and finish the downhill at the Paralympics, was probably one of my proudest moments.

It does take a lot of confidence and the belief in yourself, knowing that you've trained for so long and everything is going to be alright. You try not to think about what could go wrong. I do know what could go wrong, I've had broken legs, broken hands, all sorts. But you try to put that aside and rely on the training.

WHAT WAS YOUR FAVOURITE SPORTING MOMENT, YOUR OWN OR SOMEBODY ELSE'S?

I was really happy for Dave Ryding when he won his World Cup [in 2022] because I know how many days, how many years he's trained and trained and trained. And he just missed out in Kitzbühel the year before. So being there and watching him get up to win a World Cup was absolutely amazing. To be there watching it with his sister, because his sister's my coach, was really special.

IF YOU COULD GIVE YOUR YOUNGER SELF SOME ADVICE NOW, WHAT WOULD THAT BE?

Probably, I should have gone to the gym a bit more, to be perfectly honest. I was terrible and was not interested in doing that side of things when I was a teenager. But now I'm a bit older, I realise how important it is.

WHAT DO YOU FEEL ABOUT THE MEDIA COVERAGE OF WOMEN IN SPORT?

I think we should just be promoting it more, especially the winter sports side of things. The Winter Paralympics especially are just not covered that much, men or women. If it's not covered at all, then you're not getting any publicity, or anything to inspire the next generation.

Guide Jen Kehoe with Menna Fitzpatrick

I'm really lucky that I'm UK Sport-funded. But not everybody is and it's only after you do get the results or the medals that you get that funding. You've really got to battle through it to get to the top to actually get funded. Skiing's a very expensive sport so that makes it even more difficult.

WHAT THINGS WOULD YOU LIKE TO SEE CHANGE FOR WOMEN IN SPORT?

More publicity and for women to be able to do it as a full-time career. I know a lot of women on the football and rugby teams have other jobs as well, and for them to be able to focus on doing their sport – it's the only way that that it's really going to improve. Then girls will see that you can do it and they might want to do it as well.

WHO WOULD YOU SAY ARE YOUR ROLE MODELS IN THE WORLD OF SPORT?

Dame Sarah Storey – she's amazing. To do what she's done, so many times, as well. The determination and grit she has – it's very inspiring.

WOULD YOU SAY THOSE WERE THE MAIN QUALITIES YOU NEED TO SUCCEED IN SPORTS?

Yeah, determination to get you through all the lows, and persistence to work hard. You've also got to think: every run, every gate, you want to do better. To me, there's no such thing as perfect. You can always improve on something. Even the top guys in the able-bodied circuit who are winning, they're constantly thinking, "How can I improve? What can I do better?" That's the only way that you're going to progress.

IS THERE A PARTICULAR ORGANISATION THAT HAS SUPPORTED YOU IN YOUR CAREER?

Lots of people helped me throughout the years. For starters, the charity that got me into it, Disability Snowsport UK. They do an amazing job of getting people with disabilities skiing. Then the help from the National Lottery players, for supporting the lottery which makes them UK sports funders as well. I couldn't do it without them. I'm fully UK Sport-funded and it's the only way that I would be able to do it as a full-time career.

WHAT WOULD YOU SAY IS THE DIFFERENCE BETWEEN THE EXPERIENCE OF ABLE-BODIED SPORTS PEOPLE AND THAT OF PARALYMPIANS?

On the able-bodied circuit they get prize money and sponsorship, whereas on the paralympic side you don't get any. We may get a wheel of cheese. It's definitely something I want to see changed. I think that making the Paralympics more equal in that respect would be amazing, but that's for all Paralympians, not just women. Able-bodied people can get more opportunities too. The media is more interested. There's a lot more people going to their races, whereas for us there might be ten or twenty people and that's about it.

WHAT WOULD YOU LIKE TO SEE HAPPEN TO PROMOTE BOTH PARALYMPICS SPORTS AND WINTER SPORTS?

Each year we have a World Cup circuit and every two years we have a World Championships, but nobody knows about that because it's not covered on TV. On the able-bodied circuit, their races are streamed on Eurosport, so everybody wants to watch that but then they have no clue about us because it's not available for people to watch the paralympic side. So, first of all, having it available to watch and then for it to be promoted and get the audience in as well. There's over a billion disabled people in the world, and that's a lot of people who are not often talked about or shown as being capable of doing stuff. And we are!

KATHERINE GRAINGER

Dame Katherine Jane Grainger DBE (1975-) is a British former rower and current Chair of UK Sport. She is a 2012 Summer Olympics gold medallist, four-time Olympic silver medallist and six-time World Champion. She served as Chancellor of Oxford Brookes University between 2015 and 2020, and is currently Chancellor of the University of Glasgow.

Grainger first won silver at the Sydney Olympics in 2000 in the woman's quadruple sculls. In Athens in 2004, she won silver in the coxless pairs. In Beijing 2008 she won her third silver, again in the quadruple sculls.

At the London Olympics 2012, Anna Watkins and Grainger broke the Olympic record as they qualified for the double sculls final, before winning the gold medal. Grainger won a silver medal at the Rio Olympic Games 2016 with Victoria Thornley, after a two-year break from the sport. Grainger has won eight medals at the World Championship between 1997 and 2011.

In 2015, Grainger was part of the composite crew that won the Women's Eights Head of the River Race on the River Thames in London, setting a time of 18:58.6 for the 6.8 km course from Mortlake to Putney. Grainger also regularly raced at the HOCR in Boston in a 'Director's Challenge Mixed 8' made up of a crew containing several past rowing Olympians and in 2019 they placed 1st in this event.

WHAT WAS YOUR FIRST EXPERIENCE IN SPORT?

I grew up in Glasgow. Through primary school and secondary school I had a lot of brilliant teachers who just really enjoyed sport and PE themselves and that's a little bit infectious. We also had a local sports centre. My big sister, who is one year older, was very sporty, much sportier than I was. She joined in a lot down at the local sports club, and my mum and dad were constantly prodding me and saying, "Well, what about you then?" So every time my sister joined something, I joined as well. We did swimming, badminton and netball. We did cross-country. We had this little loch we could run around, so we could just go out and get muddy and wet. I think your influence at school-age really has an effect. I had a really positive one, so I was lucky.

WHO WERE YOUR INFLUENCES OR ROLE MODELS GROWING UP?

Growing up, it was my teachers, it was my big sister, it was the people in the years ahead of me at school who you saw doing exciting things. In my secondary school my big sister joined karate club. We'd never done martial arts before, and a bunch of my friends joined in. I think especially for girls, it's kind of safer if you're with a big bunch of friends and you all try together. Gradually, they all dropped out, but I was hooked by then. There was a brilliant art teacher at school that did it in his lunchtime, he was a very senior black belt in karate. He was so positive and so encouraging. I was his first student. He took me from white belt to black belt while I was still at school, and he always made it enjoyable, he always made it fun but challenging, and he was very, very supportive. In 2012, I got to carry the Olympic torch and as it was the home games you could also nominate someone to carry the torch and I nominated that art teacher. It was the first time I'd seen him in 20 years. When you grow-up, you think, "I probably never really thanked him enough for what he did for me." I went off and did a very different sport but I thought that what I learned from my karate teacher back at school had a huge influence on me.

HOW DID YOU GET INTO ROWING?

It was not the plan. I grew up in Glasgow. There's a big old river which would have been the obvious place to learn to row, but I didn't do it there. Then I went to university in Edinburgh. At the Freshers' Fair, I was with another friend who had wanted to speak to the rowing people, and I didn't because I wasn't interested in rowing, but I was waiting and this older girl came over and said, 'Oh, did you want to hear about rowing?' And I said no. She went away and then she came back a second time and said, "You're still here? Listen why don't you take some information, I think you'd be really good," and I said, "I'm very busy." And then she tried a third time. "I genuinely think you should come along and just see what it's like. If it's for you, you're gonna love it. And if you don't, you can walk away." There was just enough in what she said to me to make me say, "OK, we'll give it a go." So I went to the first meeting and they wanted sixteen novices and fifty-four signed up. I still wasn't keen, but I'm very competitive, so I went along and I wasn't a natural in the boat. But it's a sport in which you can get to a decent level if you're physically fit and strong. I got into the 16 and then I just had a ball. The people I met and continued to meet through rowing, they're just so charismatic and fun and challenging and inspiring. We had a great bunch of women in my first year, who are still, to date, some of my best friends. I've got godchildren through them. I've been a bridesmaid to them. Proper friends for life. That's what hooked me before the sport hooked me. During my four years at university as an undergrad, every year my rowing got a bit more serious. Then I graduated and that year I got into the British team and then the next 20 years of my life dramatically changed.

HOW DID THAT TRANSITION HAPPEN?

In my third year I overheard one of the coaches saying, "I think she could row for Scotland one day." I hadn't even thought of that and suddenly that became the ambition. That was very exciting, so I did that in my third year. Then in my 4th year, a different coach, very casually and very calmly, said, "I think you should go to the British trials." I thought that was just ridiculous because that was in an Olympic year. He was just like, "They all started somewhere. All you do is go along and you do the trial and if you don't make it, you don't make it. What have you got to lose?" He was the one that planted that seed. I went down and did the first trial and did well enough for them to be interested. And then you go to the next trial and then you go to training camp. It all rolls forward from there. The year I got in was the first year that lottery funding came into the sport. It wasn't masses, but it was enough. It was amazing, because all the women on the team had previously had very little sponsorship. Before that year, nearly

every single person on the team, apart from the top men, had either overdrafts, jobs, or loans. Some of them had all three. To be selected was massive, and then you found a way. I remember being in a meeting and the team manager was saying, "I'm sure you've all got some sort of rich uncle or aunt that could support you in this." That was the kind of environment, but it did change quite quickly because the funding started to flow in shortly after that.

LOTTERY FUNDING MADE A HUGE DIFFERENCE TO SPORT?

It attracted in some brilliant talent on the coaching side, on the medical support side. Suddenly you could pay to go on training camps, equipment could be bought. Rowing certainly became much more centralised. People have had much longer careers, because normally most people would have done it briefly and then had to stop because they had to find a way to live and pay off debts. Suddenly horizons just expanded because you could make it a career in a different way than had ever been possible before. The quality of training, the quality of everything went up, because you weren't trying to balance living and working and training. In some sports, people are still doing very early morning training and then running straight to a job, and you can't really afford to get the right food in and all these things that help you become a top successful athlete. If the funding is there to enable that, then suddenly you just leap levels of ability. Many of us spend a lot of time being very grateful for people who buy National Lottery tickets; it genuinely made a massive difference to all of us.

DID IT HELP WORKING CLASS PEOPLE TO HAVE A CAREER IN SPORT?

You still need to get onto that bottom rung, you still need to have the talent and the ability to get noticed and get pulled in, but once you're in, there's a lot more support than there's ever been, and that really does mean the opportunities are there for more people, and that that's how it should be. It's frustrating if financial barriers are put in the way, because then it doesn't feel that it's sport for all. It should be the best people who have the best ability doing it on the world stage.

WHAT WAS YOUR FAVOURITE SPORTING MOMENT, YOUR OWN OR SOMEBODY ELSE'S?

The first Olympic Games I went to as an athlete, was Sydney in 2000. They were spectacular Games, the ones at the Closing Ceremony that the President of the International Olympic Committee called the best Games ever. Until you experience your first Games, you can't quite know what it really feels like to be at an event on that scale. My first time walking in with the team in the opening ceremony was in the biggest stadium they'd ever built for the Games, a 115,000-seater, an absolutely packed-out crowd, deafening. I remember it just being absolutely joyful. I remember beaming and walking in behind the Union Jack. The biggest secret is who will finally light the cauldron. The link to tradition and history is massive: knowing this event has gone on for centuries in modern times, but going back to ancient Greek times, you feel an incredible connection with this historical event and you feel very, very insignificant in a very good way. In Sydney, it was also the 100-year anniversary of women competing at the Olympic Games. So, when the torch came in, it went past Australian Olympic champions and the final leg of the relay was female champions, which was great. Then they handed it to the final person who would light the cauldron, and it was Cathy Freeman, who was their 400-metre runner. She was the face and name of the Games. Every Australian hope was pinned on her and, because she was Aboriginal, there was always this expectation she could also unite the whole of Australia. During the ceremony, she just walks up these steps and they've got this incredible waterfall coming down into the stadium, so she walks up and she gets to the top and she's literally walking on this pool of water. She was walking on water! She was a legend before, now she's a super-legend. Then she drops the torch to the edge and the whole thing ignites into fire. She's standing on water surrounded by fire. Then the fire rises above her and goes right to the top of the stadium, and that's where the cauldron stayed. There were 150,000 people kind of open-mouthed in stunned silence.

I was back in the stadium 10 days later when she had her race. When she came in to warm up, I remember I've never seen anything like it before or since. Everything stopped. The stadium is one of those places where there are always people sprinting and javelins being thrown and high jump going on. It's hard to watch everything that's going on. But when she went up to the start line, no events carried on. It was almost this moment of respect, the moment we'd all been waiting for. You heard the whole place fall absolutely silent, everyone held their breath for her 45 seconds, whatever it was, when she won the gold. As a very new, very novice athlete at that level, watching someone take on the pressure and expectation of not just a country but the whole world, and then deliver a fantastic race, was just stunning. It was just a wonderful lesson in what is possible. And it was very cool to say, "I was there when that happened."

DID YOU FEEL THAT LEVEL OF PRESSURE DURING THE 2012 LONDON GAMES?

Massively. There's no way I could have known, sitting in Sydney in the year 2000, that 12 years later I'd be sitting at my own home Olympics with a nation expecting as well. You do wonder, when the big moments come and the big pressure comes, whether you're going to cope or not. It is incredibly helpful to know that I've sat there and watched someone do it on an enormous scale and deliver an incredible performance, and it's possible, and it is magical. You know that amazing Billie Jean King quote? "Pressure is privilege." Ultimately when that pressure comes and expectation comes and that moment in history comes, which can feel incredibly overwhelming and daunting, there's something very special about remembering we're all very lucky to be in that position.

I remember going into 2012 with Anna Watkins and people were saying, "God

it's awful being a favourite, isn't it?" It's quite nice being underdog, when no one expects anything and you can come out and surprise everyone. But if you are the favourites in an event, all it means is that you have been better than anyone else in the world. It means that you have won more races or got the fastest times. If you're the favourite, then yes, it might bring pressure with it, but it also should bring the most confidence because you're a favourite for a reason. Pressure doesn't need to be a bad thing.

WHAT WOULD YOU SAY ARE THE CHALLENGES FOR WOMEN IN SPORT TODAY?

For younger women in sport, we still lose a lot of young women in sport at crucial ages and that's hard. And I think there is a unique blend of competing distractions at that age. You've become much more self-aware and self-conscious, whether it's about body image or outfits you have to wear in sport or changing rooms. I think we're still battling that to try and get that right. When it gets to more senior levels of sport, it's getting better all the time, but there's still much lower levels of coverage, of media, of sponsorship, of money involved. It's still a challenge for a lot of women's sport, fighting in a busy market, to get coverage. The women's sport gets a tiny proportion of what you feel it could. That's got better in the time I've been involved and been aware of it but it's still far from equal.

WHAT WOULD YOU SAY PREVENTS GIRLS FROM TAKING SPORT SERIOUSLY AT SCHOOL?

It's really about asking the right questions to find out what it is that stops people. I remember going to open a new school sports hall which had amazing facilities. The female head teacher said, "You've got to come and see the changing rooms." And it was amazing actually, because they were huge, lots of individual cubicles and individual showers, and then a huge area with loads of mirrors and loads of plug points. They were losing lots of girls who used to love doing sports, and they'd asked "What is the problem?" A lot of what they said was, they didn't feel they had time after they were doing their sport to get changed, and they didn't like using the showers, especially those communal showers, and didn't have time to get their hair done, get makeup on and look ready for going back into class. If that's what's stopping some girls from doing sport, you can address that! I was really impressed. They had far more girls wanting to do sport after that. I think we need more conversations like that.

HOW CAN WE ENCOURAGE MORE GIRLS AND YOUNG WOMEN TO DO SPORT?

When I was growing up, there were the main sports and if you didn't do those, then you weren't very good at sport, that was the message. Now there's loads more. At the Summer Olympics last year, we had skateboarding and climbing and we're going to have breakdancing in Paris 2024. There should be something for everyone. Making sure the variety of options are there and letting people know about them, is very important. Some girls are competitive and enjoy that aspect, but some don't. Sport doesn't need to be competitive. There's a huge social side to it. The more visible it is, the more we've got great people telling their stories of how they go into sport, the better. We need to admit that many of us have not been good at everything. I've messed up, I've failed on very public levels, and that's OK! The wonderful thing about sport is how it tests you and teaches you. Lots of my friends of all different ages, who have maybe gone off or had kids, are finding it again now because of the social side of it, it's the connection. There's also evidence that that some sort of physical activity is stimulating for the brain and yet we forget that, the holistic health aspect.

WHAT DO YOU FEEL ABOUT THE MEDIA COVERAGE OF WOMEN IN SPORT?

We've seen horrible examples of people being really mentally affected by that negative coverage. Ultimately, it's going to stop people getting involved and we'll all be worse off for that. A lot of female sportswomen who have spoken out about how it's affected them have gotten huge amounts of support. But the ideal world is it not happening in the first place. For anyone in the public spotlight, it's inevitable, you're going to get that interest and sometimes positive stuff can come with it, and sometimes it doesn't.

There's training to be done on both sides. As an athlete, there's things you don't need to answer, things you can choose not to engage with. It's having the confidence to step up and say, "Actually, I'm not going to answer that, I'm not comfortable answering that." I think journalists have to walk this fine line, and sometimes they cross it, and sometimes they're just asking the tough questions that need to be asked. It's a constant check-and-balance. But at the same time there's certain questions you don't necessarily want to face, but you accept that as part of the job. There's an important role that journalists have that connects what we do in sport to the public. We do want it on our TV screens, in the papers, especially coverage of women's sport. You want it to be good, strong, public, visible, and really inspiring to others.

WHAT ARE YOUR HOPES FOR THE FUTURE?

I retired in 2016 from sport as an athlete and then in 2017 I was appointed in the role of Chair of UK Sport, so that's my main job. UK Sport is the arms-length government body for sport, so it takes all the public investment, all the lottery money, all the government money that comes in and it makes decisions about where it should be spent. It's a really fabulous job to have, it comes with a huge amount of responsibility which I love most of the time, but you're aware it's a job that has a big, influential part to play within Olympic and Paralympic sport. It's very demanding and I bring a lot of my experience as an athlete to it. I've learned masses since I've taken on the role as well and developed a lot of things for myself, which is really important. Every day as an athlete you are constantly trying to improve yourself and your team around you. I think in this role now, working still in sport, it feels the same, but just in a much wider landscape.

DO YOU STILL ROW?

I do still row. I've got a bunch of amazing women who all used to be part of the British rowing team, all retired now, all got jobs, families, careers, life stresses, and we have a WhatsApp group, and when people are available at the weekend we meet up down the club and we go out. There's something about physically pushing off from the bank and you leave all your stresses there and you're out in the boat, in this incredible natural environment. And the magic is still there. And we're not as fit as we used to be, but we could still make the boat feel great. There's something very wonderful about that environment. As I said about my first week at university, when I loved the women I was with and how much fun we had, it feels exactly the same with my Olympic buddies. Just great characters having fun and creating that physical energy and getting that adrenaline flowing when you're in a boat together. It's just very special.

STEPH HOUGHTON

Stephanie Houghton MBE (1988-) is an English footballer who has captained the England national team and led England to a bronze medal at the 2015 World Cup in Canada. She captained her country for eight years from 2014, won over 100 caps, and was named FA Young Player of the Year in 2008 and awarded an MBE in 2016.

Born in Durham, she made her debut at Sunderland as a striker but suffered serious injuries immediately before the World Cup 2007 and Euro 2009, recovering to play in the 2011 World Cup and Euro 2013. At the 2012 London Olympics, Houghton scored three goals in Great Britain's four games, including winning goals against New Zealand and Brazil.

At club level, Houghton helped Sunderland win promotion before moving on to Leeds United, then Arsenal Ladies in 2010 and Manchester City in 2014. She has lifted eight trophies with City: four Continental Cups, three FA Cups and the FA Women's Super League title, and has been named the Club's Player of the Year twice.

WHAT WAS YOUR FIRST EXPERIENCE IN SPORT?

Playing in the street with my dad and my friend. But my first experience of playing a game of football was at my primary school.

WHO WERE YOUR INFLUENCES AND/OR ROLE MODELS?

My parents were massive influences on my career because of the support and advice they gave me. Also David Beckham, Steven Gerrard and Kevin Phillips.

WHO ENCOURAGED YOU?

My family: my mam, dad and brother. But also my primary school, and my friends. They allowed me to do something I loved and did not judge me for it.

WHEN DID YOU KNOW YOU WANTED TO PURSUE A CAREER IN SPORT?

I always knew I would be involved in sport. I didn't expect to be at the level I am today, but I knew I would either be involved in a team, in sports science, or be a PE teacher in the future.

Ellen White and Steph Houghton holding the FA WSL trophy, August 2011.

TELL US ABOUT A PARTICULAR CHOICE THAT WAS GOOD AND ONE YOU REGRET.

Both my moves to Arsenal and Manchester City proved to be good ones in terms of winning trophies. I don't have really any regrets. If things haven't gone well then I just like to learn from them.

WHAT ARE THE MAIN CHALLENGES THAT YOU HAVE FACED IN YOUR CAREER?

Injuries; they are tough to take but I like to try and take the positives from the situation. People's perceptions in the early years were also tough. However, in terms of perception that has really changed over the last couple of years.

TELL US HOW YOU DEVELOPED AS A COMPETITOR.

I think I have been pretty competitive since a young age, especially being from the North-East and the family that I grew up in. But I love to win and I want to keep that feeling for as long as I can!

WHAT DOES A TYPICAL DAY OF TRAINING LOOK LIKE?

Breakfast, physio check in, team meeting, pre-activation, training, lunch, gym, recovery, home.

HOW DO YOU MAINTAIN YOUR MOTIVATION?

I'm motivated by wanting to improve every day and by helping my team to be successful. And by making my family proud as well

WHAT ARE YOU MOST PROUD OF?

The career I have had so far, the trophies I have won, playing for and captaining my country's team, and making my family happy when I'm playing and successful.

TELL US ABOUT YOUR FAVOURITE SPORTING MOMENT – YOUR OWN OR SOMEONE ELSE'S.

Winning a bronze medal in the World Cup. And domestic trophies with Manchester City and Arsenal.

IF YOU COULD GIVE YOUR YOUNGER SELF SOME ADVICE NOW, WHAT WOULD IT BE?

To never be bothered about other people's opinions of me. Focus on those that you trust and stick to the plan.

WHAT THINGS WOULD YOU LIKE TO SEE CHANGE FOR WOMEN IN YOUR SPORT?

I think more representation at different levels in sport. But also more opportunities to showcase individuals more across different sports.

WHAT DO YOU THINK ABOUT THE MEDIA COVERAGE OF WOMEN IN YOUR SPORT?

I think we have made a breakthrough in terms of the Sky deal for the Women's Super League this year. It's a huge step to allow more people to watch our game!

IS IT MORE DIFFICULT FOR WOMEN TO MAKE A LIVING THAN MEN WORKING IN YOUR SPORT?

At the moment, probably, still, yes, but I feel that we have made great strides in this area and women are able to make a living in a variety of areas now.

IS THERE A PARTICULAR ORGANISATION THAT HAS SUPPORTED YOU IN YOUR SPORT?

The Talented Athlete Scholarship Scheme (TASS), the Professional Footballers Association, and many more.

WHAT'S NEXT?

My focus is very much on the present, to try and enjoy playing.

Houghton in action. Photo: Getty

JULIE KITCHEN

Julie Kitchen (1977-) is a former kickboxing and Muay Thai world champion. Kitchen was born in Truro and attended St.Paul's School in Penzance, Cornwall. A shy teen, at Humphry Davy Secondary School, hockey, netball and athletics helped her to socialise and she discovered her sporting talents. She enrolled in the Sea Cadets and was awarded the honour of Lord Lieutenant's Cadet, having risen to the rank of Petty Officer by age 16. In 1993, she went on to study a course in Leisure and Tourism at Penwith College. In 1999 she gave birth to twin daughters Allaya and Amber, and joined Touchgloves Gym in Penzance to lose weight after the birth. At 23, she began kickboxing and learning the art of Muay Thai, following a strict regime of diet and training to prepare her for professional combat matches.

In 2002, Kitchen won her professional debut against Diane Fletcher from Liverpool, England. During her career she faced fighters from fifteen countries and won 14 World Championships. She was the first British woman to win a WBC title.

Her last fight was against British fighter Amanda Kelly in Los Angeles, California on 12 January 2012. She lost after five rounds but it was a split decision. She officially retired later that month and has since worked as a sports commentator, host, VIP trainer and UAE Enfusion Al Shiraa promoter.

Her daughter Amber has followed in her footsteps to become a Muay Thai boxer.

WHAT WAS YOUR FIRST EXPERIENCE IN YOUR SPORT?

After giving birth to my twin daughters Amber and Allaya, at the age of 23, I started Muay Thai as I wanted to lose my baby weight. This was my first experience of the sport I have fallen in love with.

WHO WERE YOUR INFLUENCES AND OR ROLE MODELS?

When I started, I didn't have any knowledge about the sport, I just knew that I loved it. As training progressed, I started training and sparring with Karen Ousey, a champion from Torquay who inspired me as a female. As my career developed, I travelled to many countries to gather knowledge and training from around the globe as well as learning about past greats. I soon had such a high respect for anyone involved within the sport. The 'Science of 8 Limbs' demands so much dedication if you are wanting to succeed and to step through the ring ropes.

WHO ENCOURAGED YOU?

Although my character was naturally extremely quiet and prior to having children I was very shy, I have always had a strong wish to succeed in what I am doing. No matter how big or small the task, I want to execute it to the best of my ability. I had the same feeling during training. I could motivate myself for the early morning runs, hours of training and strict diet. Of course, encouragement is always helpful and needed and I found this from my coach, my daughters, my family, and my fans as I became known in the sport. Receiving messages on how I inspired others encouraged me greatly.

WHEN DID YOU KNOW YOU WANTED TO PURSUE A CAREER IN SPORT?

When attending my first event, I was taken in by the atmosphere. Watching athletes compete after witnessing their gruelling training routine for weeks on end gave me the desire to want to compete. I never thought that it was going to be a full-time career until I reached European level. I lost my father at this time. He witnessed my European win from his hospital bed, and I told him I would carry on and reach the furthest I could in the sport. Eventually, I collected 14 World titles and became the World ranked number 1 in my weight category.

TELL US ABOUT A PARTICULAR CHOICE THAT WAS GOOD AND ONE YOU REGRET.

I never regret choices but only learn from situations which don't go the way I expected. Choices are made every second of the day which contribute to our makeup as a person. Two major choices I am extremely happy and proud of are becoming a mother and becoming a fighter.

WHAT ARE THE MAIN CHALLENGES THAT YOU HAVE FACED IN YOUR CAREER?

To begin with, being a female in a male-dominated sport proved extremely hard in terms of securing my place on the fight shows as a female and a novice. Also, living so far south in the UK meant all major shows were held hours away in the big cities. Many of my local supporters were unable to make the long trips due to their family and work commitments, which meant I wasn't a first choice for promoters to choose as my ticket sales were not the highest. With dedication and commitment to long travels, promoters began to see my worth in the ring, and fans began talking about my story which was soon printed in magazines.

TELL US HOW YOU DEVELOPED AS A COMPETITOR.

I was hungry for knowledge and thrived on winning. The feeling of your arm being raised in victory is an amazing feeling, it makes all the hard work worth it. Many sacrifices are made, such as missing out on seeing friends and family, not being able to go to a special event get together because of the strict training regime, meal plan and early nights your body requires to be the best it can be. These sacrifices and the wish to better myself helped me grow, which gave me confidence as an individual but also as a competitor.

WHAT DID A TYPICAL DAY OF TRAINING LOOK LIKE?

I used to wake up at 5.30am so I could get my running in before my daughters woke for breakfast; the runs would be between three and seven miles. I would go the gym late morning. This could involve a mixture of pad work, bag work, or sparring. Then back in the gym in the evening, generally for sparring most evenings with the males, otherwise working on my power and fitness on the pads. I added strength training with weights three times per week.

HOW DO YOU MAINTAIN YOUR MOTIVATION?

My motivation was to succeed, to prove to myself that I was capable of pushing my body and my mind to the max and achieving anything once I put my mind to it. My daughters gave me massive motivation, especially as they started to compete at a young age. When I watched them walking into the ring to compete my heart was bursting with pride and admiration.

WHAT ARE YOU MOST PROUD OF?

Firstly, winning my first European title and second, the fact that one of the shows held in Jamaica, raised money for the local school so they could add computer suites. The visit to the school to see how our sport was going to help improve the education of children and spending the day with happy children (some with no shoes on due to poverty) is an experience I won't ever forget. As a mother to young girls at the time, the visit truly hit home for me. It was a reminder to myself to take opportunities which are presented and to do your best as it can have a positive impact on others.

WHAT ARE YOU DOING NOW YOU HAVE STOPPED COMPETING PROFESSIONALLY?

I'm still heavily involved in the sport. I'm a VIP trainer, a commentator for Enfusion events, a promoter for Enfusion Al Shiraa, Abu Dhabi, a stockholder in ECE Enfusion Cage Events and a WBC Junior ambassador. I am the biggest fan of both of my daughters and a supporter of my daughter Amber, as she is finding her own path in her fight career.

TELL US ABOUT YOUR FAVOURITE SPORTING MOMENT – YOUR OWN OR SOMEONE ELSE'S.

There are so many, not only in combat sports but in every sport. I thrive on seeing people reach their goals in all aspects of life, from professional athletes on the TV to a person reaching their personal best. I believe that training in an active sport is a massive part of general wellbeing and will contribute in a positive way to other aspects of your life.

IF YOU COULD GIVE YOUR YOUNGER SELF SOME ADVICE NOW, WHAT WOULD IT BE?

Concentrate on your own path. Don't get caught up in social media. Have good people around you who support the lifestyle you have chosen and will be a positive impact in helping you on the journey. Choosing a fight career is a very gruelling path to take, you need to push your body to the max in training whilst taking physical punishment to prepare during battle. There are no short cuts. Make sure every angle is covered in training to lessen the damage to your body once stepping into the ring. Consistency is key.

WHAT THINGS WOULD YOU LIKE TO SEE CHANGE FOR WOMEN IN YOUR SPORT?

I have helped open the pathway for female fighters, which I am extremely proud of. I love to see the combat sports developing and females being given more chances. I hope in the future, more sponsors come forward to support the top women athletes within the sport so they are able to create an extra side revenue in order that they can devote their lives to full-time training.

WHAT DO YOU THINK ABOUT THE MEDIA COVERAGE OF WOMEN IN YOUR SPORT?

Over the years the coverage for females in combat sport has risen significantly due to organisations promoting female matches and showing fans that women's fights are just as technical, entertaining and brutal as the males'. Of course, there is always room for improvement, but it has advanced compared to years ago.

IS IT MORE DIFFICULT FOR WOMEN TO MAKE A LIVING THAN MEN WORKING IN YOUR SPORT?

Fight purses have had growth for females, but for sure the males are still dominating the pay cheques. If a fighter decides to make the hard decision of becoming a full-time competitor, then income cannot be relied on purely by competing. Usually, fighters turn to teaching and giving private tuition sessions which helps support them.

IS THERE A PARTICULAR ORGANISATION THAT HAS SUPPORTED YOU IN YOUR SPORT?

Throughout my career I've had many organisations and people who supported me, I wouldn't have had the career I did without being given the chance to shine, starting with the smaller local promotions to the world-renowned shows. Winning an array of World title belts under different organisations meant so much. I would always fight whenever I had an opportunity and ranged my weight up and down by 8kg so I could stay active in the ring. Taking part in Enfusion Reality opened new doors for me, such as being asked to return as the host and interviewer of the show, which then led to being asked to commentate for their live shows. I take this opportunity to thank everyone in the past who has contributed to my full career.

WHAT'S NEXT?

I am enjoying this chapter of my life, working on progressing the sport whilst training for fitness and enjoyment. Muay Thai changed my life and gave me confidence and achievements I had never dreamt of, with the gift of travelling the world and meeting people who became part of the Muay Thai family. My aim is to spread the word of this beautiful sport and help it become more mainstream in any way I can.

MEG LANNING

Meghann Lanning (1992-), nicknamed 'Megastar', is an Australian cricketer who currently captains the national women's team. She has been a member of six successful world championship campaigns, winning two Women's Cricket World Cups and four ICC Women's World Twenty20 titles. Lanning holds the record for the most Women's One Day International centuries and is the first Australian to score 2,000 Twenty20 International runs. Domestically, she is the captain of Victoria in the Women's National Cricket League and the Melbourne Stars in the Women's Big Bash League.

Lanning was born in Singapore but her family relocated to Sydney where she began playing organised cricket at the age of 10, and went on to represent New South Wales at primary school level. At 14, she made headlines by becoming the first girl to play First XI cricket for an Associated Public Schools team. In 2019, she completed her degree in Exercise and Health Science from ACU.

In 2022, she was signed by the Trent Rockets to play in The Hundred competition in UK.

WHAT WAS YOUR FIRST EXPERIENCE IN SPORT?

Playing in the school yard at recess and lunch. It was always cricket or some sort of football. Mostly touch rugby as I grew up in Sydney.

WHO WERE YOUR INFLUENCES AND/OR ROLE MODELS?

I loved the Sydney Swans growing up, so Paul Kelly was someone I loved. Once I got into cricket, Ricky Ponting was the player I wanted to be like.

WHO ENCOURAGED YOU?

My parents gave me the opportunity to be involved in sports. Teachers at my primary school were also important. They encouraged me to try out for rep teams when I was very young, I didn't even know there were rep teams to play in!

WHEN DID YOU KNOW YOU WANTED TO PURSUE A CAREER IN SPORT?

Probably when I was around 16. I got my first state contract with Victoria and that's when I thought I wanted to go as far as I could.

TELL US ABOUT A PARTICULAR CHOICE THAT WAS GOOD AND ONE YOU REGRET.

A decision that was a good one was playing a lot of my junior cricket in boys' teams. It took me out of my comfort zone but I learnt a lot.

Lanning batting for Australia against Sri Lanka during the 2020 World Cup match in Perth, Australia. The wicket-keeper is Anushka Sanjeewani.

WHAT ARE THE MAIN CHALLENGES THAT YOU HAVE FACED IN YOUR CAREER?

Taking over the captaincy of Australia at a very young age with no experience. I needed to learn on the job and understand quickly what was involved in such a role. It meant I needed to lean on others to help me and accept that I wasn't always going to get things right, and that's ok.

TELL US HOW YOU DEVELOPED AS A COMPETITOR.

I think I have always been a competitive person. It doesn't really matter what I am doing, I always want to do it as well as I can. I have always played in team sports and have loved team success and helping to achieve that.

HOW DO YOU MAINTAIN YOUR MOTIVATION?

Playing at the elite level means that you constantly need to get better. I want to be the best at what I do and there are so many amazing players out there who want the same thing. So that motivates me individually, but I love having success with the team I'm playing in. So working hard to achieve those goals are what motivates me.

WHAT ARE YOU MOST PROUD OF?

Being part of a successful Australian team! Particularly over the past five years when we have had our challenges, the team has evolved and learnt from mistakes and put on some of our best performances on the biggest stages.

TELL US ABOUT YOUR FAVOURITE SPORTING MOMENT – YOUR OWN OR SOMEONE ELSE'S.

It has to be hearing the roar of the crowd when we took the final wicket in the Final of the T20 World Cup in 2020. I never thought I would be playing in front of a crowd like that.

IF YOU COULD GIVE YOUR YOUNGER SELF SOME ADVICE NOW, WHAT WOULD IT BE?

Ask more questions. I was lucky to meet some incredible people growing up, but I was too shy to ask anything.

WHAT THINGS WOULD YOU LIKE TO SEE CHANGE FOR WOMEN IN YOUR SPORT?

I think we have made some really good progress with our National Women's sporting teams in terms of resources and media coverage, but it would be great to keep building at the domestic level and create some really good opportunities in that space.

WHAT DO YOU THINK ABOUT THE MEDIA COVERAGE OF WOMEN IN YOUR SPORT?

There is no doubt the coverage has increased massively over my time in the game. Now we are starting to be critically analysed, which I think is an important step because it means people care. There's still a way to go but no doubt there are now many female role models out there for young girls to follow.

IS IT MORE DIFFICULT FOR WOMEN TO MAKE A LIVING THAN MEN WORKING IN YOUR SPORT?

There is absolutely still a big discrepancy in how much women can earn playing sport compared to men. I think there have been significant steps forward and cricket has been leading the way. This discrepancy includes opportunities to play as well as contracts.

WHAT'S NEXT?

The Commonwealth Games provides the team with a great new opportunity. It's something we haven't been involved in before but there is a real excitement within the group to be involved.

Lanning playing for the Melbourne Stars, in a WBBL match, 2022

Photo: David Venni

GABBY LOGAN

Gabrielle Logan MBE, née Yorath, (1973-) is a Welsh TV presenter and a former international gymnast. She was born in Leeds, the daughter of Welsh international footballer and manager Terry Yorath and his wife, Christine. The family moved frequently when she was growing up due to her father's career. In 1990, Logan was placed 11th in rhythmic gymnastics representing Wales at the Commonwealth Games in Auckland. Following Durham University she began her broadcasting career in radio in 1992 and joined Sky Sports in 1996 then ITV in 1998, where she presented various fixtures including The World Cup and Champions League.

In 2004, Logan hosted *Sport Relief* for the BBC, before joining in 2007. While at the BBC, she has presented many programmes including *The Final Score, Inside Sport, Invictus Games, The One Show*. She was also a key member of the BBC's presenting team for the Olympic Games, 2014 Brazil World Cup and the 2014 Glasgow Commonwealth Games. From 2011 she presented the *Gabby Logan* show during weekdays and in 2013 *Sport Relief* from the Olympic Park as well as hosting the BBC's first ever *Sports Prom*. She lives in Buckinghamshire with her husband and two children.

WHAT WAS YOUR FIRST EXPERIENCE IN SPORT?

Sport was in my blood the day I was born. My dad flew off to play in a European quarter-final for Leeds United. I didn't really have a time without sport, everything that happened to me even as a young child was predicated because of sport, when we could go on holiday, when we gathered as a family, it was all to do with sports. As children we were encouraged to be very active and participate and to have fun with sport, which I think sometimes gets lost with young people. Especially in football, it's so serious from such a young age. There were three of us before my other brother came along, me and my sister and my brother, so we were a little sports team. We were able to play lots of sport together in the garden, make up games that involved sport. My own passion for sport and wanting to do it myself probably came from watching the Olympic Games and seeing more women doing sport, because the sporting life that I described before was male-dominated. So the Olympics was, for me, the eye opener.

WHO WERE YOUR INFLUENCES AND/OR ROLE MODELS?

When I was growing up, my dad was very much an influence because he had a professional sporting life and so did lots of his friends, so I saw professional sport more than amateur sport. When I started my own sporting experiences as a gymnast I looked up to other gymnasts who were either at my club or were international gymnasts. I also loved watching athletics. At the 1984 Olympics I loved watching Tessa Sanderson, Fatima Whitbread, Carl Lewis, and people like the American gymnast Mary Lou Retton and the diver Greg Louganis. There were lots and lots of different sports really. I'm nearly 50, and I think when I look back at my childhood, there weren't kind of standout women. If I was born in 2000, I would probably be telling you that I loved Helen Glover and Jessica Ennis-Hill, the incredible women who broke through into people's consciousness in 2012. I am a product of my age in that the sporting heroes tended to be men, so I love Daley Thompson for example. But I didn't see that as being a negative thing, that I didn't see lots of women around in sport. It just was what it was, and for the women that did break through, I was always incredibly taken by them. I had a massive obsession with Steffi Graf and thought she was an incredible athlete as well as tennis player, for example.

Denise Lewis and Gabby Logan

HOW HAS COVERAGE OF WOMEN'S SPORT CHANGED OVER THE YEARS?

We didn't see a lot of women doing sport before and now there is much more coverage. It's grown massively since 2012, which was a watershed year with women achieving at the highest level on television. I'm lucky that I cover a couple of women's sports – women's football and women's rugby. But also I cover athletics, which is one of the most equal playing grounds for sport because you have a women's 800 metre race and then the men's 5000 metre comes afterwards and then you might have a women's high jump and a men's pole vault. There's no 'Women's Day', and that's always been such a powerful thing for athletics because nobody goes, "Why are the women racing today? I just came here to see the men!" You can imagine a load of old bufties turning up at Lord's and if they were going to see the England men playing, going, "Why are the women here today? I didn't buy a ticket for the women!" Athletics has always been powerful in that respect, quite unique in terms of its early adoption of female stars. Tennis has had that opportunity as well, and golf to a certain extent, but even they were played separately. The finals for Wimbledon are on separate days and the tickets are more expensive for the men's final than the women's final. The joy now for me, professionally, is that we do bring all those stories to life and create possibilities for young people.

WHO ENCOURAGED YOU IN YOUR SPORTING AMBITIONS?

I was very lucky: when I gave up my ambitions to be a top-class tennis player and started doing gymnastics more seriously. At my club in Leeds they had two fantastic coaches: Anne Tallentire and Kathy McCreevy. They were very important. I also see this now with my own children in sport; the practicalities of it are that you have to get children from A to B all the time, move them around. So you've got to have families that want to be invested in their children's future in sport, and some people just don't see it as a priority. I think the parents' experience is a big factor. If you've got a parent who's enjoyed and loved sport, then they see the benefits that can come, whether it is in competing at a low level or it's just training. I was really grateful to my grassroots coaches and also to my mum, who was my taxi driver effectively! But it doesn't have to be the mum. My daughter wouldn't have done as much as she has without my husband's support. If you look at successful sportswomen, it's often because of the father's support; there's a different dynamic at work. There's quite a lot of high profile examples of people like Victoria Pendleton, whose dad was really instrumental in her carrying on cycling and pushing her and her brother to cycle. Steffi Graf's dad was heavily involved in her career and Richard Williams was obviously a very important man in Venus and Serena Williams' careers. It's really important for dads to feel confident about that relationship.

HOW DID YOU GET INTO THE SPORTS BROADCASTING INDUSTRY?

When I was 15 I was on Blue Peter and I thought, "Gosh, telly seems an exciting place to be and I'd like to work there." I started writing off letters and asking people for help. Just anywhere: local radio, trying to get experience, and when I was in my gap year, I'd already done a week on a national newspaper shadowing journalists on the sports desk. When I went to university, I started working for a radio station in Newcastle and I was doing the breakfast show. Nothing to do with sport, but they could see I was really into sport. They said, "Would you like to do touchline interviews?" and I just thought it was like a fun Saturday job. I did touchline interviews at Saint James Park, Newcastle United in the season they nearly won the league and it was a brilliant time to be around there. Then Sky Sports saw me and they were looking to have more women onscreen and asked me to go down to a screen test, and suddenly I found myself in sports broadcasting, which wasn't where I initially thought I was going to go, but it was an exciting, dynamic area of television and journalism. I learned a lot more on the job in that environment. And then things went from there.

DID YOUR BACKGROUND IN A SPORTING FAMILY AND AS A PROFESSIONAL SPORTSWOMAN HELP WHEN YOU WERE STARTING OUT?

Yeah, because I had a passion for it. I didn't go into it because I wanted to as a career option but my bosses could see that I had a passion for sport and they were very keen to harness that.

WHAT ARE THE MOST INTERESTING AND CHALLENGING ASPECTS OF YOUR ROLE?

It's challenging in live television when things are going wrong, trying to make sure that that doesn't come across on screen. Sometimes it's challenging when a match isn't brilliant, to address that for the audience. You have to be honest though. I think it's like anything in life, you've got to have the ups and downs. It's just an interesting field to work in because it's always changing. You start off a programme and you never really know how it's going to end and it's never the same. For example, the Six Nations Rugby this year – for the men's first three matches there was a 3-point margin or less. That's exciting, because until the very last moment, the game could move either way. It's adrenaline-fuelled. You're dealing with noisy stadiums and all those big noisy PA systems and all that stuff going on and it's quite a high-octane, adrenaline-filled environment. That's the reason to keep going back for more, I think.

WHAT ARE YOU MOST PROUD OF IN YOUR CAREER SO FAR?

Still being here really and still doing it. It's a competitive industry and there are a lot more women working in the industry now, which is fantastic and there's a lot more opportunity for people from different backgrounds, certainly to when I first started out. I'm proud to have been part of the vanguard, to have helped show what's possible.

TELL US ABOUT YOUR FAVOURITE SPORTING MOMENT, YOUR OWN OR SOMEONE ELSE'S.

It's very difficult to pick one thing, but I covered the Rugby World Cup when England won in 2003 and being on the pitch interviewing those players in that moment was so special. A lot of them were friends because my husband played for Wasps at the time and there were people who had been to my wedding! Seeing your friends win a World Championship and being that close, being the person that puts the microphone under their nose was really lovely. Obviously it's hard to interview people you know when things have gone wrong, and there are those moments as well, but that was really special. And working on the 2012 Olympics. I don't think anything will ever surpass the joy of being in that environment; it was something you just didn't want to end because every day was just a dream and there were such enormous successes for Great Britain as well. So the stories were flowing, they were easy. It was an easy work environment in some ways. It was challenging because we were working super long days doing big, complicated shows, but it was easy because the product was so good.

WHAT ARE THE MAIN CHALLENGES FOR WOMEN IN SPORT TODAY?

The main challenges are still grabbing the branding and the marketing share that women deserve. How do you keep being innovative and trying to make sure that women's sport is funded properly? It's a double-edged sword. The product has to be really good to demand the marketing budgets and the sponsorship, but without those

things it's difficult to grow. So I think what's important is making opportunity for women to play at the highest level, and they've got to have the resources behind them. Getting the hours on television is still a challenge. There are lots of innovative campaigns to get women involved in sport as well. But I think women's sport is doing well. The WSL sponsorship with Barclays is a massive success and should be seen as a huge example of what can be achieved. There are innovative ways of doing things, like the way netball, when it wanted to be onscreen, did a campaign; they funded themselves on Sky which led to more coverage of their sport, which then led to more demand for their sport. But the challenges are fundamentally numbers, whether it's financial numbers or numbers playing the game.

WHAT DO YOU THINK ABOUT THE MEDIA COVERAGE OF WOMEN IN SPORT?

It's clearly a lot better than it was, but there's still more to do. The BBC has really, really pushed hard in terms of putting women's sport in very central places in the schedules and on iPlayer, so they're making sure that there is an opportunity to watch and to be invested in it, especially over the last three or four years, major tournaments – the Women's World Cup got incredible eyeballs, 11 million for the semi-final. The Women's Euros – every match was on the BBC, which is huge. I think the change is enormous. Since 2012 we see a lot more women's sport on TV and we read a lot more women's sport in the newspapers and we hear those stories being covered on the radio. But like I said before, it's got to earn its place in a busy schedule and earn its place in a busy landscape. So we've got to keep making sure that editors and broadcasters have the right product to push, because you can't just say, "Write more about women in sport! You've got to have stories to tell, and you've got to have people to get behind.

WHAT ADVICE WOULD YOU GIVE TO YOUNG WOMEN INTERESTED IN GETTING INTO SPORTS BROADCASTING?

It is all about experience, whether you're going to a park on a Sunday morning and just watching a game of football, rugby, then you're writing up a report. How is your writing style? What are you focusing on? Know your stats, your information that you're going to bleed into your report. Have a passion for something, don't just go, "I want to work in sports journalism." You gotta have some kind of push, because there will be a lot of cold, damp, wet nights, rainy Saturday afternoons, freezing cold winter mornings, where you're outside for seven or eight hours and the sport isn't great. You've got to endure those experiences along the way and you've got to enjoy them, otherwise it will feel quite a chore. Read loads of sports biographies and find out the kind of things that make you come to life. Who is it? What is it? Where is it? It might be that you think you want to cover football, but actually it could be cycling, or it could be Olympic sport. So just try and get as much experience as you can and then if you're really serious about it, maybe do a postgrad in sports journalism, or go and apply for work experience in places. There are so many opportunities now in the industry, and so much more coverage of sport and different platforms. There's many ways to enter.

HOW CAN WE ENCOURAGE MORE GIRLS AND WOMEN TO PARTICIPATE IN SPORT?

In schools we don't have enough PE in the curriculum. Mental health is directly linked to our ability to move and be engaged with our bodies. We have a mental health epidemic coming down the track and I think we've got to try and get all the agencies to work together on this one because it's so important to keep kids as active as possible and to see sport as being something that's in their life and being motivated to keep doing it because they understand the mental health benefits. For me, that's more important than saying we need to produce another generation of brilliant footballers or brilliant rugby players. There's always something that you enjoy so it's having that possibility. It might be that you want to play badminton once a week or join a ladies netball team. Netball got a massive uptake after the Commonwealth Games success in 2018. I've got friends who hadn't played for twenty years who were going back and playing netball. Being together with a group of people who are like-minded and looking after yourself and your body is just brilliant.

WHAT'S NEXT FOR YOU?

I've got my memoir coming out, I enjoyed writing that and hope it is received well. I want to do more writing and keep doing the fun things that I do in sport, that would be great for the next ten years or so. I didn't think I'd be on telly after 40, so why not after 50? Live more in the moment and enjoy what I'm doing, that is my mantra now, rather than trying to plan too far ahead. And keep doing things that are exciting.

YAROSLAVA MAHUCHIKH

Yaroslava Mahuchikh (2001-) is a Ukrainian high jumper. She was the 2018 Summer Youth Olympics gold medalist, 2019 World Championships silver medalist, 2020 Summer Olympics bronze medalist, and 2022 World Indoor Championships gold medalist.

Mahuchikh was born in Dnipro and started the high jump at the age of 11, and at 15, she won the gold medal at the 2017 IAAF World U18 Championships in Nairobi by the largest margin in World U18 Championships history. She has continued to win championships and break records for the last five years including clearing 2.06 metres at Banská Bystrica in 2021, the highest any woman had jumped indoors since 2012. Having won the bronze medal in the high jump event at the 2020 Summer Olympics in Tokyo, in March 2022, days after fleeing the Russian invasion of Ukraine, Mahuchikh claimed the gold medal in the high jump at the 2022 World Athletics Indoor Championships in Belgrade. She had to undertake a three-day journey of 2000 kilometres by car from Ukraine to Serbia in order to compete at the championships.

Beyond sport, the Ukrainian has two big passions: animals and the environment and regularly donates money for the maintenance of a dog and cat shelter in Dnipro.

WHAT WAS YOUR FIRST EXPERIENCE IN SPORT?

I started my training in athletics when I was 7 years old, and I started to do professional high jump at 11 with my coach Tetyana Stepanova. At that time I didn't know that athletics would be my future and that I would compete on an international level. After the under-18 World Championships, when I won and jumped to 1.92m, I decided to start my preparation for the Olympics in Tokyo. In 2020, I had support from my family, my coach, and I achieved this result and so I have a bronze medal.

WHO WERE YOUR INFLUENCES OR ROLE MODELS?

At first, I started athletics thanks to my older sister, because she was doing athletics. She has a silver medal from the European Championship in karate. I started doing karate and athletics, but I liked athletics more and I do athletics now. Then, of course, I watched the jumps of high-jumper Blanka Vlašić, she did beautiful jumps, and beautiful dancing after jumps!

WHO ENCOURAGED YOU?

My family supported me every time. When I was going through my first training camp for three weeks and it was too hard to study at the same time, I told my family, "Maybe I can just do school, because it's too hard to do athletics as well." But they said, "No, you can do it. You can do lessons and athletics. You must think about the future and be able to focus on several things in life." For the first few years they didn't believe me, but when they saw that I really loved athletics they supported me.

At Doha in 2019. Photo: EOC

HOW OLD WERE YOU WHEN YOU KNEW THAT YOU WANTED TO PURSUE A CAREER IN SPORT?

I think it was at 15, after the under-18 World Championships when I won, that I understood that I wanted to do it professionally and I wanted to prepare for the Olympic Games.

TELL US ABOUT A PARTICULAR CHOICE THAT WAS GOOD AND ONE THAT YOU REGRET.

I think in our life we shouldn't regret anything because every trouble, every situation, gives us experience for the future. It feels good that I believed in myself and continued to do athletics. In school, when the teacher said, "It's only a hobby, that's all," I believed in myself and continued to train and to show good results on the international level.

HOW DID YOU DEVELOP AS A COMPETITOR?

I remember my first Diamond League. I was 16 and I was going to Rome without my coach. But my manager said, "It's experience for you for the future." I was very excited but I came last. It was a bad result, but I understood that it was for the future. Now I compete at the Diamond League with the other girls and I understand what the Diamond League requires in its competition.

WHAT WERE THE MAIN CHALLENGES THAT YOU HAVE FACED IN YOUR CAREER SO FAR?

I think every day is a challenge, because you must wake up for morning training. And when you're tired, you must go to second training, but you understand that, in competition, if you train hard, competitions will be easier. A lot of athletes like competitions because you only run once, you only jump once and you do not have to work out!

WHAT DOES A TYPICAL DAY OF TRAINING LOOK LIKE?

If I'm at training camp, it's wake up, breakfast and go to the first training. That's one-and-a-half to two hours. After that, I go back to the hotel, it's lunch and maybe a little sleep. After this we're going to second training and then we come back to the hotel and truthfully, after that I don't want to do anything, I just want to lay on my bed. But I go out to dinner and after dinner I'll do a little bit of studying. I'm studying Physical Education because I want to be a coach.

HOW DO YOU MAINTAIN YOUR MOTIVATION?

I know that training is hard but I realise that I must do it because I am competing on an international level. I must get results for my country and show that its sportsmen and women are very powerful people. In training camp, I watch other athletes and they work hard and it motivates me to work hard too.

WHAT ARE YOU MOST PROUD OF?

Of course it was winning the bronze medal from the Olympics in Tokyo, and then winning a gold medal at the indoor championships. For me that's more important than the Olympics because I won it during this difficult time when my country is fighting to protect its independence. It was so unbelievable! It was wonderful because my people were so happy when they saw that a Ukrainian girl had won the World Championship.

WHAT IS YOUR FAVOURITE SPORTING MOMENT— YOUR OWN OR SOMEBODY ELSE'S?

I think it was at the Youth Olympic Games. There were some children on the Ukrainian team, a lot of games and it was such a good atmosphere. I think that's the best memory from my career. I'm proud to represent my country in competition because I want to show the world that the Ukrainian people are strong and that they never give up in any situation.

IF YOU COULD GIVE YOUR YOUNGER SELF SOME ADVICE, WHAT WOULD THAT BE?

I think I would say that you're doing alright, and in every situation, to believe in yourself. Don't look to other people to give you advice. They might say, "You can't do it, it's not for you," but if you believe in yourself, you still need to do it.

WHAT WOULD YOU LIKE TO SEE CHANGE FOR WOMEN IN SPORT?

I don't know what we can change, but I know that for women it is harder than for men. Women go through pregnancy and childbirth so it's more difficult to retain peak fitness and come back from that. But girls are powerful!

WHAT DO YOU THINK OF THE MEDIA COVERAGE OF YOUR SPORT?

There's lots of media interest in sports in Ukraine. We have a lot of media attention after all our competitions. They interview all the girls who compete. It's very good. Now it's become a major part of sports coverage. I think it's more popular than it was five years ago.

IS THERE A PARTICULAR ORGANISATION THAT HAS HELPED YOU?

I'd like to thank the Ukrainian Athletics Federation and my long-term partner PUMA. They help us because when we are training, we go to training camps in other countries. In Dnipro we have a school of athletics where you can train from being a small child until you are a teen. I grew up with this school.

WHAT'S NEXT FOR YOU?

For me the most important competition this year was the World Indoor Championships and next it will be the World Outdoor Championships and the European

Championships. I want to compete and win, and of course I'm continuing my preparation for the Olympics in Paris in 2024. I'm currently in Turkey and then we are going to a competition in the USA, the Diamond League. After that we're coming back to Germany, because there are supporters there.

ARE YOUR FAMILY BACK IN UKRAINE OR NOT?

My father, my grandma and our two cats are still in Ukraine. But my mother, my sister and her two-year-old daughter have gone to Poland to be with my cousin. Soon they are coming to Germany so we'll meet up there. I'd like to go back home as soon as possible and I really want to continue my preparation for the World Championships at home. I don't know when that will be because the military are still fighting to protect our country; it's very sad because a lot of people are dying at the moment. A lot of children have lost their parents and it's a really terrible situation for them. But my country is strong and I hope that as soon as possible we will win.

Competing at Doha 2019. Photo: WAO

50 WOMEN IN SPORT

EVE MUIRHEAD

Eve Muirhead OBE (1990-) is a a Scottish curler who won a gold medal at the 2022 Winter Olympic Games in Beijing as part of Team GB. She grew up in Blair Atholl, and started curling when she was 8 years old at a rink in the village of Pitlochry trained by her father, also an international curler. She began her career by winning four World Junior Championships and has won the European Championship title in 2011, 2017 and 2021. She made her Olympic debut in 2010, winning a bronze medal at Sochi 2014.

Muirhead was awarded the BBC Scotland Young Sports Personality of the year in 2009 for her achievements in curling. She modelled at the fashion show Dressed to Kilt in 2010 and became an ambassador for Piping Live!, a festival dedicated to playing the bagpipes, which she also plays, competing in four World Championships. There is a portrait of her with broom, clubs and pipes at the National Galleries in Edinburgh. Muirhead also plays golf and reportedly turned down the chance to become a professional golfer with the offer of two scholarships from American universities. Muirhead opened The National Curling Academy in Stirling, her home town, in 2017. She was awarded an OBE in the Queen's Birthday Honours list, June 2022.

WHAT WAS YOUR FIRST EXPERIENCE IN SPORT?

My dad was a high-class curler, he toured the world. He'd been to several World Championships and European Championships, and he definitely passed his experience on to me. I remember I was about 8 years old giving curling a go for the first time. I think I had trainers on with milk cartons stuck to the bottom and a tiny little brush which my dad brought me back from Canada!

WHO WERE YOUR INFLUENCES AND/OR ROLE MODELS?

My dad influences me and he's someone that I've always looked up to for advice. A role model of mine is also Jessica Ennis-Hill. I was lucky enough to see her down in London at the 2012 Summer Games.

WHO ENCOURAGED YOU?

My family and my teammates, I think they're two parts of my curling career that have definitely helped me and pushed me forward. My teammates have got me to where I am today and there have been lots of them, but each one has definitely brought different qualities. We make sure we're all the best and we encourage each other.

WHEN DID YOU KNOW YOU WANTED TO PURSUE A CAREER IN SPORT?

I knew I wanted to pursue my career in sport when I was young, when I was still at school. I never, ever missed PE. I never gave up on any challenge we were given. I always wanted to win and I think when I turned my hand to curling and golf I realised that I had that sporty side to me and I had a big opportunity to do well.

TELL US ABOUT A PARTICULAR CHOICE THAT WAS GOOD AND ONE YOU REGRET.

Taking up curling, trying to be as good as I can. I've put a lot of work into the sport of curling. I've trained very hard. I've never given up and I definitely believe that that's a choice, the best choice I've made. A regret of mine? I do have a slight regret that I didn't attend university, only in terms of missing that social aspect and meeting more people. I might have missed out on a few years of fun, of meeting new friends. But then again, I made the choice that I wanted to be a curler, and I guess I was at my first Olympics at university time.

TELL US HOW YOU DEVELOPED AS A COMPETITOR.

I developed as a competitor through a lot of challenges, I think that's the best way to describe it. Every single game that I lost, I always wanted to learn why I lost. I always wanted to get better and I never forget about it. I have probably lost as many games as I've won, if not more. I think focusing on how you can become better is one of the main challenges to becoming a good competitor.

WHAT DOES A TYPICAL DAY OF TRAINING LOOK LIKE?

A typical training day for me would be two ice sessions and a gym session and then around that you'll have your physio, your nutrition meetings, your catch up with people. So I'd usually be on ice starting about 8:00am for about an hour and a half on my own or paired with one other person. We then carry on into a team session running until about 12.30 and then, in the afternoon, we do our gym session. Three times a week we do strength and conditioning and the other two-to-three times we do cardio-based intervals. I do CrossFit-type sessions too.

HOW DO YOU MAINTAIN YOUR MOTIVATION?

To maintain motivation, you definitely have to set goals. I think that's one thing I've done well over the years, setting myself small goals to reach and once you reach them you then set yourself some new goals. I think that's probably kept me motivated to do better even in the gym. Every time I step on ice I always have an outcome I want to achieve in that session.

WHAT ARE YOU MOST PROUD OF?

I'm definitely most proud of winning that gold medal. I've worked very, very hard for that. I'm also very proud of my teammates for helping all of us get that far. It's taken a lot of hard work over the last six months in terms of missing out on qualification at the World Championships last year and then having to go through the qualifier to even get to the Olympics. I'm very proud of them too for basically just not giving up.

TELL US ABOUT YOUR FAVOURITE SPORTING MOMENT – YOUR OWN OR SOMEONE ELSE'S.

My favourite sporting moment is definitely stepping on that podium with the Olympic gold medal around my neck, and hearing the national anthem play was something very special. That's really when it hit home that I had won the gold. A lot of people saw that I got emotional. I think that's just because I was so relieved. I was just so emotional that the journey I'd been on to get there had paid off.

IF YOU COULD GIVE YOUR YOUNGER SELF SOME ADVICE NOW, WHAT WOULD IT BE?

If I could give my younger self advice, it would definitely be to slow down. I think over the last couple years since Pyeongchang 2018 I've just taken a small step back and focussed more on myself and on getting me to 100% before focusing too much on everything else. I think if you go at 100 miles an hour every day, all day, it doesn't work. That's one thing that I'd give my younger self advice about, just to take a step back and figure out all the options before jumping in at the deep end.

WHAT THINGS WOULD YOU LIKE TO SEE CHANGE FOR WOMEN IN YOUR SPORT?

I would like to see more young women involved in sport. I think we need to focus a lot on the grassroots and help develop sport, especially curling. Curling is one of those sports that gets a lot of limelight once every four years, but I'd like to increase that and get as much coverage as possible right through every single year.

WHAT DO YOU THINK ABOUT THE MEDIA COVERAGE OF WOMEN IN YOUR SPORT?

The media coverage is getting better for sure, and I've always believed that what I can do to help that is be successful. During the Olympics it was excellent, but we need to keep that coverage going all year round. Curling is not a huge sport in terms of size when you compare it to rugby, football, or golf, but I'd like to see it continue to grow.

IS IT MORE DIFFICULT FOR WOMEN TO MAKE A LIVING THAN MEN WORKING IN YOUR SPORT?

I wouldn't say there's any difference in terms of women and men within curling. I'm definitely one that is all about being fair and equal, but curling is one of those sports that in the majority of events, prize money is the same and jobs are not given to any particular male or female whatever role it is.

IS THERE A PARTICULAR ORGANISATION THAT HAS SUPPORTED YOU IN YOUR SPORT?

We've been very lucky to be funded by UK Sport and the National Lottery over the years and that's what's allowed me to become a full-time curler. I'm also always very proud to say I'm part of Team Red Sky. Those guys have helped me for the last 15 years to become the person I am, become a better person. I've also been very fortunate with many sponsors over the years that have helped me have a better lifestyle, helped me have a better quality of life with such things as eating a proper dinner; you can just spend that little bit more and get good quality food.

WHAT'S NEXT?

I have two more tournaments to go this season. I've got the last Grand Slam of the season, the Players' Championships in Canada. And then back home for a couple days before I fly out to the World Mixed Doubles Championships in Geneva. Another World Championships to go. So that's exciting. I'd love to be able to do European gold, Olympic gold, and a World mixed double gold. There's a long way to go before that, but that's what's next for me. And then of course, enjoying the summer. I'm looking forward to getting a holiday and it would be nice to switch off from curling for a little while.

Liz Nicholl CBE. Photo: World Netball

LIZ NICHOLL

Liz Nicholl CBE (1952-) is the former Chief Executive of UK Sport, and current President of World Netball. Nicholl was born in Barry, Vale of Glamorgan, Wales, the sixth of seven children. Her father was a schoolteacher who coached his school's sports teams. She played netball as a centre and wing attack, and represented Wales in international netball competitions including two World Championships with 22 caps between 1975 and 1979.

She was appointed as Chief Executive of England Netball in 1980, serving for more than 15 years over two tenures. She was also director of the 1995 World Netball Championships held in Birmingham. Nicholl joined UK Sport in 1999, and was CEO from 2010-2019. Under her guidance, Team GB significantly improved their performance at international sporting events, including record performances at London 2012, Sochi 2014 and Rio 2016. In Rio, the UK finished second in the medal table, taking home 214 medals across both Olympic and Paralympic competitions. This was an increase on the team's incredible medal tally at the London 2012 Games.

In 2000 she received an MBE for services to netball, an OBE for services to sport in 2005, and a CBE for services to sport in 2015. A year later, in 2016, she was awarded the Sports Journalists' Association award for services to elite sport and in 2019, a Lifetime Achievement award from the British Sports Industry.

WHAT WAS YOUR FIRST EXPERIENCE IN SPORT?

I come from a big family of seven children. Anne, Margaret and Theresa came first, followed by Mike and Tim, then me and Patrick. My mother was a midwife and my father a primary school teacher in Barry. Both parents were very keen on sport and my father led much of the after-school cricket and football competitive sport activity for the boys. The opportunities for girls to play sport in school were very limited. I was envious of the boys, but I had access to footballs and cricket equipment and from a very young age I played with my brothers and other boys from school in the local park. I was very competitive! I discovered netball at Grammar school in Cardiff and soon realised that my ball handling skills were transferable, and I really enjoyed winning. I played netball for my school, for Cardiff schools and South Wales school girls.

WHO WERE YOUR INFLUENCES AND/OR ROLE MODELS?

During my school years, I felt myself growing in confidence through sport as a player and when given responsibility as a captain and at times an umpire. I noticed articles in my local Barry paper about those from a nearby school who played netball for Wales. One, Jennifer Williams, lived around the corner. I was also aware of the long jumping-success of Lyn Davies who trained at Maindy Stadium in Cardiff, a venue that I had competed in at inter schools' events. They both made the possibility of achieving success feel real. When I was leaving school to go to Nottingham University a PE teacher from another school said, "Don't lose touch with Welsh Netball" and I thought then "she thinks I could play for Wales one day."

I played at an international level for six years from 1975. I gained 22 caps for Wales and played in two World Championships, in New Zealand in 1975 and in Trinidad in 1979. These opportunities gave me a glimpse of the administration of sport at an international level and I knew then that I wanted to work in sport.

WHO ENCOURAGED YOU?

Another key influencer for me was Sue Campbell or Baroness Sue Campbell DBE as she is now. I went to University in Nottingham to study Chemistry. Sue Campbell lived in Nottingham, played for England and was the coach to the English and British Universities Netball teams. I captained both. She was an inspirational coach and my skills and confidence developed further. I travelled back from Nottingham for Wales trials and was selected one year prior to the 1975 Netball World Championships.

Sue knew that I wanted to work in sport and pointed me towards the Loughborough Masters degree course in Recreation Management. Towards the end of 1977 she made me aware of a job opportunity in inter-university sport and my career took off from there. I have never forgotten the support and advice Sue gave me. I was very fortunate to have such an incredible coach and mentor at a critical stage in my career development.

HOW DID YOU GET INTO THE SPORT INDUSTRY?

My first job out of university was as the first full time General Secretary of the Women's Inter Varsity Athletic Board (WIVAB) organising inter-university competition in 16 sports for women students across 40 universities in England and Wales. This role gave me the opportunity to engage with other sporting organisations at a national level. In 1979 WIVAB merged with the men's organisation, the Universities Athletic Union. Whilst I was offered a number two role, I decided to take my chances and was delighted to be appointed as the first full-time CEO of England Netball.

WHAT ARE THE MOST INTERESTING AND CHALLENGING ASPECTS OF YOUR ROLE?

I have been so lucky throughout my career to take on roles that feel very significant in terms of providing opportunities that make a difference to the lives of others. When with WIVAB and England Netball, it was all about providing opportunities for women and girls to play, compete and succeed through sport. When with UK Sport, the organisation's commitment to providing equal support to athletes of equal talent transformed selection processes and the potential for more athletes of both genders to win Olympic and Paralympic medals.

Now in my role as President of World Netball, I can see the huge potential for our sport to grow internationally and contribute to creating a better world through connections, communities, collaboration and sharing. My Board is focusing on increasing our global reach and resources; driving game development and worldwide delivery of thrilling world class events; and harnessing the power of Netball to change lives through the creation of a new Foundation. We are hugely dependent on our voluntary workforce, and I never cease to be amazed by the care and commitment that is evident every day.

WHAT ARE YOU MOST PROUD OF?

I am proud of the way so many people in organisations across the British sporting system worked together to help athletes succeed. I am also very proud to be part of the Netball family. Now, as the President of World Netball, the global Governing Body for the sport, with 76 Member Nations across 5 Regions and 20 million participants, I am loving giving back to the sport that gave me so many opportunities. I am also a Board Member of the Barclays FA Women's Super League.

In the 20 years that I worked for UK Sport, the government agency responsible for actively investing National Lottery and Exchequer funding in Olympic and Paralympic sports to drive and showcase medal success to inspire the nation, I worked alongside some incredibly talented individuals and never stopped learning. I started out as Performance Director and in the intervening years my role developed to Director of Elite Sport, Acting CEO for a period, then to Chief Operating Officer and finally Chief

Executive from 2010 to my retirement in 2019.

It was an amazing journey, from a 'dream' that the UK could be a top nation in world sport, to the journey through the winter and summer Olympics and Paralympics from Sydney 2000, through London 2012 to Pyeongchang 2018. My retirement in 2019 was to enable the new CEO to take responsibility through Tokyo and through the investment decisions for Paris 2024 that follow.

From 1980, I was Chief Executive of England Netball for 16 years, managing the dual responsibility of England Netball CEO and Championship Director for the World Netball Championships 1995. I took a career-break of four years from 1982-86 to have and to raise my daughter and son. In those four years I took on voluntary positions with Welsh Netball and was delighted when England Netball re-recruited me in 1986.

WHAT THINGS WOULD YOU LIKE TO SEE CHANGE FOR WOMEN IN SPORT?

Women's sport is on the rise but is still lagging way behind men's sport. The Olympic/Paralympic and Commonwealth Games provide a gender balanced focus every couple of years and at long last the major men's sporting codes of football, cricket and rugby and their sponsors, broadcasters and media in the UK are embracing, resourcing, and showcasing their women's game. But for sports like Netball more resources and commercial partnerships are needed around the world to grow the sporting opportunities it provides, increase professionalisation, to showcase more competition products more often and to shine a brighter and more frequent light on the fantastic women leaders, administrators, coaches, athletes, and officials who are role models in my sport and across a much greater range of sports.

TELL US ABOUT YOUR FAVOURITE SPORTING MOMENT – YOUR OWN OR SOMEONE ELSE'S.

My favourite sporting moments relate to London 2012 – being in the middle of Trafalgar Square in July 2005 when London was announced as the bid winner and then, as CEO of UK Sport, being able to witness almost every one of the 65 Olympic medals and 120 Paralympic medals that followed. I was particularly moved at the sight of so many families bringing young children with disabilities to the Paralympic Games to focus on the ability of the athletes. What an inspiration!

WHAT ADVICE WOULD YOU GIVE TO WOMEN INTERESTED IN ENTERING YOUR INDUSTRY?

The advice I would give to young women that want to get into the sport industry is never give up, don't hold yourself back, set any personal doubt about your ability aside, follow your dreams, take every opportunity to gain relevant experience or a qualification, seek feedback from those you respect, take on leadership responsibilities when you have the chance as they will help you grow in confidence, reach out to others in the industry, apply for roles that you might think are beyond your reach and you might surprise yourself. In general, I think there are far fewer barriers now for women seeking employment in the sports industry and the Code for Sport Governance is helping to reform the industry ensuring publicly-funded bodies have a good gender balance on their Boards.

HOW CAN WE ENCOURAGE MORE GIRLS AND YOUNG WOMEN TO PARTICIPATE IN SPORT?

I think a key to encouraging more girls and women to participate in sport and activity is having an enjoyable first experience in early years. An experience that is positive and builds confidence about capability. So, ease of access in schools and in the local community is important. High cost is a deterrent and so affordability must be considered. An element of fun is important as is going with friends and/ or the opportunity to make new friends. What I see in Netball is the wonderful example of how athletes who have children are enabled to return to play at the very highest level with exceptional support being provided within the Netball community. It makes me proud of my sport.

WHAT ARE YOUR HOPES FOR THE FUTURE?

My hope for the future is that gender equality becomes more widespread around the world and that we will see and feel the impact of many more men advocating for this positive change.

Nicholl at Congress in Liverpool, during the Netball World Cup 2019, where Nicholl was elected as President of World Netball. Photo: World Netball

CELIA QUANSAH AND MEGAN JONES

Celia Quansah and Megan Jones are both professional rugby players who were selected to be part of Great Britain's Rugby Olympic team at the Tokyo Olympics 2020. The couple has been dating for a long time, and are LGTBQ+ activists.

Celia Quansah (1995-) is an English rugby sevens player. She was born to an English mother and a Ghanaian father, and grew up in Twickenham. She participated in athletics, winning the long jump event at the 2011 School Games, and represented England internationally in heptathlon. Whilst at university, she took up rugby and was invited to join the England Sevens programme for 2018-19, and played for the winning GB team at the 2019 Rugby Europe Women's Sevens Olympic Qualifying Tournament.

Megan Jones (1996-) is a Welsh and English rugby union player. She debuted for England against New Zealand in 2015. Despite being a Welsh-speaker and growing up in Wales, Jones made her XVs debut for England in July 2015, playing against New Zealand in the Rugby Super Series that year. Selected for the English squad for the 2017 Women's Rugby World Cup in Ireland, she scored the side's opening try against Spain. Jones joined the England Sevens programme full-time but both men's and women's teams were made redundant in August 2020. She signed for Wasps Ladies as a fly-half in 2020. In 2021, she returned to Rugby XVs as an invitational player for England in the 2021 Women's Six Nations Championship.

HOW DID YOU FIRST GET INVOLVED IN SPORT?

CELIA: I am from a very sporty family. My sister was a British gymnast and my brother played rugby at a fairly high level. I started looking up to my sister and tried out gymnastics from the age of 3. Then throughout school I tried loads of different sports. At 11, I started doing athletics and at secondary school we got access to rugby but when I left school, I went to an athletics academy and I thought I was going to go to the Olympics as an athlete. That's what I had always dreamed of. I did heptathlon, so seven events over two days. Jessica Ennis was my hero growing up and I actually got to compete against her at the British Championships one year in hurdles, which was pretty cool. I just loved sport. I loved everything about it. I loved how you got to meet different people that you probably wouldn't meet otherwise. When I went to university I hadn't played rugby since school but I was falling out of love with athletics a little bit. I went to university at Loughborough and one of my friends started playing rugby and she told me, "Come on, you should try it. I think you'd be really good. We loved it at school." I'd always wanted to, but I'd never had the opportunity to play because I was always focused on athletics. So I just tried and I absolutely loved it and haven't looked back since. The team aspect of it is something that I didn't know that I needed.

MEGAN: I'm a bit different. I've been playing rugby since the age of 5 or 6. I was born and bred in Cardiff. Rugby is big there; there's a lot of passion and pride to be Welsh and playing rugby. My brother was playing, he's four years older than me, and I said to my dad that I wanted to go down and play with him. He said "No, I'm not letting her." My mum eventually told him, "Take her down." Of course, I went, and my dad was in awe. I think he was shocked more than the other parents, and then he built a huge community around it. So I think that really made me want to stick in it as well, because my dad was really

Jones facing a tackle.

interested in it and wanted me to do well because he was enjoying it from a spectator point of view. At the age of 6, I was playing with the boys. I was the only girl and I had to battle my way in. But I earned a lot of respect just because of the way I played; it wasn't really about gender.

The realisation that I was a little bit different, was when I was 12 and I applied to get into the Cardiff School boys' team. I eventually got in. I actually overtook one of the boys whose dad was the coach. It shows that it doesn't matter who you are, because what you do and how you perform on the pitch is what counts. I think that was the bit that really grabbed me. I loved the sense of respect and euphoria I got playing rugby and, similar to Celia, being in a team sport was really important to me.

At high school I shied away from it. I was trying to find my feminine side. I used to love running around the schoolyard but when I got to year eight, year nine, I was kind of like, "I need to stop getting muddy now, I need to be a bit more of a girl." Which is quite sad really, looking back on it. My high school was actually really supportive of sport but it was all the generic, hockey, netball, stereotypical sports for women and girls. When I was 16, I made the jump to come over to England because women's rugby in Wales was quite poor and then I got my first cap when I was 17 for England. My mum is from Bristol so I haven't looked back.

DID YOU HAVE OTHER PEOPLE BEYOND THE FAMILY WHO WERE ENCOURAGING YOU TO DO SPORT?

CELIA: My PE teacher was Mr. Watson; he's someone that sticks out to me as a big role model and someone who really encouraged me from a young age. When I went to secondary school, Miss Kemp was the one that brought rugby into the school. I always looked forward to PE and games. I just knew that I could get out there and do what I was good at. Afterwards, coaches were important. I started off at Saint Mary's and my coaches there obviously inspired me and then as I got a bit older and I moved on to heptathlon I was coached by Eldon Lake, who is the father of one of my best friends. These are all people that have massively inspired me along the way. And of course my parents, who have literally driven me up and down the country taking me to training sessions every week. They have supported me financially. You don't get paid as a youngster at all; you're the one that's paying. When you look back now you think, "God, I would never have been able to do any of that without them." My parents have been so supportive and when I got selected for the Olympics that was just really special because it was something that I could give back to them. They were so proud, it was so lovely to see.

MEGAN: My coach, Owen Smith from Cardiff 'Quins, was massively influential when I transitioned into the women's game. Same with Stuart Kibble. He was another coach there. They really took me under their wing. I used to do extra sessions and they would go out of their way. They never got paid for any of this, it was solely off their backs because they saw potential, and they really wanted you to prosper. That's really nice to look back on. So now I'll try and give back as much as I can. I had a Teachers Assistant in primary school who created our rugby team. I think she saw there was quality in our year. I remember she went out of her way. I think she was really keen to get us playing as much sport as possible. In high school, Mr. Jones, he was a geography teacher and also the boys' PE teacher, but he bought me a pair of Welsh cut-off gloves. No one wears them now, they're quite Brian O'Driscoll-esque. They've got no fingertips, they've just got grip. But it was the thing.

WHO WERE YOUR ROLE MODELS?

CELIA: Jessica Ennis was a big one, and Kelly Holmes. I remember I met Kelly Holmes at St Mary's. It's funny that they're both people that have a resemblance to me. When I look back on it now, I don't know that it was ever a conscious thing, but they were probably the two role models that I felt were kind of close to me and accessible.

MEGAN: All mine were male. The Welsh rugby players: Stephen Jones, Shane Williams, Dwayne Peel. It was the year 2008, when they won the Grand Slam. Women's rugby was not on TV, it's only just coming on now! You'd have to read it in the newspaper and then go and find it. I remember going to watch one of the women's Six Nation games, England versus Wales, but we only knew about it because it was in a newspaper article and my dad decided, "Right, let's go." I didn't know any of their names. Maybe Non Evans, she was one of the biggest in the Welsh women's game, and she also did judo and was a weightlifter. She was inspirational. But it was mainly those boys. The only role model I had was when I was 16 – it was Danielle Waterman, our coach. I went on to play alongside her, she was pretty influential and inspiring as well.

WHAT ARE THE MAIN CHALLENGES THAT YOU'VE FACED IN YOUR CAREERS SO FAR?

MEGAN: In high school, people made comments. I think if I didn't have my dad and people around me trying to thicken my skin, I would have had a really tough time. You know the classics: I used to get called a man, lesbian – not that that's offensive – but just loads of things. Just because of the sport I played and how I held myself. I'm maybe quite masculine in comparison to other girls. The feminine side I found challenging in terms of having to display that to people and show them that I am feminine, when actually you don't have to show that, you can just show who you are. Obviously, later on you understand that it's OK to be yourself, but when you're still developing it can feel really horrible.

CELIA: I had the same thing at school and I didn't even really play rugby. But because I was muscly, I constantly felt a bit out of place, and you would get comments all the time and even if they didn't necessarily mean it in a negative way, it was always pointed: "Your arms are really big," or "You're really muscly," or "Look at your legs." I've been called a man and all of those things as well, and I've always been quite a girly-girl, so for me, I really struggled with that.

Quansah making a dash

MEGAN: Your femininity feels attacked, right?

CELIA: Yeah, and that's something that I struggled with massively, even sometimes now. It's funny when I'm in sports kit, I'm like, "Yeah, get my muscles out as much as possible," then sometimes I'll be in a dress or something and I'm like, "OK, my arms feel a bit out there," and it's so crazy! That's just been instilled in me since I was tiny. But you grow up, like you said, and you learn to love yourself for who you are. But when you're young and you have all these negative comments coming at you, it does get in your head. It's quite worrying, because being fit and healthy was not considered beautiful.

MEGAN: The way being 'healthy' is marketed is so wrong! It's all skinny; it's not muscly. Some of my friends even now are like, "I want to go to the gym but I don't wanna get too big," and I'm like, "Are you joking? To get big you have to lift an extortionate amount a week, quite heavy weights and do quite a lot of reps, and have done it…

CELIA: For years!

MEGAN: But it's that concept of, "I don't want to be really muscly. I want just to be skinny. I'm just gonna do cardio and not eat." But there are so many ways to train.

HAVE YOU BEEN TROLLED ON SOCIAL MEDIA ABOUT YOUR LOOKS?

CELIA: I wouldn't say so necessarily though I've seen it loads on other people's, and we haven't got a massive following. Quite a lot of our followers are really positive.

MEGAN: And they support women's sport.

CELIA: But you see some of the comments on other people's posts which are ridiculous.

MEGAN: People do still comment like, "Women still playing rugby?" The abuse is about rugby, not body image, but just women playing rugby or football.

CELIA: And always being compared to the men, that's the one thing that we get a lot, especially on social media. And you think, "Well, we're literally like ten years behind the men, maybe more," and they try and compare us and it's just so frustrating.

WHAT DO YOU THINK ABOUT THE MEDIA COVERAGE OF WOMEN IN YOUR SPORT?

MEGAN: Well, it's hard because obviously their lens is male, probably white male, as well. A lot of their lens is only from what they've experienced or what they know, so education is the biggest thing that we can do to help everyone. All of us are always learning. We need as much awareness and visibility and calling people out as possible, and sometimes just positive confrontation. It might just be a case of saying, "Look, you can't really say that. This is how you should probably say it." And then that actually helps bring about a solution.

CELIA: Sometimes people say things they don't even realise they've said, but when you do call them out on it and they hear it repeated back to them, then they say, "Oh OK, I didn't realise it sounded like that, I didn't realise it came across like that."

MEGAN: One instance that sticks out to me is when a BBC journalist congratulated Andy Murray on being the first tennis player to win two Olympic gold medals and Andy Murray reminded him, "No, actually, Venus and Serena Williams. have won about four each." Allies like that are amazing.

HOW DO YOU FEEL ABOUT YOUR PERSONAL RELATIONSHIP COMING TO THE FORE IN THE COVERAGE OF WOMEN'S RUGBY BECAUSE YOU'RE OFTEN INTERVIEWED TOGETHER?

MEGAN: We've had a lot of positive feedback, positive comments about sharing our story and just being in an open, public relationship. I think a lot of that went hand-in-hand with journalists in interviews wanting to get two for the price of one, essentially.

But for us it's really positive, because all it is, is a natural representation of what we are doing, we're just putting it out there a little bit more. I don't think there's any controversial take on it. It's no different to office jobs, it's always the case that these things happen sometimes.

WHAT WOULD YOU LIKE TO SEE CHANGE FOR WOMEN IN YOUR SPORT?

MEGAN: Oh so many things. Biggest thing? You know that Real Madrid-Barcelona women's game in March 2022? 91,000 spectators for a women's game. I would love that for a women's game of rugby. Sell-out crowds for a World Cup match! 2025, they're bidding for a home Rugby World Cup for the women, so maybe that'll be possible. I'd love to see people wanting to come and watch it, really enjoying themselves, and just taking it in.

CELIA: For me, there are so many things, but I would love to see someone say, "Look, I'm gonna put this amount of money into the women's rugby and see what we could do with it." For example making the Allianz Premiership professional now, rather than saying, "In ten years time it will be professional." How far could we then be in ten years time? It's almost like you need someone to just take a risk with it now, and I don't even know how much of a risk it really is because…

MEGAN: There's so much money out there now.

CELIA: Yeah, it could just be so much further ahead in ten years' time. It's like, why are we waiting? Why don't we do it now? Then you'd get more visibility and get more youngsters coming through. They won't get to the age of 20 like me and say "Oh, I think I want to start playing rugby now," they'll be playing it from the age of 5 like Meg did, which is rare.

MEGAN: Do you know what I'd love to see? A female head coach or a female director of Rugby England or something like that. I'd love to see how many females there are on the board as well in terms of suit and ties. I don't think there's many. I'm sure there's qualified coaches and people like that, but I always say, boys look after boys. But why don't girls look after girls?

WHAT IS YOUR PROUDEST SPORTING ACHIEVEMENT?

MEGAN: The biggest one for me was getting into the Cardiff Schools boys' team because it made me think anything is possible. You can work anywhere and you could do anything as long as you just put your head down and crack on and that's something that's really stuck with me. Whenever I had a trial, I just thought back, casting my mind back to that and I just thought, well, look, bottom line is, if I do everything I possibly can, then the outcome is going to look after itself.

CELIA: I think mine was being selected for the Olympics. From such a young age, I'd just always known that I was going to go to the Olympics. It does sound weird because there's not many people who get to go as a track athlete. But as I was growing up, that was something that I always, always wanted, and that's something I was always pushing for. But it always seemed a little bit out of reach. Then when I was selected for a completely different sport, which obviously I didn't expect, I was so proud of myself. And like Meg said, it just shows that anything is possible. If you really, truly believe that you can do it and you work hard enough for it, you can do it. As I said, I was also so happy for my family and to be able to sort of give something back to them because they've put so much time and effort and energy into me.

WHAT MAKES A GOOD COMPETITOR?

MEGAN: Purpose. I try not to stick with the fact I'm just a rugby player because then you're boxing yourself in. If you can find purpose in your own identity, in what you want to achieve, I think that's powerful. It also encourages the people around you, bringing people with you along the journey. So being really purposeful in your identity, I think that's my big one.

CELIA: I think perspective is a big thing and I've learned a lot recently. I'm injured at the moment, and you have to step back and really look at the bigger picture and think, "Actually, I've got this. I'm so grateful for this. I've got this that someone else doesn't have." It's just really important to remember how privileged we actually are to even be in this position.

DO YOU THINK IT MAKES A DIFFERENCE HAVING A TEAM TO HELP MOTIVATE YOU AND INSPIRE YOU AS WELL?

CELIA: Yeah, massively. When I first came over from athletics it was something that I struggled with, having to take into consideration everyone around me. It sounds silly, but as an athlete all you have to focus on is you and you know that your training isn't going to affect anyone else. But now if I ever had a down day and I said, "I really, really can't be bothered to do that," a running session for example, there's not a chance in the world that I wouldn't do it, because I know it's going to affect the rest of the team. As an individual athlete, I feel like it was harder to get that motivation because I'd only be cheating myself. Having a team around you to motivate you during home training weeks or during lockdown was a massive thing. It is something that I never thought that I needed until I came into a team sport.

MEGAN: It's definitely that accountability aspect. Even taking sport out of the picture,

Joy after qualification for the Olympics. Photo: RFU

you still want to feel accountable for something that you're involved in, and that's the same within a team, it's a community. People share confidences with you and you get to balance each other out so you get to lean on each other.

IF YOU COULD GIVE YOUR YOUNGER SELF SOME ADVICE, WHAT WOULD IT BE?

CELIA: I would just tell myself to keep believing in myself, and, "Keep doing what you're doing and one day it will happen for you." Because there are so many things along the way that dip in and out and you get distractions, you get the negative comments from people, but just keep believing in yourself and that you're doing it for a reason and it's going to pay off.

MEGAN: Mine would be, "Be vulnerable." Because when I was growing up I was always, not quite reserved, but I was always a bit closed off until I really trusted someone, which I think is natural, right? But if we can be more vulnerable with people then I think there's more room to grow and I think if I had done that sooner I would have understood empathy and sharing more as well.

IS THERE A PARTICULAR PERSON OR ORGANISATION THAT HAS SUPPORTED YOU?

MEGAN: The National Lottery funded us. It's so amazing. My nan was like, "I've started buying the National Lottery scratch card." We are employed by England but during the pandemic our contracts were taken off us. The National Lottery stepped in and funded us for the prep up until the Olympics, so that was really important. We literally could not have done it without them. We wouldn't have had the training facilities, the programme, access to coaches, staff, physiotherapists. So yeah, that's a big one. Also, Celia's mum and dad for letting us stay here! That's an organisation surely?

CELIA: To be fair, they sorted us out, didn't they? After the pandemic we were left with nothing really and so we moved in with my parents and we've been here since.

MEGAN: Family's community – it always comes back to community, the little teams around you. That generosity is so amazing, but I think it also highlights the stark disparity between us as international rugby players. The international rugby players on the men's side don't have to live with their parents because of the renumeration that they get. So one of the things we want to see change is equal pay for the men and women's teams.

CELIA: Just having a professional premiership so we are paid to play. Megan and I are very lucky, we're contracted through England, but a lot of the girls have full-time jobs. They're doctors, teachers, dentists. They come and train in the evening and play semi-professional at the weekend. It's very frustrating, it's so hard to balance both.

MEGAN: They come straight in from work to training at half-five, they're there till 9:00pm and then they gotta wake up at 6.00 in the morning. I can't wake up till like 11:00am the next day if I train that late! The recovery time is just not possible. And that's the power of love of the game.

WHAT IS NEXT? WHAT ARE YOUR HOPES FOR THE FUTURE?

We've got the home Commonwealth Games in Birmingham at the end of July, so that will be amazing. We've never had a home tournament, we don't have a London leg which the boys have for sevens. So it's really special because not everyone can travel to Dubai, or South Africa, all these lovely places. And we need to qualify for the Rugby World Cup Sevens, which is in South Africa in September. We've got loads of little World Series in between. We call them little World Cups, which they essentially are. It's the same teams which we play every couple of months. Then the Olympics, Paris 2024.

CELIA: And for us personally, we're looking to buy a house at the end of this year, which will be lovely. And we love travelling. We want to see the other side of the world, if we can at some point. When we go to tournaments we only get two to three days to explore so we'd love to go and do it properly, wouldn't we?

MEGAN: It's hard because there are so many rugby events coming up. We still play Wasps, and 2025 is a home World Cup for Fifteens. We'll take it as it comes. Don't hold yourself down to anything, whatever happens, will be.

Quansah facing opposition from the Harlequins women's team.

ARIES SUSANTI RAHAYU

Aries Susanti Rahayu (1995-) is a professional sport climber from Indonesia. A Muslim who wears hijab when she climbs, she has been nicknamed 'Spiderwoman' for the incredible way she can scale a climbing wall. Rahayu came to international attention in 2019 for breaking the world record for speed climbing. She is the first woman to climb a speed wall in less than seven seconds. Rahayu has also won numerous medals at the Asian Games, the Asian Championships and the World Cup.

As a child, she practised climbing trees near her home and in local parks. In 2007, she was introduced to sport climbing by her teacher when she was still a junior high school student. In 2017, she competed in the Climbing World Cup for the first time, and garnered a silver medal at the World Cup in Xiamen. In the 2017 Asian Championships in Tehran, she was awarded a bronze medal.

In 2018, she got her first gold medal at the International Federation of Sport Climbing (IFSC) World Cup in Chongqing. Then, she achieved a bronze medal in Tai'an and two more gold medals at the World Cups in Wujiang and Xiamen, in China. At the end of the 2018 season, she was second in the overall ranking in the speed discipline. In the same year, at the Asian Championships in Kurayoshi, she came third after she made a false start in the semi-final.

Forbes Magazine included Rahayu in its 2019 Asia 30 Under 30 list.

WHAT WAS YOUR FIRST EXPERIENCE IN SPORT?

My first experience of competing in sport was at school doing athletics and I wasn't that keen. It wasn't until junior high school that I discovered sport climbing.

WHO WERE YOUR INFLUENCES AND/OR ROLE MODELS?

My role models in life are definitely my parents, especially my mom. Working abroad in Saudi Arabia was definitely not easy for her, but she did it for the good of the family. She taught me not to be afraid to fight for what I want and to pursue my dreams.

WHO ENCOURAGED YOU?

Apart from my parents, Hendra Basyir, Indonesia National Sport Climbing Team Coach is the one who always believed in me. Not only to become a world champion, but also to break the existing world record. I practised very hard and sometimes I was close to giving up. But in 2019 I made it to become the first woman in history to scale a speed climbing wall in under seven seconds!

WHEN DID YOU KNOW YOU WANTED TO PURSUE A CAREER IN SPORT?

I started to think about my sports career when I was in the second grade of senior high school. I took part in my first junior national competition in 2008 and won a silver medal. After that, I chose to focus mainly on my sporting achievements.

TELL US ABOUT A PARTICULAR CHOICE THAT WAS GOOD AND ONE YOU REGRET.

In 2017, I was invited by my coach to join the National Athletes training for the Asian Games 2018. Although, I was chosen as a reserve, I was very grateful. I trained really hard to improve and be part of the team and was finally selected to take part in the Asian Games 2018, where I won a gold medal. At that moment, I realized that I had made the right decision. I didn't really notice that I was missing out on friendships or things like that at school. My life was all about training for sport climbing.

WHAT ARE THE MAIN CHALLENGES THAT YOU HAVE FACED IN YOUR CAREER?

I had to let go of all the normal things about being a teenager in order to focus on my sporting career. Following a busy daily training schedule and being far away from my family was hard when I went to competitions abroad, but I soon realized that that was a necessary cost for an athlete who really wanted to achieve great things. Now the toughest challenge is how to keep my focus and get the best results in every competition.

TELL US HOW YOU DEVELOPED AS A COMPETITOR.

When I was kid, people often underestimated me and my family. I'm someone who doesn't like to be beaten. So, there is no choice for me, but to win. And, Alhamdulillah, [Praise be to God], I've succeeded, beyond what I ever imagined.

WHAT DOES A TYPICAL DAY OF TRAINING LOOK LIKE?

I prepare different activities each day. In sport climbing, you can't stop training for a few weeks, because it's hard to regain momentum. So every day I do weightlifting, jogging, running, a fitness session, and of course climbing on the climbing wall! Sometimes I have a day off, occasionally two, if I've been training extra hard.

HOW DO YOU MAINTAIN YOUR MOTIVATION?

Every time I want to give up, I always look back to see how far I've come already. Then, I remember what my mom told me: "Don't waste the opportunity that God has given you... lift your head up and be proud of your achievements!"

WHAT ARE YOU MOST PROUD OF?

What I'm really proud of in my career is that I could make a difference to my parents' lives and that I can bring respect to Indonesia in sports internationally. I'm proud that I achieved this as a Muslim woman, wearing hijab, as Muslims are a minority in sport.

TELL US ABOUT YOUR FAVOURITE SPORTING MOMENT – YOUR OWN OR SOMEONE ELSE'S.

My favourite moment is when I broke the world record, winning at the Asian Games, and also being the world champion. Those are moments that I'll never forget, especially as I had injured my hand prior to competing in Xiamen and was worried about my ability to compete at all.

IF YOU COULD GIVE YOUR YOUNGER SELF SOME ADVICE NOW, WHAT WOULD IT BE?

I'd say: "Thank you for being strong since you were a child. Thank you for being independent when you were far away from your parents. Thank you to my body for being strong and tough!"

WHAT THINGS WOULD YOU LIKE TO SEE CHANGE FOR WOMEN IN YOUR SPORT?

There are no racial or gender issues in my sport. I'd really like to see sport climbing spread out and become popular around the world, especially in Africa, since they currently only have a few participants.

WHAT DO YOU THINK ABOUT THE MEDIA COVERAGE OF WOMEN IN YOUR SPORT?

Since the Asian Games 2018, the Indonesian media has given more attention to sport climbing, both the competitions and the athletes. And more people have joined the sport, which is exciting. Of course, we have to be prepared if our personal life comes under the media spotlight too.

IS IT MORE DIFFICULT FOR WOMEN TO MAKE A LIVING THAN MEN WORKING IN YOUR SPORT?

The Indonesian government gives lots of support to their athletes. They give an allowance for both men and women athletes, equally. In sport climbing, it's generally harder for male athletes because they have more competitors out there.

IS THERE A PARTICULAR ORGANISATION THAT HAS SUPPORTED YOU IN YOUR SPORT?

The Indonesian Sport Climbing Federation (FPTI) is the main body for sport climbing.

WHAT'S NEXT?

Although I'm no longer a member of the National Sport Climbing Team, I'm still involved in the sport. I'm currently part of the Regional Sport Climbing Team in Jawa Tengah, where I focus on training young local athletes and developing climbing sports in the region.

Rahayu celebrates after a winning climb. Photo: Eddie Fowke IFSC

JAWAHIR ROBLE

Jawahir Roble, (1995-) also known as Jawahir Jewels or JJ is a Muslim Somali-born British football referee who wears a hijab on the pitch. She grew up in north-west London with her parents and eight siblings.

In 2013, with Ciara Allan, a development officer at her local Football Association, they launched the Middlesex FA Women's League with a new Desi division for girls. In return for refereeing games regularly, Middlesex FA funded Roble's training to become a qualified referee.

In 2017, she was selected for a Respect Award, in recognition of her volunteering work for the education charity Football Beyond Borders (FBB) and with the Middlesex FA, coaching FBB's first women's team, as well as for achieving a Level Six refereeing qualification. She is also an FA Youth Leader.

In 2014, aged 19, she wrote: I have a dream that one day my fellow Muslim sisters will happily play sport. My aim is to engage young Muslim girls in sports from the age of 8 years to 15 years. My overall aim is to promote football as a tool to engage young girls and then to run workshops that help develop team-building skills, boost confidence and also promote a healthy lifestyle.

WHAT WAS YOUR FIRST EXPERIENCE IN SPORT?

My first experience in sport was back when I was in Somalia. I would play football with the kids in the neighbourhood, kids in school, with my brothers. We had a massive courtyard in the house so we would also play inside.

WHO WERE YOUR INFLUENCES AND ROLE MODELS?

Growing up, when I was in Somalia, I had no one. The way I stumbled across football was just literally seeing the boys play and also wanting to play. There wasn't a superstar in Somalia that I looked up to, but moving to the UK when I was 10 years old, I got a bit more understanding of how football works, with all the leagues. I was like, "Oh wow, so you get to see more people playing." I watched Rachel Yankey play so I had her as my inspiration growing up. Football was always something that made me look forward to things.

DID YOUR PARENTS ENCOURAGE YOU?

My parents actually said, "Don't play football." They were like, "That girl will grow out of it one day and hopefully she will just do something more ladylike." But I kind of said to myself, "That doesn't make sense. This sport makes me happy and my parents are actually telling me not to do it. So I don't know what's happening. But until we get to the bottom of it, I'll continue." Because I didn't see anything wrong with it. I kind of encouraged myself. I motivated myself, because I had a lot of passion for it.

WHEN DID YOU KNOW THAT YOU WANTED TO DO SOMETHING WITH SPORT AS A CAREER?

I used to take one of my brothers to football when I was about 13. I liked the structure.

I loved all those nice parents. The best experience ever. There were so many nice people out there. It wasn't wasted time either, because you get to understand how coaches operate, how the teams are linked. You have to study the game because that's the only way you enjoy it more. You need to know why a decision is given, instead of getting frustrated at things that you don't agree with. To be a referee, you have to keep your cool. You have to stay calm and try not to take sides.

I always wanted to be a football player and represent either Somalia or England Ladies. And that didn't go according to plan. My parents didn't want me on the pitch playing football. I thought maybe I could be on the coaching side because there's less running involved. I was like, "OK, coaching is my next big thing." Then I stumbled across refereeing.

WHAT MADE YOU THINK YOU HAD THE RIGHT PERSONALITY FOR BEING A REFEREE?

Good question. I would say the fact that I'm outgoing, I'm talkative. I'm a people person, I love meeting new people. The only thing that made me think twice about it was the travel, because I don't drive. I'm still learning to drive. I was like, "How do I get to these games?" I don't care if people shout at me and say "Oh, who's this referee? Are you blind? Are you crazy? Why are you doing this?" I bring that player over and say, "Excuse me, respect me. I'm not getting money, I'm volunteering." Most of the time when I was starting off, I was volunteering.

When I'm refereeing, I always tell them to enjoy the game. Even though I am there to control the game, I don't see myself as the boss, because if I don't respect them, if I make myself bigger than them, then they won't respect me. As a referee you have to be humble. They can see that you are the authority person. But you have to carry yourself with a lot of respect, because respect is given when you're giving it to other people. Even though I can send them off, I don't feel like I'm there to tell them what to do. Often there's a fine line of telling them, "Be respectful to each other."

WHAT ABOUT WHEN YOU HAVE TO SEND PLAYERS OFF?

You have to have confidence. Some of them won't go! I'm like, "You are off!" I give them the red card and then people say, "The referee just sent you off, are you gonna take that?" Their friends will encourage them to argue so I have to stay assertive, I have to look like I'm very confident with my decision. That way they will be like, "Okay, she's not going to change her mind, this girl's made her decision. I'm just gonna leave the pitch." But if I feel like 50/50 about it, players can tell when you're not confident and then they'll argue with you more.

HOW DO YOU DEAL WITH BAD BEHAVIOUR?

The abuse that I get – you can't stop it. A lot of people have told me it comes with the game. It shouldn't come with the game. Even though you don't agree with a decision, go to the referee and say, "I don't agree, give me a reason why you made that decision," instead of screaming at the referee's face, making the referee feel small. I have to keep reminding players, "I made the decision. And this is what I see. I am not on anyone's side. How am I going to benefit from it?" And then they're like, "Yeah, ref', okay."

HOW DO WE ENCOURAGE OTHER YOUNG WOMEN TO GET INVOLVED IN SPORT?

I run my own session every Sunday morning. I'm always telling these girls, "Enjoy playing football," because when I was young I used to hide it from my parents. I was always playing behind their back. I say to them, "You're getting your parents to bring you. You're getting your uncles and aunties to bring you, your whole family knows you play football. Enjoy that because I never had it. Also, if playing doesn't work out, you can be a referee. There's so many sectors in football."

Now I'm educating others, I'm letting them know, there are so many things you can do within football. It would be fantastic to have more women referees, wouldn't it? And to get them to the top games. That's my dream honestly. Now I'm on the Women's National League, the Women's Super League, so a few steps closer.

ARE THERE OTHER WOMEN REFEREES WHO'VE MADE A NAME FOR THEMSELVES?

Yes, Bibiana Steinhaus, she's from Germany and she was the first female to referee the Bundesliga. Rebecca Welch was first female referee to referee the EFL and then you've got Sian Massey-Ellis, she's the only female assistant referee in the Premier League to this day. All these ladies at the top show me that if I work hard and I stay persistent, and motivated, I can also reach there one day.

WHAT'S YOUR FAVOURITE SPORTING MOMENT?

I would say the England men playing in the European Championships in 2021. That final was the most nerve-wracking I've ever watched. Honestly, that really made me upset. So sad. I was like, "We've come so far!" At the same time, that was the best moment ever, because I was so proud of how 11 players united the whole country. Everyone was watching football! There were so many fans who had hope, and everyone was together, everyone watching, the streets were fully decorated with flags, families were going to each other's homes, we got snacks, everyone was in the England kit. I think that was so amazing.

WHAT DO YOU THINK OF THE RACISM TOWARDS THE PLAYERS WHO MISSED THE PENALTY SHOTS?

That was so sad because people are missing the bigger picture, how much they've achieved and then a penalty miss is what you're gonna remember. Imagine all this build-up that these players have done. Everyone was working so hard. I bet the keyboard warriors, if they were told to take that penalty, they wouldn't even touch the ball. That's how nervous they would have got. Young Saka did so well. He's scored so many good goals. One little mistake is what everyone is gonna remember, which is very sad. I think it's just a few people that ruin the football for everyone.

WHAT DO YOU THINK ABOUT THE MEDIA COVERAGE OF WOMEN IN SPORT?

Honestly, since the Women's World Cup there has been so much coverage: Sky Sports, BT. We're seeing women's sport, women's football especially, on Sky Sports. That's a big deal! That's a massive achievement. And now we have five tournaments coming up, we have the Euros coming up. Now imagine how many things are going to happen for the women's game. I can't wait! I'm here for it.

DO YOU THINK THAT THERE'S A NEW AUDIENCE DEVELOPING TO WATCH THE SPORT?

Yes, there is. If you go to women's games, it's family-orientated. You can take your niece to football and she will not hear a lot of abuse. It's so much better. The female players, when they're finished their games, will come up to the fans. They will sign stuff. It's such a nice family day out.

We just need more people to invest in the women's game and believe in it. The reason why it didn't take off before was because female players had to have two jobs, three jobs. As an athlete how can you reach your potential if you're working in so many jobs? But if you're told just to play football and don't worry about anything else then of course, you're gonna work hard. You're either playing or you're at the gym: you're gonna work super hard. So knowing that most of these female players are going full time, it's just the best news. The quality of football will improve. More people will come to the stadiums because the games will be more entertaining. It will be more physical, more skills. It's just a matter of time.

ARE ETHNIC MINORITY GIRLS BEING ENCOURAGED TO PLAY FOOTBALL NOW?

Yes, I think that the film *Bend it like Beckham* fired a lot of people up, especially for ethnic minority girls who were not allowed to play football, like me. I was like, "That girl is so me! You're going to a wedding, and you're fully dressed, you've got makeup on, and then underneath you've got football boots on and your football kit. That's literally me!" Oh my God, I think that was a movie I could relate to so much.

We need more role models. Maybe me being there will help, "If JJ can achieve it, then we can too." Growing up, I started to understand what a role model is. Then I was like, "Rachel Yankey is doing this, Sian Massey-Ellis is doing this. Rebecca Welch…" Now I know where I'm going. I want to reach the Women's Super League. I go, "Who is on the Women's Super League? Who's actually achieving this now?" then I see: "Oh she's there?" Imagine a young girl who wants to start refereeing asking, "Who's there?" And she'll see me.

WHAT ARE YOU MOST PROUD OF?

I'm proud of staying true to who I am and just having a lot of self-belief. We need more advocates, like Ian Wright – he's a big fan of women's football. We need more allies to come out and say, "The women's game is actually very good and people should watch it more and support the game."

KATE SHORTMAN & IZZY THORPE

Kate Shortman is a talented young British artistic swimmer who made her senior and junior European Championship debuts in 2016, and her first World Championship final in 2017. She is a multiple national Solo and Duet champion at both senior and junior level. First stepping onto the podium with Bristol Central for Team Free gold in 2011, Shortman won her first clean sweep of Solo, Duet and Team titles at the 2012 ASA National Age Group Championships in Gloucester. She repeated the treble in 2014 and 2015 before lifting the Shacklock Trophy for the first time in 2016 after winning Solo and Duet gold as well as Free Team silver with City of Bristol.

Teaming up with Isabelle Thorpe, Shortman made her World Championship debut, finishing 16th alongside Thorpe in the Free Duet, as well as making the Free Solo final on the way to a 12th place finish. At her second senior European Championships in 2018, Shortman finished ninth in the Free Solo and 11th with Thorpe in the Free Duet.

The 2019 season brought Shortman her first individual FINA World Series medal with a bronze medal in Barcelona, which was followed up with reaching the Solo Tech and Free finals at the 2019 World Championships in Gwanju, in addition to a 14th place finish in the both the Duet Tech and Free with Isabelle Thorpe.

In 2017, Isabelle Thorpe made her senior international debut in 2016, competing with the British team at the French Open in Paris, then the European Championships in London. In 2016, the pair competed at the European Junior Championships in Rijeka, finishing 10th in the Duet, while Thorpe also helped the British squad to top 10 finishes in the Team and Free Combination events. Thorpe combined with Shortman to great effect at junior international level, finishing eighth against some of the top European nations at the Mediterranean Cup in 2015, then improving to fifth in 2016.

She also won the Solo title for her age group in 2013 and lifted the prestigious Shacklock Trophy in 2013 and 2014. Thorpe built a fine record at national age group level, winning Team gold for five consecutive years between 2011 and 2015 and Duet gold alongside Kate Shortman for five straight Championships between 2012 and 2016.

WHAT WAS YOUR FIRST EXPERIENCE IN SPORT?

IZZY: I started off in gymnastics when I was quite young, 3 or 4, just going to a gymnastics centre and playing around. I started synchro as I got a little bit older. But I had to decide at about 12 whether to do synchro or gymnastics, and I ended up doing synchro. Gymnastics was my main introduction to sport, and it's a very intense sport as well, so it's quite a big one but definitely really fun.

KATE: I first got involved with speed swimming. Loads of my family did it, though my mum did synchro. That's how I got into it, but my dad, my uncles, a lot of them did swimming. So I got into that at about 5 and then at about 7, I did synchro.

WHO WERE YOUR INFLUENCES AND ROLE MODELS?

IZZY: My mum was a big influence because she was still involved in the sport and had done it in the past. Also, for me a massive one was Tom Daley, because I was seeing him from such a young age, diving and doing so well and being so successful. It was really inspiring for me just to think, "OK, it is possible from a young age to be at a high level in sport."

KATE: I would say similar for me. My mum and my older sister did sync as well and that definitely inspired me and it just naturally happens that you get involved with it.

WHEN DID YOU KNOW THAT YOU WANTED TO PURSUE A CAREER IN SPORT?

IZZY: I think for me that transition between gymnastics and synchro was when I realised that I did want to pursue synchro to a high level. I had to do one or the other.

KATE: I would say after London 2012. We knew a lot of girls that were in the Olympic squad for synchro and we'd seen them progress and I think for both me and Iz, when we saw that competition we were just so inspired and it definitely made us want to pursue something in professional sport. I'd say that's probably one of the turning points for me, watching the Olympics and thinking, "Oh my gosh. One day I could be there."

IS BRISTOL A HUB FOR SYNCHRONISED SWIMMING?

IZZY: At the moment it's the National Centre for Synchro in Great Britain. Before that, there were a lot of girls coming up through the programme that were quite good in Bristol. I guess they've just had good coaches and left quite a legacy.

WHAT ARE THE MAIN CHALLENGES THAT YOU HAVE FACED SO FAR IN YOUR SPORTING CAREERS?

IZZY: For me, personally – injury. I've had quite a few injuries along the way. I'm currently injured so that's a bit annoying. But getting over that and still being able to compete at a high level and at the Olympics has made me realise how strong I am as a person, and more determined to carry on. I had a hip problem and I got told by a doctor, "You know, there's Usain Bolt and then there's everyone else, and unfortunately, you're just like everyone else and you're not going to make it." And then I was like, "Right well, I'm gonna show him." I was 13 years old then and I went to the Olympics. I showed him.

KATE: For me, touch wood, I haven't had any really serious injury so far. My biggest challenge has been fitting in school work with synchro and also just life in general: a social life, time to relax, academic commitments. Managing all of that is actually very stressful when you're part of an elite sport that requires over 40 hours a week of training. It's something I've had to overcome. We've both had to get more organised and be really efficient with our time. I guess you learn through years of doing it.

HOW DO YOU MAINTAIN YOUR MOTIVATION?

IZZY: I mean, it *is* hard! At times it does get really difficult. Especially at the moment, at university it's quite different to school. 'A' Levels were really difficult, but we had a lot of support from the school. Going to university and trying to fit in a social life as well, because you're living with new people, is really difficult. Like Kate said, you just have to be really organised so you can stay on top of it. As soon as you let it slip and you get a little bit too tired or a little bit under

Thorpe training with weights

the weather, it's really hard to get back on top. So for us, staying on top of it, I think that's the main way to keep motivated. Otherwise it does get really tricky.

KATE: I'm quite lucky because I go to the University of Bath, which is really supportive because it's a high performance centre for sports. There's not too much difference between being at school and being at uni in terms of the level of support I've received. But it is difficult: things you don't think of, like making food or the travel to get to the pool, take up a lot of time.

IZZY: We definitely rely on each other a lot because we know each other so well. We're like sisters, we've gone through a lot of things together in life, so we have each other to lean on. I know that Kate's

someone I can trust and she'll always be there. We met when we were 7 and we've been doing a duet since we were 10 years old. It's been a really long time.

KATE: I would say exactly the same. Also, I feel like it is a very specific lifestyle and it's a very niche thing to be doing. Not a lot of people understand what it takes so to have another person who understands everything you're going through, because we do essentially live kind of the same life, is always good.

WHAT ARE YOU BOTH MOST PROUD OF IN YOUR CAREERS SO FAR?

IZZY: Obviously, the Olympics. That has been my dream since we went to see the girls in London 2012 compete. Achieving that even after Covid, which made it even more difficult, just to get there and appreciate the hard work we've put in, was an incredible experience. I can't even put it into words.

KATE: The Olympics is a huge one. Nothing will ever top that. The whole journey was just insane. It really did live up to everything. You would probably think, "Oh, after a five-year build-up, it's going to be a bit anticlimactic when you actually get there," but it was everything we'd dreamed of and more.

TELL US ABOUT YOUR FAVOURITE SPORTING MOMENT, YOUR OWN OR SOMEONE ELSE'S.

IZZY: The Olympics! But qualifying for the Olympics is probably another one. There were very high tensions at the qualification tournament between all the countries. We

just had to do the routine, nail everything that we had practised in training, and we did that! Then afterwards we gave each other the biggest hug and it was really emotional. Knowing that everything had paid off was really great.

KATE: I would agree, but I'll give another example. When we were at the Olympics we were sat in the Team GB lounge and we were watching the diving finals when Matty Lee and Tom Daley won the gold. Honestly, it was such a special moment. I think they were against the Chinese who normally win. It was like Team GB can really do it against all the odds. Everyone was so proud of them, and really excited.

IF YOU COULD GIVE YOUR YOUNGER SELF SOME ADVICE NOW, WHAT WOULD IT BE?

IZZY: For other people who are going through it at a young age: "Just stick with it and try to stay positive." Even if you face things like injury or mental health or schooling issues, or just going through a hard time, I think that sport really helps with that. Even though it seems like a lot, pushing through, it really benefits you on the other side.

KATE: Sometimes you have to sacrifice a lot to do the training but if you can push through it when times are hard, it makes the experience much more worthwhile.

WHAT THINGS WOULD YOU LIKE TO SEE CHANGE FOR WOMEN IN YOUR SPORT?

IZZY: I think there's quite a lot. For women in sport, it's difficult with things like body image and mental health and a lot of people critiquing you. Especially in the sport we're in, where you're always in a swimming costume and you're getting judged on the way you look, the way you're swimming. It's really easy to forget what the main goal is and remember that your body is actually helping you. Women shouldn't be shamed about looking too muscular. Their body is the reason that they're doing so well in sport.

KATE: I feel like there's a certain stereotype or image of girls, especially on social media and in magazines, and it's impossible to live up to that. When you have the added pressure of a swimming costume, it can be quite daunting for some girls to stay in the sport when they feel worried about what they look like. Swimming helped us to be proud of our bodies for what they do for us and how strong we are.

HOW DO YOU DEAL WITH NEGATIVE COMMENTS ON SOCIAL MEDIA?

IZZY: It is hard to deal with that kind of stuff, but knowing that so many other girls are going through the same thing and showing online that it doesn't matter what you look like, helps us. In swimming, you are naturally going to have broader shoulders because that is just what happens, and it's positive, it's helping you succeed in your sport. It's important to remember, too, that the people writing these comments are probably not doing anything with their life. You're the one who is going to the Olympics, making your dreams a reality. It's just about trying to get past that initial thought.

KATE: Seeing examples of women with a similar body type to me really helps, and it reassures you that you're doing the right thing. You don't need to look a certain way or look like someone else, or try and fit into what you think you should look like. If we could be pioneers for that, if that inspired even one person, I would feel so proud.

DO YOU HAVE ANY FEMALE ROLE MODELS IN THAT REGARD, IN THE WORLD OF SPORTS?

KATE: I follow a couple of gym Instagram accounts that promote normal, healthy physiques and sporting athletes.

IZZY: I definitely follow a few people on Instagram as well, who promote body positivity around being athletic and strong. Or, if you're having an off day, you're going to fluctuate, and it's normal for that to happen. For people to be promoting that in a positive way is such a good thing, because for all these young girls who are on TikTok and Instagram and Snapchat these days it's important for them to see that and not feel like they have to fit into a norm.

WHAT DO YOU THINK ABOUT MEDIA COVERAGE OF WOMEN IN YOUR SPORT?

KATE: It's a shame that we don't get as much media coverage as other sports but I don't know if that's due to the fact that it's all females. I think it's just a not very popular sport or it's a very small sport, so not that many people are involved with it. The fact we don't get much attention means that we can't grow and expand. That is a shame for our sport.

Kate Shortman (left) and Izzy Thorpe (right)

50 WOMEN IN SPORT

IZZY: It's a minority sport and not a lot of people know about it. I've spoken to loads of people, especially since moving to uni, they've been like, "What is synchronised swimming? Don't you just wear flower caps and push off the bottom of the pool and do handstands?" It makes it harder for people to get into the sport and to take it seriously.

KATE: When you do show people videos of it, they are like, "Oh my God, this is completely different to what I thought it was. Oh my gosh this is so cool!" I feel like there's a lack of knowledge and awareness of the sport.

IZZY: The main media attention for most sports is during the Olympic Games, that is when most people are watching sport other than football and more mainstream sports.

IS THERE A PARTICULAR ORGANISATION THAT HAS SUPPORTED YOU IN YOUR SPORT?

IZZY: We've not had an awful lot of support throughout the years. It has been us as GB Synchro or our club, just trying to promote it and get our name out there. We've had various people along the way come and help us, especially towards the Olympics. Our swimming costumes for the Olympics were sponsored by a company called BEU and their costumes are made out of recycled plastic which was amazing. We could also promote awareness of plastic pollution at the same time, which is something we're quite passionate about and so that was good. But we haven't had loads of support.

KATE: We did YouTube videos recently this year with the Global Triathlon Network and also with Nile Wilson. They help to raise the profile and also it was really fun.

WHAT THINGS WOULD YOU LIKE TO SEE CHANGE FOR WOMEN IN YOUR SPORT?

KATE: I feel like it's a really good environment for girls to be in. It gives you a lot of confidence. It's predominantly girls that are in synchro, so it's a really positive and safe environment to be in. It's like a family because it's quite small as well. Sometimes you see reports of synchronised swimming being made fun of, which obviously is not ideal, that is really not the message that we want to be promoting. I think the more people that hear about it and see it, the better it is.

IZZY: I'd like to get the message across about the perception of body image and giving that positive message that it's OK to look muscular, especially to young girls. We did a campaign with an underwear company Bluebella, it's about 'Being strong is beautiful.' It's trying to promote that especially to young girls, because a lot of young girls drop out of sport. The reason that girls give up sport is mainly due to a lack of self-confidence and concerns about body image.

WHAT'S NEXT?

IZZY: This year we have the World Championships in Budapest, then the senior European Championships in Rome.

KATE: We're just trying to improve our rankings and see how far we can go and improve from the Olympics and anything we've done before. At the last World Championships, we didn't make the final, but we were really, really close to making the final. So if we can make a final this time, that would be amazing.

Photo: L.I.J. Cieslikowscy

BARBARA SLATER

Barbara Slater OBE (1959-) is the Director of BBC Sport. She is a former gymnast who represented Great Britain at the 1976 Olympic Games in Montreal.

Slater's father, Bill, was a professional footballer who played for England, won the Footballer of the Year award in 1960, and won three Football League titles with Wolverhampton Wanderers. Her uncle, J J Warr, played for the England cricket team. As a gymnast, she won the Champions All, British Championships.

Slater appeared in the children's TV series *Out of Bounds*, before working for ATV Sport. She joined the BBC in 1983 on a Trainee Assistant Producer scheme graduating to the sports department. Slater worked her way up to become head of sports production, and helped produce programmes for events such as Wimbledon, The Open and Masters Golf, the Commonwealth Games, horseracing, and the London Marathon. In 2009, she was promoted to Director of BBC Sport, the first woman to hold the position. In 2013, she won back the broadcasting rights of the FA Cup, and was responsible for the sport broadcast coverage of the 2012 Summer Olympics, held in London. Slater was awarded the Inspirational Woman prize at the Women in Film & TV Awards in 2012 and appointed OBE in 2014 for services to sports broadcasting.

Slater far left, front row, at 1976 Montreal Olympics

WERE YOU INVOLVED IN SPORT BEFORE YOU TOOK ON YOUR CURRENT JOB?

I always consider myself lucky that I came from a sporting family. I had a father who was an international footballer. He played for England in the 1958 World Cup and he was captain of Wolves (Wolverhampton Wanderers) when they won the FA Cup trophy in 1960 so he was steeped in it. I had an uncle who played for England in cricket, so sport was always an important element of our lives.

My father worked at Liverpool University; they had a big swimming pool with diving boards and I did some diving with a local club too. Then my father moved jobs to Birmingham and they didn't have any facilities for diving so I took up gymnastics instead. There was a really good club at school and I was encouraged. I went from there to eventually compete in the Olympics in 1976, which was actually the same competition as Nadia Comăneci when she scored a perfect 10. As I got to a more competitive level we really struggled to find the expertise and the coaching so my dad actually trained me. When I left university, ITV had the broadcasting rights to gymnastics in the UK and they wanted someone to advise and do some commentary. Having that experience under my belt I applied to the BBC on one of their training schemes. This was right back in 1983. I've been at the BBC ever since.

It really wasn't easy for a woman back then, and I consider myself very lucky to have got my place. As I had been an athlete that was an enormous benefit because nobody could say that I didn't have a genuine passion or knowledge and therefore I think that was an extraordinarily good thing. I don't think you need that today, but I think then it was important – it gave you credibility. It was just a very different organisation and it really is an incredibly different environment in which we now work, but it wasn't always easy. What I think is interesting is the new generation coming in mustn't take that for granted. You've still got to be really vigilant and determined that there is equality of treatment. I don't think there is any job in the BBC that couldn't be

Competing at 1976 Montreal Olympics

done by a woman and I would not have said that when I entered the business.

WHAT HAVE BEEN THE MOST INTERESTING AND CHALLENGING ASPECTS OF YOUR ROLE?

It had never really entered my head, this idea that I might be second class in the sphere of sport. It hadn't been my life experience until I joined and then it came as a bit of a jolt and maybe it was a good thing because I wasn't really gonna buy into that, was I? I've always tried to focus on doing a good job and that was the best way to deal with those early days: to be really good at what you did, to make sure you were incredibly well-researched, make sure you knew what you were doing. You took the extra time to be really knowledgeable so that you became an important part of the team. I think that once people get to know you and they lose that initial bias that they might have, suddenly you are part of the team and you are treated as an equal.

DID YOU FEEL THE NEED TO DO MORE THAN YOUR MALE COLLEAGUES TO PROVE YOURSELF?

Maybe it was having had the background in gymnastics which is all about striving to do things better, to do a more complicated move, to land something. Maybe that sporting discipline was rather instilled and I took it through to the workplace. There was just a sort of determination to always do well. I remember being in some of the outside broadcast trucks and watching the directors in action thinking, "Gosh that's got to be one of the best jobs in the world!" To be there and trying to catch that unfolding story of a sporting event. You start off on three cameras, some small event, then you gradually increase. I think probably the most complex production I ever did was the Open Golf Championship where there's 60 cameras and an unfolding story all around the golf course with a lot of the action happening simultaneously; that's a very complex production. You work your way up through increasing complexity in the productions that you do and I absolutely loved it. It was a really challenging but incredibly exhilarating and enjoyable role and I think I was just driven by a real passion for the job.

I think sport builds confidence too. So I think there are many transferable skills that you build up in the field of play that you can take through to the workplace and I've always been a great believer in the benefits of sport and the change that it could make and that it can be incredibly empowering and has real value. And that doesn't matter whether you're a participant at grassroots level or at elite level, I still think you can learn extraordinary life lessons through sport.

WHAT WAS YOUR FAVOURITE SPORTING MOMENT, EITHER YOUR OWN OR SOMEBODY ELSE'S?

I probably have to plump for Nadia Comăneci's perfect 10 in gymnastics, I think that would have to be one of them. There's quite a list. The extraordinary achievements of 2012 would also have to go very high up the list. I think that was a transformational moment for women's sport because we had so many inspirational role models and

Comăneci competing at the Montreal Olympics

we saw an enthusiasm for sport across the board. When you can fill Wembley with 80,000 people watching a women's football match, that's quite something. The 2012 Olympics was pivotal for women's sport because it presented much more of a level playing field and you cheered just as much for Jess Ennis as you did for Mo Farah. It was truly inspirational those games, for a lot of girls as well as boys.

WHAT DO YOU THINK ARE THE MAIN CHALLENGES FOR WOMEN IN SPORT TODAY?

I believe we do have a degree of gender equality in certain spheres of sport, so if you look for example at the Olympics, the Commonwealth Games where you really do have a very equitable split of medals. I try and make sure that there's an even spread for the really pinnacle moments, and a lot of thought and care goes in.

We actually see that reflected in our audiences as well, we find that events like the Olympics, like the Commonwealth Games this summer, like Wimbledon, where you've got a high degree of gender parity, we get a very even split in terms of our audiences. It's often where the really big audiences in broadcasting come from is where you've got universal appeal.

I think for the team sports there's been a kind of legacy issue in that for example men's football, men's rugby, men's cricket had a very big head start. But I think we're seeing that changing. Certainly in women's football I think unbelievable strides have been made. You really do see a transformation in attitudes and the governing bodies of sport are seeing the opportunity and the growth potential of women's sport.

You could say there's a degree of saturation in terms of some of the men's events but there's still quite a lot of growth opportunity within the women's. For example the women's World Cup that was covered in 2019, the numbers just grew round by round and ended up with the women's semi-final achieving an audience of nearly 12 million. That was the second most-watched programme of the year of any genre, not just for sport but drama, entertainment, news, comedy. It debunked once and for all this myth, "Well, there's not much interest women sport." What's also interesting was the audiences generally skewed slightly younger so there really is a changing attitude coming through, we're seeing a new generation with a different attitude and that's great. The women's football really tapped into that.

Slater in the studio. Photo: BBC

DO YOU HAVE ANY FIGURES ABOUT THE PROPORTION OF MEN TO WOMEN VIEWERS?

There is a skew towards male viewers but it's changing. The ECB launched the cricket event, The Hundred, last year. They really embraced the women's game, it was very much a major part of the whole approach that was taken and again I think we saw some great success. I remember some of the women players playing in front of really big crowds and just how exhilarating that was and how great the atmosphere was and I think it's a great example of a governing body recognising the opportunity that women's sport presents.

WHAT WOULD YOU SAY YOU ARE MOST PROUD OF IN YOUR CAREER?

There's no question that if you want to have instant buzz after something then it would be directing something like the men's final at Wimbledon or the final few hours of the Open Golf. I mean, that is just a fantastically exhilarating experience. Then you move more into a managerial role where your responsibility is more in terms of oversight and wanting to make sure all the many pieces are put together. You might have an overview of how the team perform and how the team come together. Probably the great example of that would be the 2012 Olympics because there was a team within the BBC that organised that. In overall charge was Roger Mosey who ran the whole pan-BBC operation but clearly what we did in Sport was a very important element of that and in my role as the Director of Sport, that would have to go down as an absolute highpoint. I would say that the BBC played an important role in the transformation of the coverage of women's sport. With the Women's World Cup, the exposure and high-profile scheduling was a major contributor to the extraordinary audience interest and the impact that it made.

WHAT DO YOU THINK OF THE MEDIA COVERAGE OF WOMEN'S SPORT?

I'm not sure I see that as necessarily a gender issue. I think there might be wider issues around what the players want to do, what they see their role as, whether they feel that the press is always fair on them. I think there is a quite a lot of research now which would say that women athletes are described sometimes in a different way to men athletes. With men athletes it's often very much personal achievements, women athletes it can be more, "Well, it was a great team effort." I hope sport can be a trailblazer in leaving some of that behind. Yes, those biases continue now but I hope there is a greater vigilance and the more that it's called out the better things will become.

WITHIN THE BBC, ARE WOMEN NOW COMING INTO PRODUCING ROLES ACROSS ALL GENRES?

Without question. I think some of the blocks that were there in the past have truly gone. I mean, when I entered the industry the idea that a woman would run a sports department, would have seemed impossible. But obviously it's not and I sincerely hope that there will be women who will follow in those footsteps and occupy very senior roles not just at the BBC but across the sports industry and the sports broadcast industry as a whole.

HOW CAN WE ENCOURAGE MORE GIRLS AND YOUNG WOMEN TO PARTICIPATE IN SPORT?

I think making sure there are role models for them. If you can see it you can be it. I think that's really important. Again I think we're seeing progress being made and if I look at the broadcast industry I would point to the extraordinary role models that we see in some of the presentation teams, some of the reporters, and that's a very powerful message. I really believe we make a judgement upon the quality of the journalism, of someone's presenting abilities, and our attitude is very gender neutral.

WHAT DO YOU WANT TO SEE CHANGE FOR WOMEN IN SPORT GOING FORWARD?

Again I would say the parallels with the broader society: equality of treatment. In some sense we have it, but there's probably truth that it isn't yet universal and that's what we'd love to see. We won't have to write books like the one you're planning to write because that won't be necessary, but unfortunately it still is.

WHAT ARE YOUR PERSONAL HOPES FOR THE FUTURE?

To continue to see the fantastic progress that I think has happened since that 2012 Olympics, that last decade, that that same momentum continues, and that we are on an upward trajectory that will ultimately see genuine gender parity.

BBC Studio on top of containers at the Olympic Park, 2012
Photo: Ian Patterson

BIANCA SMITH

Bianca Smith (1991-) started her 2nd season as a minor league coach with the FCL Red Sox in 2022. Prior to the Red Sox she was an Assistant Athletic Director and Assistant Baseball Coach/Hitting Coordinator at Carroll University for two seasons. Smith has also coached at Case Western Reserve University (where she earned her dual JD/MBA in sports law, sports management, and organizational behavior) and the University of Dallas, as well as working in Baseball Operations in the front offices of the Texas Rangers, the Cincinnati Reds, and MLB's Commissioner's Office. While at Case Western Smith also worked as the Athletics Compliance Assistant, Teaching Assistant for the undergraduate Sports Management course, and Assistant General Manager for the Northern Ohio Baseball Club of the Great Lakes League.

Smith has also coached for the Youth Academies of the Rangers and the Reds and worked as a summer youth baseball coach for the Milwaukee Brewers. In 2017 Smith also attended and completed MLB's Scout School.

Smith grew up in Texas and attended Colleyville Heritage High School, before graduating from Dartmouth College in 2012 where she played varsity softball and club baseball. While at Dartmouth, Smith also worked for the varsity baseball team among a variety of other sports-related projects.

Smith is the first African American woman to serve as a coach in a professional baseball organization and has received sponsorship from Nike, among others.

WHAT WAS YOUR FIRST EXPERIENCE IN SPORT?

My mom introduced me to baseball when I was 3 or 4 but I also started playing soccer and dancing at around 3 years old. I also did karate.

WHO WERE YOUR INFLUENCES AND/OR ROLE MODELS?

I looked up to my parents a lot, mainly for their drive to work hard, be the best, and live their lives, all while having kids.

WHO ENCOURAGED YOU?

My dad has been my biggest supporter since I was a kid.

WHEN DID YOU KNOW YOU WANTED TO PURSUE A CAREER IN SPORT?

I decided I wanted to work in baseball my sophomore year of college.

TELL US ABOUT A PARTICULAR CHOICE THAT WAS GOOD AND ONE YOU REGRET.

Every choice I've made has led me to my dream job and I've been able to learn from each one, so there isn't one particular one that's better than others, and I don't regret any of them.

WHAT ARE THE MAIN CHALLENGES THAT YOU HAVE FACED IN YOUR CAREER?

The hardest part was getting people to take me seriously enough to give me a chance.

TELL US HOW YOU DEVELOPED AS A COMPETITOR.

It came naturally, honestly. As an athlete growing up in an athletic and competitive family, I was always taught to try my best and to try and get better to achieve my goals. So I was always competing against someone else or myself.

HOW DO YOU MAINTAIN YOUR MOTIVATION?

I look back at where I started and how far I've come. If I can do everything that I've done in just 29 years (since I was 29 when I was hired by the Red Sox), I can't imagine what I can do with another 29 years as an adult.

WHAT ARE YOU MOST PROUD OF?

Every time I connect with a player and can help them achieve a goal or task I'm proud.

TELL US ABOUT YOUR FAVOURITE SPORTING MOMENT – YOUR OWN OR SOMEONE ELSE'S.

That's easy: both times the New York Giants beat the Patriots in the Super Bowl!

IF YOU COULD GIVE YOUR YOUNGER SELF SOME ADVICE NOW, WHAT WOULD IT BE?

Learn Spanish sooner!

WHAT THINGS WOULD YOU LIKE TO SEE CHANGE FOR WOMEN IN YOUR SPORT?

I look forward to when it's no longer a big deal when a woman is hired in a previously male-only position, or when they actually do the job they're hired for.

WHAT DO YOU THINK ABOUT THE MEDIA COVERAGE OF WOMEN IN YOUR SPORT?

There needs to be more coverage of women playing baseball, not just working in baseball. Coaches and staff are meant to be in the background, not the spotlight!

IS IT MORE DIFFICULT FOR WOMEN TO MAKE A LIVING THAN MEN WORKING IN YOUR SPORT?

Absolutely. It's hard enough to get into baseball, whether you're a woman or not, but when you take into consideration trying to have a family, women are often pressured to put their family first and that tends to push us back in our careers. For those of us on the field, if we decide to have kids, we have to deal with pregnancy and post-pregnancy issues on top of that. Not to say that men wouldn't help out, but as a society we're not raised to expect men to put their careers on hold for family; just women are.

WHAT'S NEXT?

I keep on coaching and eventually make it to the majors!

Smith with the 2021 FCL Red Sox Outfielders. Photo: Junior Zamora

ZOE SMITH

Zoe Smith (1998-) grew up in a sporty family in Bournemouth, and enjoyed competitive swimming, tennis and football which she played at a high level within the women's league. She studied and obtained a BSc Hons degree in Sport Science and Psychology and had plans to go on and study a PGCE in Physical Education. Before the car accident which led to the amputation of her left leg in 2015, she had recently returned from an around the world trip visiting over a dozen different countries.

She took up surfing at The Wave in Bristol in 2021, inspired by seeing a video of an amputee surfer in the England squad called Pegleg Pennett. She was soon recruited by the England paralympic surf team and with some coaching on the waves in Cornwall, finished fifth in her class at the World Para Surfing Championship in California, narrowly missing out on a medal.

She now attends Para Surf competitions all over the world and recently took part in the Access Surf Hawaiian Adaptive Surf competition, at Queens Beach Waikiki.

Smith is currently self-funded and looking for sponsors to enable her to carry on competing. She lives in Bournemouth with her two dogs.

WHAT WAS YOUR FIRST EXPERIENCE IN SPORT?

I remember playing sport since I was a toddler. I grew up in a sporty family and enjoyed most team sports available to me.

WHO WERE YOUR INFLUENCES AND/OR ROLE MODELS?

I don't remember ever being particularly influenced by anyone outside of my family until I was a bit older. My dad was, and still is a keen sportsman and my parents would take me and my siblings off to play football, tennis, swimming, or go horse riding on the weekends. As I grew up, I was interested in alternative sports. Basketball, baseball, bodyboarding, water sports and scuba diving. I like to test the limits and enjoy sports that raise your adrenaline. My biggest competition for the entirety of my childhood was my brother. He was good at all sports and excelled at a few.

WHAT ARE THE MAIN CHALLENGES THAT YOU HAVE FACED IN YOUR CAREER?

As an amputee athlete my main challenge has been engineering and designing a prosthetic that will allow me to move and balance in the water. Not only is it extremely expensive to own a water activity leg (my current prosthetic costs 10k) but practically there are a lot of adaptions to consider as well. The weight of the leg, its manoeuvrability through water and finally its capacity to stay firmly attached in powerful surf! This is an issue I'm still working on at the moment with my prosthetics team. Ultimately, I need my equipment to work to enable me to have the same chance of performing in the water as the next able-bodied person.

TELL US HOW YOU DEVELOPED AS A COMPETITOR.

I started my surfing career only very recently and did so at The Wave in Bristol. It's a perfect environment to start learning to surf as it's very safe, contained, and there are water safety measures all around you. From there, I began working with the Team England adaptive coaches at my local beach break in Bournemouth and then ultimately further afield in Cornwall. I've also taken myself off to some different locations such as Sri Lanka, Lanzarote and Portugal to experience some different waves and surf for intense and concentrated periods of time. In the World Championships in December, I placed 5th in the below knee amputee category and 3rd overall out of the amputees competing. Hopefully this year with advanced training and time I will make my way into the medals. Time will tell!

WHAT DOES YOUR TRAINING DAY LOOK LIKE?

I try and surf at least three times a week depending on conditions. Obviously, my local break is not always going to be working so sometimes this involves a decent amount of travelling to and from surfable conditions. When I'm not surfing I not only exercise

At the English Adaptive Open, 2022. Photo: Phil Williams

to be surfing fit (concentrating on my paddling and upper body resistance training), but I also mind-surf and work on my surfing theory. Competitions can be won and lost by reading the ocean correctly and it's definitely something I need to work on as a newcomer to the sport.

HOW DO YOU MAINTAIN YOUR MOTIVATION?

Surfing makes it incredibly easy to stay motivated. You do have to work through some injuries, knock-backs and the inevitable plateaus in performance but ultimately, for me, there's nothing more liberating, exhilarating and plain fun as surfing. It's playful, creative and exciting. It's also scary and super rewarding when you do it well. I'm also competitive against myself and my last surf. When I identify a weakness, I make sure I work on it and push myself to be better. At the end of a session, I write down my highs and lows and do my best to work through what went wrong and how I could have been better. I also try very hard to celebrate the successes. If, during a session, I've caught one great wave and ripped then that should be worthy of remembering.

WHAT ARE YOU MOST PROUD OF?

I'm proud of and grateful for my resilience. Three years ago, when I wanted to go into the ocean on holiday to swim, I had to crawl on my hands and knees because I did not have a prosthetic that was waterproof. Walking was challenging, let alone the concept of surfing. Then, when I started surfing, I realised that I have a very real residual fear of pain. We all do I think (it's human nature) but post-accident my sense of reckless abandon has been tamed somewhat by a fear of reliving pain. I work through that on a daily basis in the surf when I feel myself falling, or catch a wave wrong, and find myself looking over the falls! Mental toughness is important in all sports but in adaptive sports it's imperative.

TELL US ABOUT YOUR FAVOURITE SPORTING MOMENT – YOUR OWN OR SOMEONE ELSE'S.

Recently, I have celebrated Kelly Slater winning at Pipeline. At his age to still be on top of the game and winning is very inspiring. Also, of course, competing at last year's ISA World Para Surfing Championships was a lifetime high for me. My first heat in particular was just fun. I was new on the scene so had very little pressure externally aside from that which I had placed on myself. I was well supported by my team and knew if I could just get out there and catch a few waves I'd progress. I stuck with my coach's game plan and came away with second in the heat. It was just an amazing privilege to surf for my country and alongside some incredible amputee women who were great surfers. A celebration of overcoming adversity for sure!

IF YOU COULD GIVE YOUR YOUNGER SELF SOME ADVICE NOW, WHAT WOULD IT BE?

Don't put your feet on the dashboard!!

WHAT DO YOU THINK ABOUT THE MEDIA COVERAGE OF WOMEN IN YOUR SPORT?

The coverage of women in sport (not just surfing) frequently represents female athletes as women first and athletes second. Coverage of the women surfers in the recent WSL footage of the world tour has once again been dominated by references of their age, family life, who their husbands are, whereas the male surfers are depicted as standalone athletes, determined and other-worldly. There is always a stronger emphasis on appearance for female athletes. During Pipeline one of the female athletes was asked why she was surfing in leggings as opposed to tiny bikini shorts. When it comes to female surfers, the most publicly successfully women are the most media-marketable because of their appearance.

However, in 2019, the WSL as the leaders of the $10 billion surfing industry began offering equal prize money for all its events, making it one of the few professional sports leagues to achieve pay equity. Women's sponsorship may still be quite behind and still very much based around male patriarchy but things are slowly improving.

IS IT MORE DIFFICULT FOR WOMEN TO MAKE A LIVING THAN MEN WORKING IN YOUR SPORT?

Yes, I believe it's harder for female athletes across all sports to make a living from competing. We are underrepresented within the media, unless overtly sexualised, and underfunded. In any arena where women's performance can be directly compared to a man's we often struggle to establish ourselves as 'the greatest'. All too often our successes are attributed to male collaborators: coaches, partners, idols. Women have a constant fight to be given the same opportunities and playing field as their male counterparts. Just last week when I was in Sri Lanka there was a local surf contest open to both male and female competitors. At the end, the top three men were all financially rewarded by the competition's sponsors and the women were simply awarded with smiles and claps!

The women in that competition were all incredible surfers and surfed under the same conditions, time and rules as the men. As I was leaving Sri Lanka, there had been so much disapproval about the blatant inequality on display, I heard that the organisers were in the process of scraping together some money to present as a peace offering.

IS THERE A PARTICULAR ORGANISATION THAT HAS SUPPORTED YOU IN YOUR SPORT?

Surfing England have been great at supporting me and championing my development. I have also just returned from a holiday with Wild and Free Adventures where I had the privilege of being coached by the Sri Lankan Ticket to Ride team. An incredible female-led team of coaches who went out of their way to support an adaptive athlete. The head coach Nikita Robb, an ex-WSL competitor, is the best surfer I've ever seen in the water and a total inspiration. Regarded as the best surfer in Sri Lanka, she out-surfs all the men on the island and is a total badass.

WHAT'S NEXT?

My primary focus will be on the ISA World Championships in California in December.

Smith riding a wave at Newquay, Cornwall, 2022. Photo: Sarah Bunt

MARIA TOORPAKAI

Born in 1990 in South Waziristan, Pakistan, Maria Toorpakai is a professional Pakistani squash player. Using the name Genghis Khan, she disguised herself as a boy for the first 12 years of her life in order to participate in competitive sports with the support of her Muslim parents. She won the all Pakistan U-16 boys weightlifting championship in Lahore but then took up squash, becoming the national champion and the first Pashtun girl in international tournaments, turning professional in 2007.

The President of Pakistan bestowed the Salaam Pakistan Award upon her but threats by the Taliban forced her to spend the next few years in hiding. In 2009, she won a bronze medal in the World Junior Women's Squash Championship and double silver medals in the South Asian Games. In 2011, she arrived in Toronto, Ontario, Canada to train with Jonathon Power and has since resided in Canada. In 2016, her memoir, *A Different Kind of Daughter: The Girl Who Hid from the Taliban in Plain Sight* was published and the film about her life *Girl Unbound: The War to be Her* directed by Erin Heidenreich, was premiered at Toronto International Film Festival. A vocal advocate for women's rights in Pakistan, she has set up a foundation encouraging families to educate girls and allow them to play sports in Waziristan, Pakistan.

WHAT WAS YOUR FIRST EXPERIENCE IN SPORT?

Growing up we had some local sports. I come from the tribal regions on the Afghan border. There were girls wrestling with each other, kite flying, marbles, dodgeball. It was fun to be involved in such things. Also hunting! We wouldn't hunt ourselves because we were too young, we would just go along to watch the men.

WHO WERE YOUR INFLUENCES AND/OR ROLE MODELS?

When I was young, we lived in the mountains, people were really far away from each other. My dad would buy second-hand books and teach himself, and then teach us. My dad would teach my sister then I would listen and I would understand what was happening. My sister was very inspired by Benazir Bhutto, the first female Prime Minister, and by the United Nations, and she wanted to become the UN Secretary General. She would go to all the debating competitions and talk about girls' rights to education or other rights for women. So my dad always supported me, and my sister was my role model. I wanted to be like her, to talk like her.

My mom was also very supportive. She would always talk about kindness and bravery. My mom was a teacher and she started teaching and running girls' schools, but there were no girls coming to the schools so my mom would take me from village to village. I'd hold her hand and go to different people's houses where she would ask them to allow their daughters to come to the school. I'm very blessed in that way.

WHEN DID YOU KNOW YOU WANTED TO PURSUE A CAREER IN SPORT?

It all happened accidentally. I didn't choose anything, it's just destiny. When people say that in Islam, God doesn't want women to do this, I'm like, "You can go to court against God! Go ask God directly. Do not ask me because God put me there." Whatever I did in childhood, that was all God. My first sport was weightlifting. I called myself Genghis Khan when I competed in an all-boys championship in Pakistan, and I came second!

Then I saw some squash courts and wanted to play, but there were no girls playing squash at the time. The boys were wearing shorts, jumping and diving and getting the ball and people were clapping and cheering. I was like, "This is what I wanna do!" So I got into that and luckily my dad supported me. I feel that it is destiny. I'm the only girl who made it out from that region in that way.

WAS THERE ONE CHOICE THAT YOU THOUGHT WAS GOOD AND ONE THAT YOU REGRET?

I don't think I have any regrets because I believe that whatever happens in life, it's written, it has happened, and we have to come out of those challenges, deal with it rather than feeling regret. The best decision I made was when I had threats from the Taliban in Pakistan and I couldn't really leave the house so I had to make a decision about whether I should go back to squash or not. And if I did go, then it wouldn't be safe for the other children. I didn't want to be the cause of something happening to other kids. But I did not lose hope. I love myself. I fully accept myself the way I am and I always look for solutions, so I started emailing all over the world offering my coaching with one condition, that I would only be a part-time coach so I could go on training myself as well. I was emailing by day, and all night I would be training in my room. I knew that when you have the purpose and you constantly tell the universe that you're not going to stop, things start happening eventually, and they did happen.

WHAT WERE THE MAIN CHALLENGES YOU FACED AS YOU TRIED TO CREATE A CAREER FOR YOURSELF IN SQUASH?

I was the only girl in that area playing squash. I was nothing like other girls. I had short hair, I was wearing shorts and everybody was surprised. It was always a problem for them to just enter me into the tournaments. I felt like everybody was questioning whether I'm a girl or not. It's the system, patriarchy; some people don't want you to play so they create hurdles or they won't give you the right information on how to enter the tournament, how to become a professional player, how to train. I had no other training partners so the only people I could train with were boys of my own age. But men would come on court and start harassing me, and some actions were completely unacceptable. It taught me about the many ways they can try to stop you, all those men. But I think God made me this way and I can stand up and fight for myself. I'm not shy, I'm not scared and I have trust in myself. So when I was facing all those struggles, a kind of mental torture, I wasn't acting very feminine. But the way I would talk, everybody would listen, and I would call them 'Brother.' I would look into their eyes and they would understand that they can talk to me, they can really explain things and they can be friends with me, and things started changing.

Now with young girls, in the society they come from, they wear the burka and then in the camps they take off the burka and wear tracksuits and pants. I tell them, 'Be real whether you are in a village or whether you are in a camp. Tell your parents this is what you wanna do. It's not about being one way in front of your parents because you're scared of them and then in another place you are completely different. You should be everywhere the same, whether in public or at home.'

HOW DID YOU DEVELOP AS A COMPETITOR?

Now I teach in Toronto and sometimes the kids ask me about my competitions. And I laugh. I'm like, 'You guys have it easy because you can play with each other and get experience of competing with somebody else.' I was always competing against myself, so that was an issue, but other than that I trained all my life. I would watch the kind of drills the boys would do together, and I would create those drills for myself. I would practise hitting a ball for hours and hours and hours to get perfection, and I would run, do the core movements, visualise those drills and imagine that I am on the podium and winning. I did not have a lot of knowledge, because I did everything myself. My nutrition wasn't good. When I came to Canada I had a lot of injuries. I played all my tournaments in pain. I had no idea of the benefits of different exercises. But I think I still did well given the situation.

HOW DID YOU KEEP YOUR MOTIVATION UP?

I don't want to paint everything in black and white because my country survives because there are good people out there, so there were some people who actually helped me. The Pakistan Squash Federation thought that they should give girls a chance too. I was lucky that they started taking part in different tournaments at that time, so I played at the Asian Junior event, I played at the Asian Games. I played at the British Juniors many times. I travelled for tournaments and I felt more and more motivated and excited. It was really beautiful to see the different parts of the world and realise how girls lived there and how they trained. And I'm no different from them! I thought I was very unique but I soon realised that there are other people like me. Then coming to Canada, I was very focused. I'm adaptable. I just wanna be free. I wanna travel. I know that I'm kind and when you're kind good things start happening.

At the South Asian Games, 2016

WHAT WOULD YOU SAY YOU'RE MOST PROUD OF NOW?

I'm glad I never stopped and I don't want to stop. I didn't give up. That's the most important thing for me. I always brought happiness to my parents, a smile to their faces. That's something that always keeps me happy. And the journey continues through my Foundation, the goal is there, the vision is there, and every day is definitely exciting.

WHAT IS YOUR A FAVOURITE SPORTING MOMENT, EITHER YOUR OWN OR SOMEONE ELSE?

Winning a bronze medal at the World Juniors was very unique. I was training in my bedroom and that was my only chance to travel and play that tournament because I would be a senior after that. So I wasn't expecting a win or anything, but I just wanted to participate. I was also in so much pain. But when I went there I won my first match! Second match, third match, fourth match! Somebody came to me and they're like, "We need you to do the dope test." I'm like, "What does that mean?" They said, "You were in the semi-final and semi-finalists have to do that." I'm like, "I'm in the semi-final. Wow!" Other than that, right now I think a lot of exciting things are happening. If you watch the Olympics, Winter or Summer, a lot of countries are pocketing medals. In the women's events, all the women are bringing medals home, this is very exciting. Canada is home to me now and I just love this country. It's so beautiful. I feel peace and happiness and acceptance here. I think this deserves all my loyalty. And for that reason, when I see their women winning, like in the hockey they got a gold medal, in the soccer they got a gold medal at the Olympics. It just makes me very happy.

IF YOU GAVE YOUR YOUNGER SELF SOME ADVICE WHAT WOULD IT BE?

Well, I think it looks very lame if I say that I really like my past and I really like my present. I just don't hold grudges and I don't have regrets. I always listened to my dad whenever he gave me advice about society, because anything could have happened to me. Many times I was attacked, but luckily nothing happened to me because I always listened to my dad and I trusted in his wisdom.

WHAT WOULD YOU LIKE TO SEE CHANGE FOR WOMEN IN YOUR SPORT OR FOR SPORT IN GENERAL?

A lot of people don't take sport seriously. Right now in the West maybe it's becoming important for everybody, but there are girls and boys who are not interested in sports. But sport is fun, it brings joy and it's a good activity for your brain and for your body. It also introduces us to our own strengths and weaknesses in a very quick way. So if your child is playing sports you know they would understand their own limits and the limits they should push for. There is this quote from Pope Francis that I really like: "If we start challenging ourselves in life, we will be better humans." So to people I would say that in sports, it's not about winning or losing, it's not about those laurels or those trophies or awards or money. It's more than that. You have to look deep inside, at who you are and what you can do. And once you are a strong person mentally and physically, you can actually bring change to your surroundings.

WHAT DO YOU THINK OF THE MEDIA COVERAGE OF WOMEN IN YOUR SPORT?

I think that women are still fighting for rights, equality. Whether it's Canada or the USA or the West or East, anywhere. The system has those kind of holes that we need to fill in. Recently, the US women's soccer team won the equal pay lawsuit. That's a step forward. But the women's gym is still smaller than the men's gym. The women's locker rooms are smaller than the men's locker rooms; the media attention for women, the time on air is less, compared to that of men. The sponsorships are less. People say, "The sponsors don't want to support women's sports." It's not that. In the past few years or so, it has changed a lot. Now there are many more women spectators whereas before some countries were not allowing women to go to watch sports. Now we are showing that women do play sports and a lot of girls want to watch them and they now have role models in the sports world. The media has a strong role to play.

ARE THERE ANY ORGANISATIONS THAT HAVE HELPED YOU OVER THE YEARS?

In Pakistan the major sports are cricket, hockey and squash. They come under the jurisdiction of the armed forces. Squash comes under the Air Force. Of course, Pakistan has a history of men's squash, but women were only just introduced at the time I started. It was exciting to go through that journey. But the fight continues. Even with the Pakistan Squash Federation, when I won a championship they said, "Oh Maria, you saved us," because the men's squash was not successful at that time and they wanted some good news in the media. I said, "You're telling me that I saved you but you're not even thinking about what you can do for women's squash rather than for men's?" So that is a systemic kind of patriarchy and the mindset of our system.

WHAT'S NEXT?

Right now I'm working on a sports school for women and girls of my region because that is where my roots are and a lot of Afghan refugees have arrived in Pakistan now. I think it's a great opportunity for me to help them and also for people around the world to help them too. The school will give them a good education and quality sports. We have prospective land, close to Islamabad Airport because I want to bring international coaches and trainers in so that our people can really learn from them.

If there are any individuals out there who really believe in me and believe in this cause and in this vision, I would appreciate if they could reach out because I do need support, skills and financial support to make this a reality.

www.mariatoorpakai.org

Misty May-Treanor and Kerri Walsh Jennings of Team USA volleyball celebrate after defeating Brazil, Beijing Olympics, 2008. Photo: Craig Maccubbin

INDEX

A

Adams, Nicola 28, 40, 47, 76-77
adaptive surfing 215
Alcott, Chemmy 94-100
Allit, Mary 24
archery 12-14, 35-36, 112
Ashe, Arthur 55, 69, 91
athletics 16, 18, 22, 27-28, 31, 60, 68-69, 114, 147, 157-158, 163-166, 178-179, 185, 212

B

badminton 58, 84-85, 105, 136, 162,
Bannister, Roger 26
baseball 212-214, 216
basketball 17, 54, 62-63, 66-67, 101-6, 111, 114, 116, 216
BBC Sport 29, 37, 57, 83, 206
Beckwith, Agnes 12-13
Berners, Juliana 11
Besford, Pat 26
Biles, Simone 29, 90-91
Blackmore, Rachael 82-23
boxing 28, 46-47, 76-77
Bueno, Maria 27
Buttrick, Barbara 27, 46- 47
Buxton, Angela 27,45

C

Carr, Cat 101-106
Carter, Amanda 229
Challis, Ellie 107-112
Chaplin, Shelley 229
Christiansen, Sophie 39
climbing 52, 3, 112, 141, 188, 189-191
Coachman, Alice 22
Coe, Sebastian 31
Cookey, Pamela 113-118
Cottee, Kay 51
Couch, Jane 28
cricket 84, 99, 152-153, 155, 174, 176, 206-207, 209. 226,

cycling 37-38, 86-87, 158, 161

D

Dartchery 36
Dean, Christopher 56-57
Dearing, Alice 119-124
dell Valle Frias, Soledad 77
Diame, Fatima 33
Didrikson, Mildred 17
discus 22
Dingle, Carolyn 26
Dive, Mollie 22,24,65,105
Dixie, Florence 13
Dod, Charlotte 17
Dow, Ruth 24
dressage 39,87
Durack, Sarah 14-15

E

Ederle, Gertrude 15
Edwards, Tracy 125-129
Elek, Ilona 17
El Moutawakel, Nawal 28, 62-63
Pierce-Evans, Sophie 16

F

fencing 17-18, 22-23, 39, 58-59
Fairclough, Polly 27
Fitzpatrick, Menna 130-134
Fletcher, Jenny 15, 147
Heyhoe-Flint, Rachael 24-25
football 105, 108, 120, 123, 133, 143-144, 146, 153, 156-158, 161-162, 172, 174, 176, 182, 192-197, 204, 206-209, 216
Freeman, Cathy 20, 68-69

G

Gibson, Althea 27, 44-45, 72
Golden, Diane 38
golf 14, 17, 45, 158, 168-169, 172, 206, 208-209
Grainger, Katharine 135-142
Grand National 14, 82-83, 206

228

INDEX

Amanda Carter & Shelley Chaplin at the 2012 Summer Paralympic Games in London.
Photo: Australian Paralympic Committee

Grand Slam 27, 30, 38, 45, 54-55, 72-73, 172, 181
Guttman, Ludwig 35
gymnastics 48-49, 90-92, 156, 158, 179, 199, 207-208

H
Haig, Mary Glen 23
Hamilton, Bethany 34
Hard, Darlene 27, 36, 45
Hartel, Lis 26
Heine, Jutta 27
Henie, Sonja 16
high jump 18, 21-22, 139, 158, 163-164
hockey 16, 24-25, 92, 114, 147, 180, 224, 226
horse riding 216, 229
Houghton, Stephanie 143-146
Hudson, Amy 24
Hyman, Dorothy 27

I
Iranian women's youth football team 24

J
jennings, Kerri Walsh 227

Johnson, Mamie 43-44
Jones, Katya 28
Jones, Megan 178-187
Jujie, Luan 58-59
Jousseaume, Andre 26
Joyner-Kersee, Jackie 60-62

K
kayaking 22
Kenny, Laura 86-87
King, Billie-Jean 45, 54-55, 139
King, Ethel 16
Kitchen, Julie 147-151
Blankers-Koen, Fanny 18
Kostelić, Janica 74-75

L
Lanning, Meg 152-155
Latynina, Larisa 48-49
Leather, Diane 26, 27
Leslie, Lisa 66-67
Lewis, Denise 28, 29, 114, 118
Chojnowska-Liskiewicz, Krystyna 50-51
Logan, Gabby 156-159
Lumsdaine, Gemma 35

At the 2013 US Open. Serena and Venus Williams defeated Silvia Soler-Espinosa and Carla Suarez Navarro. Photo: Edwin Martinez

M

MacArthur, Ellen   70-71
Mahuchikh, Yaroslava 163-167
Marie, Eva   29, 30
Marta   31, 80-81
Maughan, Margaret 35, 36
May-Treanor, Misty   227
Mayer, Helene   17
Millan, Isabel   40, 77
Mirza, Sania   29
Mitchell, Jean   22
Molchanova, Natalia 64-65
Morgan, Alex   4, 29
Morgan, Connie   43
muay thai   147
Muirhead, Eve   168-171

N

Nehwal, Saina   84-85
Nemati, Zahra   39
Neidhart, Natalia   29

netball   105, 114, 116, 136, 147, 161, 162, 173, 174, 180
Nicholl, Liz   173-177
Noel, Susan   26

O

Olympics   14-20, 21-29, 31, 35, 39, 47-9, 57, 69, 87, 91,94-9, 108, 120-1, 135-143, 157-169, 171-179, 180-87, 199-211, 224, 227
Ourahmoune, Sarah   77

P

Page, Louise   28
Pak, Pong Sik   22
Paige   29
Paralympics   29, 35-39, 131-4, 175
Patrick, Danica   231
Philips, Gladys   24
Preis, Ellen   17
Pressley, Toni   81
Preston, Beryl   22
Princess Anne   22
Pritchard, Winifred   22

INDEX

Q
Quansah, Celia   178-187
Queen Alexandra   14
Queen Elizabeth II   22-23

R
Raducanu, Emma   32
Rahayu, Aries Susanti   188-191
Rapinoe, Megan   31, 78-79
Ren, Cancan   77
Riggs, Bobby   55
Roble, Jawahir   192-197
rowing   135-142
Rudolph, Wilma   18-19, 27

S
sailing   14, 22, 51, 70-71, 125-129
Sanderson, Tessa   28, 157
Semenya, Caster   30-31
Shortman, Kate   198-205
skating   14, 17, 56-57
skiing   75-75, 94-100, 108, 130-135
Slater, Barbara   206-211
Smith, Bianca   212-214
Smith, Zoe   215-219
soccer   78-79, 102, 212-3, 224, 225
sports presenter   94, 120, 156
squash   26, 220-226
Stone, Toni   42-43
Storey, Sarah   37-38, 133
surfing   34, 215-219
swimming   12, 15-6, 22, 36-36, 88-9, 108-112, 119-124, 136, 198-205, 207, 216

T
Tabei, Junko   52-53
tennis   13-15, 26-7, 30, 32, 38, 44-5, 54-5, 69, 72-3, 95, 158, 183, 216
Grey-Thompson, Tanni   36
Thorpe, Izzy   198-205
Toorpakai, Mari   220-226
Torvill, Jayne   56-57

U
UK Sport 23, 131, 133, 135, 172, 173, 175, 176

V
Vergeer, Mary   38
Vick, Mary Russell   25
Vonn, Lindsey   3, 100

W
weightlifting   190, 220, 221
Wellington, Chrissie   32
Whitbread, Fatima   28, 157
Williams, Jean   11, 21
Williams, Serena   30, 45, 72-73, 158, 183
Williams, Venus   72-73
Wimbledon, 13-4, 27, 30, 45, 54, 58, 72-73, 209, 210
Women's Islamic Games   23
wrestling   29, 221
Wylie, Mina   14-15

Y
Yee, Alison Yu Chui   38-39
Yuanhui, Fu   88-89

Z
Didrikson Zaharias, Mildred   17
Zorn, Trischa   36

Danica Patrick, racing driver, 2017.
Photo: Camping 500

MORE GREAT BOOKS FROM SUPERNOVA

978-0-9932207-8-4

£24.99

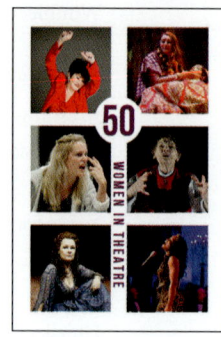

978-1-913641-05-4

£24.99

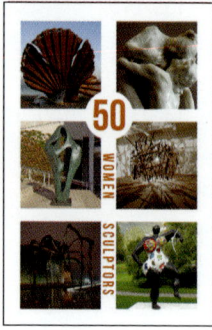

978-0-9932207-7-7

£24.99

Supernova Books is an imprint of
Aurora Metro Books
www.aurorametro.com

NOV 2022